Confronting Social Issues

This is a volume in
EUROPEAN MONOGRAPHS IN SOCIAL PSYCHOLOGY

Series Editor: Henri Tajfel

EUROPEAN MONOGRAPHS IN SOCIAL PSYCHOLOGY 28
Series Editor: HENRI TAJFEL

Confronting Social Issues: Applications of Social Psychology Volume 1

Edited by

PETER STRINGER

University of Nijmegen
The Netherlands

1982

Published in cooperation with
EUROPEAN ASSOCIATION OF EXPERIMENTAL
SOCIAL PSYCHOLOGY
by
ACADEMIC PRESS
A Subsidiary of Harcourt Brace Jovanovich, Publishers
London   New York
Paris   San Diego   San Francisco   São Paulo
Sydney   Tokyo   Toronto

CALIFORNIA SCHOOL OF PROFESSIONAL PSYCHOLOGY LOS ANGELES

ACADEMIC PRESS INC. (LONDON) LTD.
24/28 Oval Road
London NW1

United States Edition published by
ACADEMIC PRESS INC.
111 Fifth Avenue
New York, New York 10003

British Library Cataloguing in Publication Data
Confronting social issues.—(European monographs
in social psychology; v. 28)
1. Social psychology
I. Stringer, P.   II. Series
302   HM251

ISBN 0-12-673801-7

LCCCN 81-68017

Photoset by
Paston Press, Norwich

Printed in Great Britain by
Thomson Litho Ltd, East Kilbride, Scotland

European Monographs in Social Psychology

Series Editor: HENRI TAJFEL

E. A. CARSWELL and R. ROMMETVEIT (*eds*)
Social Contexts of Messages, 1971

J. ISRAEL and H. TAJFEL (*eds*)
The Context of Social Psychology: A Critical Assessment, 1972

J. R. EISER and W. STROEBE
Categorization and Social Judgement, 1972

M. VON CRANACH and I. VINE (*eds*)
Social Communication and Movement: Studies of Interaction and Expression in Man
 and Chimpanzee, 1973

C. HERZLICH
Health and Illness: A Social Psychological Analysis, 1973

J. M. NUTTIN, JR
The Illusion of Attitude Change: Towards a Response Contagion Theory of Persuasion,
 1975

H. GILES and P. F. POWESLAND
Speeck Style and Social Evaluation, 1975

J. K. CHADWICK-JONES
Social Exchange Theory: Its Structure and Influence in Social Psychology, 1976

M. BILLIG
Social Psychology and Intergroup Relations, 1976

S. MOSCOVICI
Social Influence and Social Change, 1976

R. SANDELL
Linguistic Style and Persuasion, 1977

A. HEEN WOLD
Decoding Oral Language, 1978

H. GILES (*ed*)
Language, Ethnicity and Intergroup Relations, 1977

H. TAJFEL (*ed*)
Differentiation between Social Groups: Studies in the Social Psychology of Intergroup Relations, 1979

M. BILLIG
Fascists: A Social Psychological View of the National Front, 1979

C. P. WILSON
Jokes, Form, Content, Use and Function, 1979

J. P. FORGAS
Social Episodes: The Study of Interaction Routines, 1979

R. A. HINDE
Towards Understanding Relationships, 1979

A-N. PERRET-CLERMONT
Social Interaction and Cognitive Development in Children, 1980

B. A. GEBER and S. P. NEWMAN
Soweto's Children: The Development of Attitudes, 1980

S. H. NG
The Social Psychology of Power, 1980

P. SCHÖNBACH, P. GOLLWITZER, G. STIEPEL and U. WAGNER
Education and Intergroup Attitudes, 1981

C. ANTAKI (*ed*)
The Psychology of Ordinary Explanations of Social Behaviour, 1981

W. P. ROBINSON (*ed*)
Communication in Development, 1981

J. P. FORGAS (*ed*)
Social Cognition: Perspectives in Everyday Understanding, 1981

H. T. HIMMELWEIT, P. HUMPHREYS, M. JAEGER and M. KATZ
How Voters Decide: A Longitudinal Study of Political Attitudes extending over Fifteen Years, 1981

Contributors

GLYNIS M. BREAKWELL: *Nuffield College, Oxford, England.*

ANTHONY N. DOOB: *Center of Criminology, University of Toronto, 130 St. George Street, Toronto, Canada.*

MURIEL DUNAND: *Faculty of Psychology, Catholic University of Louvain, 20 voie du Roman Pays, Louvain-la-Neuve, Belgium.*

J. RICHARD EISER: *Department of Psychology, University of Exeter, Exeter, England.*

PETER ELLIS: *Department of Social Psychology, London School of Economics and Political Science, Houghton Street, London WC2, England.*

GEORGE GASKELL: *Department of Social Psychology, London School of Economics and Political Science, Houghton Street, London WC2, England.*

GINETTE HERMAN: *Faculty of Psychology, Catholic University of Louvain, 20 voie du Roman Pays, Louvain-la-Neuve, Belgium.*

JACQUES-PHILIPPE LEYENS: *Faculty of Psychology, Catholic University of Louvain, 20 voie du Roman Pays, Louvain-la-Neuve, Belgium.*

AUGUSTO PALMONARI: *Faculty of Political Science, Institute of Sociology, University of Bologna, Via Belle Arti 42, Bologna, Italy.*

JONATHAN POTTER: *Department of Sociology, University of York, York, England.*

PETER STRINGER: *Department of Social Psychology, University of Nijmegen, Netherlands.*

RENÉ VAN DER VLIST: *Department of Social and Organisational Psychology, State University of Leiden, Hooigracht 15, Leiden, Netherlands.*

BRUNA ZANI: *Faculty of Political Science, Institute of Sociology, University of Bologna, Via Belle Arti 42, Bologna, Italy.*

Preface

If applied social psychology received a boost in the late "sixties from student demands that psychology should be more 'relevant' ", the impetus today comes from a different direction. We now have series devoted to *Advances in Applied Social Psychology* and *Progress in Applied Social Psychology*. In an era of economic recession it is not surprising to find an increase in research which appears to have a practical payoff. But an impetus undoubtedly comes as well from dissatisfactions with the purely gestural field studies which marked so much of the reaction against laboratory experiments.

The contributions in this and the companion volume are not intended primarily to report on the results of recent research. As the title suggests the authors wish rather to offer a number of different *viewpoints* on the endeavour of pursuing a social psychology which is oriented towards societal problems and application. The reader will not find a definitive statement on the nature of applied social psychology. It is clear from these pages that there are quite diverse pursuits, interests and arguments which social psychologists are willing to put under the label "applied". The temptation to categorize and legislate has been resisted out of respect for a range of individual differences in motivation.

This volume has been divided, after the event, into three parts, which variously and approximately deal with (i) metatheoretical and theoretical issues, (ii) substantive research on three or four contemporary societal problems, and (iii) a more specific discussion of the role of social psychology in relation to the social services.

Each part is introduced by a discursive section which points to some of the general issues which it raises. Readers are invited to use these introductions as a rough means of rapidly orienting themselves to the contents of the book. They should not be taken as a complete synthesis of its arguments. Some, but not all, of the issues which are raised in these introductions are derived from exchanges among the authors at two workshops which were arranged to discuss the papers.

The workshops were held during 1979, in January at Cartmel in Cumbria, and in October at Rye in East Sussex. We are grateful to the European Association of Experimental Social Psychology for sponsoring the meetings; and to the Social Science Research Council for making them financially possible. The encouragement and advice of Henri Tajfel helped these volumes to fruition.

October, 1981   PETER STRINGER

Contents of Volume 1

III
Studies on social services

Contents of Volume 2

I

Theory and Practice

Introduction

A number of common threads connects the three chapters in the first part of the book. All of them discuss the nature of applied social psychology and the relation to it of theory or theoretical social psychology. Not surprisingly these issues recur throughout the book. Emphasis is also given to the importance of realizing applied research within a specified and appreciated socio-historical context. This often entails much more prior, descriptive work than psychologists are used to doing.

Applied can be differentiated from theoretical research in its focus on dependent or independent variables rather than on lawful relations between them. But the term "applied" suggests more than that: that research results will actually be applied to a problem outside of purely theoretical concerns; or, at the very least, that they be potentially of application. Instances of research where results are actually being applied are often referred to by a special phrase, "action research". That the phrase had to be coined is an indication of how far most "applied" research is from practice.

The great majority of so-called applied social psychology conducted in academic settings is not applied in any overt or concrete way. The label is assumed because of the researchers' superordinate concern with issues or problems which are readily recognized in contemporary society. The source of questions to be examined is different from the source of theoretical questions, but the destination of the answers is the same. Most applied research cannot be justified in terms of *applicability*, since that would entail an awareness, which is rarely demonstrated, of criteria for successful application. Who might apply research results, under what circumstances, and with what outcome is not a part of the agenda of an applied social psychological study. More generally, we have very little formal information indeed about the uses, of whatever kind, to which social psychological knowledge is put. From research on other social sciences, one would guess that it serves a diffuse "enlightenment" or "preparatory" function rather than acting as a specific input to policy decisions.

Academic researchers are by definition rarely able to carry out the "in-house" research which, it has been found, is most likely to be

applied by organizations. If they wish to study problems plucked from
the outside world, they have to justify their work in conventional
academic terms. They should add to the store of knowledge, for example, and publish research results in acknowledged journals. They have
to live with colleagues who do just that. One consequence is the incan-
tation that applied need not be separated from pure research. Despite
all that van der Vlist and Potter say in the first part of this book, the
authors of several subsequent chapters insist that no boundary can be
drawn between the two domains.

One way in which the boundary is erased is by recourse to Lewin's
famous dictum about the practicality of theory. Theory can certainly
offer economies of structure and direction to a piece of applied research.
And applied research can make a critical and positive contribution to
theory evaluation and development, as several of the present writers
propose. Ellis's chapter later in the book gives an example of testing
competing theoretical positions in an applied setting. But there are
some hard questions still unanswered. Are there particular demands of
theory in applied work? Are broader theories needed? Are some existing
theories inherently more applicable? In the study of a complex problem, does more than one set of theoretical propositions have to be called
into play?

There is no reason to believe that theoretically founded applied research is any more likely to be useful. It may academically be of high
quality and have an impact on the discipline. But unless there is some
congruence between the academic Theory and the theory or theories of
the practitioners whom one hopes to help or influence, there is unlikely
to be any practical outcome.

With this in mind, Breakwell's refusal in her chapter to distinguish at
all rigorously between Theory, model and theory is salutary. Much of
her argument appears to be countering an excessive adherence to one
particular theory or a particular area of social psychology. A persistent
adherence is the hallmark of the scholar. For a practitioner it is a set of
blinkers. It is an obstacle to communicating with anyone who does not
have a similar cognitive framework or who refuses to adopt it because
he does not agree with its assumptions and implications. It may be possible in time to educate people to think in terms of, say, exchange
theory. But for the solution of a proximate social problem one has to
speak the same language as the decision-makers whom one is trying to
help, or anyone else who is caught up in the context of the problem.

Discovering what that language is will be one of the tasks preparatory to the research. Others include an analytic description of the social, economic and political characteristics of the problem area, both for their own sake and to help in problem-definition. On occasions it may be enough simply to have carried out the descriptive preparation. There is rarely a single or absolutely optimal solution to a social issue. Policy-makers are adept at balancing political and other considerations to arrive at a feasible solution. They are often best helped by an analysis of the problem area and its background. Descriptive research is treated as a poor cousin to explanatory research. But whatever their relative epistemological status, description can be just as demanding, rigorous and valuable a goal.

Behind this disdain is an unwillingness on the part of social psychology to study the natural history of the phenomena in its field. While aping the other sciences, in this respect it has failed. If sociobiology is attractive, in part it is because we have elaborate and formal descriptions of the social life of animals. If people want descriptions of their own social life, they turn to journalists, novelists and historians rather than to social psychologists. We shall return to this point when discussing the topics dealt with in the second part of this book.

There is another reason for encouraging descriptive work. The problems which the social psychologist is invited to tackle may be insoluble with his resources. A complete analysis and resolution might stretch beyond the problem's life-span. The problem may be manifestly too complex to investigate without colossal expenditure. In these cases descriptive research might enable society to understand and adapt to the problem more clearly, and, in particular, to appreciate the senses in which it is not soluble by rational, scientific means.

Underlying each of the three chapters in the first part of this book is a disquiet about our ignorance of how social psychology "works". Van der Vlist offers his contribution as a prolegomenon to the systematic and empirical study of this question. Potter is actually engaged in such a study, a small part of which is described here, while Breakwell goes further, in anticipation of the empirical results, by offering social psychologists some guidelines for application and practice. (The reader might incidentally like to ponder on the relevance of Breakwell's propositions, from the perspective of the one whose practice is described by Potter's case-study.)

One intriguing aspect of the question "how does social psychology work?" is our attitude to what counts as a communication of social psychological ideas. It was due neither to accident nor idleness that this volume and its companion came to be composed entirely of contributions by academics and about academic work. Social psychological practice, independent of academic strings, is rarely found in the literature. The gate-keepers of the written word in journals and books help to restrict the definition of applied social psychology. Practice and its results is sometimes recorded in mimeographed reports of very limited circulation, but it generally tends to be invisible from the academic viewpoint. Presumably social psychological practitioners occasionally communicate with one another. But their more probable isolation must have consequences for the nature of their practice. If applied social psychology is to be about application, we all need more accounts of their operation.

The very particular attention which we give to the written word was well illustrated by the proceedings of the two workshops held to discuss the contents of this book. As scientific discussions they were not especially unusual, but a number of features are extremely interesting. Participants were often prepared to introduce their papers in significantly different terms from those which they had put on paper. In re-drafting their contributions they generally made very few changes which can be directly attributed to points which other people had made. Although the discussions were a highly complex social process, very little of that is recorded here. Of course there cannot be and is not a hard and fast barrier between the formal, written and informal, conversational transmission of ideas. But it is curious that those who study social processes should not have reflexively found ways to reveal it in the forms which they make public.

Opening up what is generally not recorded may be resisted for a number of reasons. A transcript of our discussions may be of interest to nobody but ourselves and those studying the social aspects of science. But if we are interested in the application of social psychology, this secrecy about informal processes withholds highly pertinent information. The conventions which designate what is "the literature" are damaging to the diffusion of practical knowledge.

In the search for parity with other branches of psychology, social psychology has recently transferred its preoccupation with sophisticated operationalizations in the laboratory to a new respect for theory. Some of the demands of applied social psychology may shock that respect. It is not that there is a dislocation between theory and practice. There may or may not be. What may be shocking are the suggestions made here that one's theoretical framework may be chosen for one by the situation of the research, and that in the process of applied work theories are necessarily transformed. Of course, neither event is unusual. In non-applied research there are very clear contingencies dictating people's choice of theory and theoretical issue. And precisely the aim of research guided by the principle of falsification will be to see theory modified. What may be shocking is the removal from the academic sphere of control of these operations. The applied researcher in effect allows others than the scientific community to make crucial decisions for him. It is in that respect rather than through the choice of "real life" questions to study that applied research can incorporate the researcher into society.

Several chapters in the second volume of this book will expand on these points in quite radical ways. For the moment one may wonder whether or not they might be significant for mainstream social psychology as well. Two other parts of van der Vlist's arguments certainly are. He suggests that applied social psychological studies may not be quite as definitive as we would like to believe. On the one hand, they are generally no more than crudely indicative of the state of affairs represented in their results; on the other, even crudely indicative results are subject to a cultural relativity.

The argument deserves to be expanded. (Though one should not perhaps go as far as Herbst persuades van der Vlist to go. If each person is a behavioural universe on his own, a *social* psychology becomes very difficult to imagine.) Very many social psychology studies have to be crudely indicative because of the impossibility of controlling situational variables and subjects' interpretation of and reaction to the experiment. This is particularly so in the light of the unrepresentative character of most subject samples. The implications are that we should be prepared to do many more replicative studies, and that research strategies be formalized for "triangulating" on the question at issue.

In cross-cultural research, similar strategies have been recognized. One device is systematically to permute the cultural identity of subject and experimenter. The point of interest then becomes, not the emergence or otherwise of universal laws, but the difference in results between subject-cultures, between experimenters and the interaction between the two. Having admitted that the results of a study on, say, blood donation may be culture specific, one should focus essentially on the differences between cultures as such. In an applied setting one presumably has a general interest in learning from other cultures.

Even within cultures the same strategy may be adopted. Different viewpoints on an applied problem should be determined by prior research and separate studies then conducted both from and between those viewpoints. The women of Amsterdam may not react in the same way as those of Leiden to a cancer screening programme; and the two populations may have a pertinent perspective on one another's position. In such a fashion one begins to learn in what sense one's results are crudely indicative and in what sense they reflect the particular sociohistorical context of the parties to the research.

1

Social Psychological Theory and Empirical Studies of Practical Problems

R. van der Vlist

Theoretical and applied research differ in their objectives

Theoretical or fundamental research in the social sciences (and perhaps in the other sciences as well) is predominantly interested in relationships between certain concepts or variables. Being a social psychologist I shall illustrate this with an example taken from an introductory textbook on "the science of social psychology" (Berkowitz, 1975, p. 8). In a paragraph entitled "what social psychology is" Berkowitz explains that:

> ... social psychologists have looked into *the conditions governing* whether or not people help those in need of assistance, are *influenced* by what they see and read in the mass media, *conform* to the views of the others around them or resist these opinions, *react violently* to a provocation, or come to like or dislike the persons they meet. Social psychologists have also investigated many other topics including how attitudes can be changed, the influence of leaders on their groups, and vice versa, why people vote as they do in elections or do not bother to vote at all, what makes some groups more productive than others ...

And he adds to this:

> ... the discipline's major attention has been on the formulation and testing of theoretical propositions explaining a person's reactions to particular social stimuli under certain types of conditions. (p. 9)

This textbook example asserts that theoretical research attempts to formulate (nomothetic) laws concerning the relationship between variables related to scientific concepts. Applied research, on the other hand, either tends to focus on the *independent* variable (what are the consequences of X) or on the *dependent* variable (what are the causes of Y). It is seldom that particular relationships between X and Y are studied in applied research.

Applied research which focuses on the independent variable is well known in the form of evaluation studies in which the effects of certain phenomena are studied. The ultimate goal of such studies is to make a decision with respect to the independent variable. Such a decision will

usually be based on many different kinds of effects; and not on one particular relationship $X \rightarrow Y$. When applied research focuses on the dependent variable the research is almost never limited to one possible cause of Y. On the contrary, in order to be practical and useful the research will deal with many causes and consequently with many theories. Where theoretical research tries to increase knowledge about a theoretically interesting relationship, applied research serves as the basis for decision making with respect to a concrete dependent or independent variable. This fact in itself makes it more difficult to benefit from theoretical research (or theory) when doing applied research. If one tries to use theoretical insight the result is that a rather complicated research design has to be used. An example may clarify this point.

In 1975 all women in Leiden (the Netherlands) of age 35 and over were called up to be screened in a breast-cancer screening programme. Slightly more than 30% of the relevant population failed to respond. The Institute of Social Medicine of the University of Leiden decided to find out why so many women failed to respond. The results of such a study could be important in future screening programmes (Spruit and Van Kampen-Donker, 1976).

One of the theoretical notions that seemed promising for such a research-project was Leventhal's (1970) research on the relationship between fear and behaviour (persuasion). In several experiments Leventhal and his colleagues demonstrated that the relationship between fear and behaviour is complex, and that the available data probably require a complicated model that Leventhal termed "the parallel response model". (Leventhal proposed that a fear-arousing message evokes emotional reactions as well as adaptive behaviour. But whether the individual engages in fear control or in (problem-solving) danger control, or both, depends on personality variables and the effectiveness of the recommendations.)

This being the case, it is not clear why over 30% of the relevant population did not respond in the Leiden study. Everybody received the same message and the same instructions. Although fear level (as well as personality factors) may have influenced persuasion it is likely that this is not the whole story. It is probably important also to study the impact of the fear-arousing message in more detail. This implies that other theories must be consulted, since Leventhal's model does not deal with this factor. At the same time it is quite evident that still other theories or theoretical notions must be consulted. (Is it possible, for example, that some of the potential respondents missed, or did not understand, the original call?) The conclusion is that applied research which deals with either a particular dependent variable or a particular independent variable can lead to a very complicated design in which many theoretical notions have to be combined. It is understandable that quite often a less complicated and less theoretically-based design is preferred.

The application of theory: bridging a conceptual gap

THE NEED FOR INTERMEDIATE RELATIONSHIPS

As stated before, theoretical research in social psychology is directed at the formulation of "nomothetic laws" between variables of a conceptual nature. Social-psychological science (or any science for that matter) never focuses on concrete phenomena, but on the analysis of a conceptual representation of phenomena. These scientific concepts are of a higher level of abstraction than concrete phenomena. On the other hand, applied research always tries to increase useful knowledge with respect to concrete phenomena proper, or phenomena of a very low level of abstraction. Phenomena such as "sickness absenteeism among school-teachers in elementary schools in the Netherlands in 1977", or "behaviour with respect to preventive health screening in Leiden in

1975", or "number of working days lost in Rotterdam due to strikes in 1979", may be the concern of particular applied research projects. They cannot, however, be treated as scientific concepts. This implies that applied research, interpreted as *"the application of nomothetic knowledge"*, should bridge the gap between theories using scientific concepts and concrete phenomena which are of particular concern in a given applied research project. This is always a difficult process.

For instance, when Y is a concrete dependent variable, and U, V, W and X are scientific concepts and possible independent variables, intermediate variables must be found (U_1, U_2, U_3, and V_1, V_2, V_3, etc.) which are more directly related to the concrete dependent variable. The following figure illustrates this point:

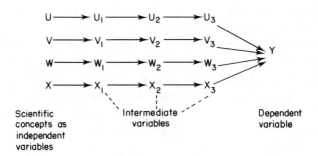

In the last instance the relationships between these intermediate variables (U_3, V_3, etc.) and the dependent variable Y are often of an *"evident"* order. This is not a disadvantage; on the contrary, the lack of such "evident" relationships should not be trusted since it suggests the operation of "magic". An example taken from applied research will illustrate this line of thought.

Research in the Dutch sea-fishing industry, dealing with the causes of differences in the amounts of fish caught between fishing vessels (van der Vlist, 1970), ventured the hypothesis that there might be a positive relationship between "distribution of influence" (a concept from Tannenbaum, 1961) and amounts of fish caught (the concrete dependent variable). How could this relationship be explained?

A number of observational studies aboard fishing vessels suggested, among other things, the following (simplified) intermediate model:

(1) Amount of fish caught per unit of time depends in the first place on the fished area per unit of time.

(2) Amount of fish caught per time unit is, in the second place, dependent on the "quality" of the fished area (in the sense of rich or poor fishing grounds).

(3) Other things being equal the ship which is using fishing grounds in a more efficient way, will catch more fish.

With this intermediate model we may conclude that a theoretical concept (e.g. "the distribution of influence") can only be linked with the dependent variable when it can be linked with one or more intermediate variables of the model.

Tannenbaum's concept "distribution of influence" may affect the dependent variable because "distribution of influence" implies the occurrence of problem-solving communication between the skipper and his crew. This problem-solving communication may focus on the question of which fishing grounds to choose in certain (given) circumstances (for example, being somewhere at sea, in a certain period of the year and on the way home). This process would link Tannenbaum's concept to the dependent variable in the following way:

greater distribution of influence $\longrightarrow$	more frequent communication of a problem-solving nature $\longrightarrow$	superior decisions $\longrightarrow$
(X)	(X_1)	(X_2)
	better fishing grounds $\longrightarrow$	greater amounts of fish caught
	(X_3)	(Y)

Because other variables are much more important with respect to Y (engine capacity, via fished area per time unit; and differences in all kinds of equipment, via quality of fishing grounds), we can also conclude that Tannenbaum's variable has only a minor effect on the dependent variable—which was indeed the case.

When "evident" relationships (such as the one demonstrated) cannot be traced, the relationship between the theoretical concept and the dependent variable is of a "magic" nature. And in puzzlement, one might well wonder "How is this possible?"

A NEGATIVE EXAMPLE: FIEDLER'S CONTINGENCY THEORY OF
LEADERSHIP EFFECTIVENESS

If we look at social psychological (or social scientific) theories on the
one hand, and applied research on the other hand, we may see that
theories are not always stated properly in conceptual terms (as they
should be) and that applied research does not always specify the relationships between scientific concepts and concrete variables. We may
find mixtures of almost everything. An example is Fiedler's contingency theory of leadership (Fiedler, 1964, 1967). Fiedler's theory
suggests that there is a relationship between group performance and a
leader attribute (Least Preferred Co-worker score or Assumed Similarity between Opposites). The nature of this relationship is assumed,
however, to be contingent on the "*situation*". This "situation" is
specified by three dimensions: "affective leader-group-relations"; "task
structure"; and "position-power" of the leader. The "*situation*" may
vary from favourable to (very) unfavourable for the leader. Among all
these concepts, only the LPC-score is clearly operationalized. "*Affective
leader-group-relations*", as a variable, is sometimes identified with a
sociometric acceptance index (in earlier studies), sometimes measured
as "*group-atmosphere score*" (in later studies). The concept "*task structure*"
is quite difficult to grasp. Though it is not clearly operationalized a task
is seen as more structured when the task itself defines an order from
above (as in assembling a rifle). The concept "*position-power*" is measured by a check-list in which aspects such as status of the leader, sanc-
tion power, etc. are mentioned. Some of these are given weights of five,
and others only a weight of one. (The rationale behind this differential
weighting is lacking.) The dependent variable "*group-performance*" is not
defined or described in general terms; it might mean quite different
things.

Fiedler's theory was developed partly in a theoretical way, and partly
via applied studies in an *ad hoc* manner. Although in a number of studies
in the United States Fiedler's theory appeared to receive support, one
might wonder why. Fiedler has always been very vague as far as the behavioural consequences of a high or low LPC-score are concerned. However, any relationship between this attribute and group performance
can only be demonstrated by specifying the behavioural or motivational consequences of such an attribute and the impact of these conse-

quences on task-relevant conditions for the workers or the behaviour of the workers when performing the task. Fiedler has never shown how his theory could work in concrete settings, in the sense which I explained. He has given only correlational evidence.

When Fiedler's theory was tested in the Netherlands (van der Vlist, 1970; Doerbecker and Vos, 1976; Vos, 1979), it was not supported. Van der Vlist (1970) used Fiedler's model in a study in the Dutch sea-fishing industry in an attempt to account for differences in amount of fish caught by different vessels. With his co-workers he undertook about 20 observational journeys and studied 78 ships in detail (looking at interviews with skippers, fishermen, owners; results over the last few years, etc.).

The "*situation*" on board the ships, in Fiedler's sense, is favourable or very favourable for the leader (the skipper): the "position power" is high, "group-atmosphere" is predominantly positive (only teams with a relatively good group atmosphere stay together) and the task is relatively "structured". In such a context, the correlation between LPC and group performance should be substantially negative (between -0.30 and -0.60). In fact some positive but not statistically significant correlations were found. This result could not be due to a restriction of range of the independent variable as the variance in LPC-scores was evident.

Doerbecker and Vos (1976) and Vos (1979) tried to use Fiedler's model with respect to the effectiveness of volley-ball teams. Their research is very interesting since they did, in fact, conduct a "*natural experiment*". In 1971–1972 the Dutch Volley-ball Association (NeVoB) decided to restructure the top of its league. Instead of four districts with 12 teams in each league the objective was to create two classes of 12 teams each and to down-grade the other 24 teams. One of the hypotheses was that the coach of a team (as a leader) would have some influence on the team's results in the competition to follow. This influence should be especially important in the situation studied because other relevant variables (e.g. playing-force) would be relatively equal or constant.

Doerbecker and Vos have severe criticisms of LPC as a psychological attribute. No significant relationship was found between LPC and success in any of the conditions. The authors criticize LPC as a psychological attribute of the leader because of the lack of stability of this variable over time. It also appeared that the relationship between LPC-scores

and task—and/or social emotional leadership was practically non-exis-
tent, though Fiedler (1967) has suggested that LPC-scores can be related to these concepts.*

The fact that Fiedler's theory failed in both cases could be due either
to an insufficient measurement of the "situation" (the technical and
social context of Dutch sea-fishing) or to the irrelevance or vagueness of
the LPC-score as a leader attribute (sea-fishing as well as volley-ball).
In both cases the theory is not applicable because of shortcomings in
the theory itself.

ON THE RELATIVE IMPORTANCE OF CROSS-CULTURAL APPLIED RE-SEARCH

Theoretical research does not focus on concrete phenomena but on a
conceptual representation of these phenomena and applied research, to
be successful, must bridge the gap between relevant theoretical concepts and the concrete variables that are of central importance in the
applied study. Thus, a comparison of empirical investigations of social
problems in cross-cultural studies or cross-situational studies, may be
irrelevant if concrete variables cannot be clearly linked to theory in a
similar way. A few examples may make this clear.

One can compare sickness-absenteeism studies conducted in the
United States, in the Netherlands and, for instance, in Israel. But it is
quite probable that the dependent variable (absenteeism) is a completely different variable in these three countries because the phenomenon is embedded in totally different settings. Therefore, one might well
ask what the advantage of such a comparison could be. Any study in
this field should start with a careful in-depth analysis of the dependent
variable as it is manifested within a specific context (e.g. social security
regulations, law, effects on income, unemployment threat, etc.). Only
from such an in-depth study might it become clear that absenteeism
may be linked to theory in different ways depending on the situational
context.

* It is interesting to note that there were some significant relationships between leadership style and the "success" of teams. In highly cohesive groups a negative correlation
was found between task leadership and success (-0.49, $n = 18$, $P < 0.02$). In low cohesive groups this correlation was positive (0.43, $n = 17$, $P < 0.05$). These results are
compatible with a contingency model. However, the operation of such a model would
be limited to a quite narrow range of situations.

Another example is the cross-cultural comparison of empirical studies of blood-donor motivation as the basis for decision-making with respect to the recruitment of more donors. A Dutch study on this policy problem, undertaken by Stammeyer and Staallekker (1977) revealed that in The Hague more than 90% of newly recruited donors had altruistic motives such as helping other people and relieving suffering. Oswalt and Hoff (1975) did research on the same problem in a small town in the State of New York and reached the conclusion that ". . . altruism was the basis for 16% of the donors" (Oswalt and Hoff, 1975, p. 70). The difference in results is very impressive. This may be partly due to differing techniques in data gathering. Oswalt and Hoff coded (first?) answers to the question "What motivated you to donate blood the first time?". Stammeyer and Staallekker made a distinction between the immediate cause or decision to donate blood (on the basis of something that happened) and the motive behind this behaviour. Both studies used check-lists on which respondents could indicate the applicable response. This procedure may have affected the answers. Whether this different procedure can account for the impressive differences in results must be doubted. Donating blood in a "community in upstate New York" is different from donating blood in The Hague. Unlike the United States, the Netherlands provides no financial compensation for blood donors. In most cases not even travel expenses are returned. This fact in itself makes blood-donating behaviour in the U.S. different from blood-donating behaviour in the Netherlands. It is very likely that the motivation behind the behaviour is totally different and that the optimal recruitment policy of new donors will differ as well.

The foregoing examples suggest that when conducting applied research at least two basic rules must be kept in mind:

(1) The best approach to the problem is to start with an in-depth study of the relevant concrete phenomena on which the research is focusing (a "grounded-theory-phase" in the design). It is only on the basis of such an in-depth study that it may become apparent which body of theory may be fruitfully applied to the problem in hand.

(2) Studies conducted elsewhere (in other cultures, in other situational settings), though apparently dealing with the same practical problem, should be treated with caution. Such studies are certainly informative, and they may be interesting, but they are not automatically relevant and most of the time are only crudely indicative.

Is there a fundamental difference between "policy research" and "discipline research"?

In the second section of this chapter it was explained that the objectives of theoretical and applied research differ. On the basis of a few examples it was shown that applied research focuses either on a (set of) independent variable(s) or on a (set of) dependent variable(s) in order to facilitate policy-decisions. Theoretical research is predominantly interested in certain *relationships* between conceptually based variables with the intention of furthering theoretical knowledge. On the basis of this difference applied research will often necessitate a complicated design, since many theoretical notions have to be incorporated in a particular research project.

Other authors have, however, come to different conclusions. For example, Coleman (1972) states, "It is important to distinguish sharply between a methodology that has as its philosophical base the testing and development of theories and a methodology that has as its philosophic base a guide to action". The distinction he makes between "discipline research" and "policy research" being, respectively, "conclusion-oriented" and "decision-oriented", coincides with the distinction I made. However, Coleman decides that this implies that ". . . A fundamentally different methodological foundation is needed for policy research than exists for discipline research". (Coleman, 1975, cited by v.d. Vall, 1978.) Since Coleman based this conclusion on the study of a single case (van de Vall, 1978), it would not be too difficult to discard this conclusion.

Recently, however, the Dutch-American sociologist, van de Vall and his co-researchers (van de Vall and Bolas, 1977; van de Vall *et al.*, 1976; van de Vall, 1978) have given new strength to Coleman's ideas. They analysed 120 policy research projects carried out in the Netherlands between 1960 and 1970: 40 projects each in the fields of industry, town and country planning, and social work and public health. Van de Vall used a focused design in which research reports were first of all analysed and then semi-structured interviews were held with the researcher and the responsible policy-maker of each project. The evaluation of policy impact was based either upon interviews with the policy-maker (van de Vall *et al.*, 1976) or interviews with the researcher as well as the policy-maker (van de Vall, 1978). This study focused on the policy impact of research or the degree of research utilization, for which a special measure was developed (The OPI: Overall Policy Impact Score). It appeared that research projects that started with "nomothetic" or "formal concepts" (theory based) had significantly less policy impact than when the project started with qualitative techniques, such as participant observation or in-depth interviewing, and then developed "grounded" concepts of a low level of abstraction.

Van de Vall refers to earlier publications (Lazarsfeld *et al.*, 1967; Glaser and Strauss, 1967) which also concluded that formal concepts should be avoided in policy-research and replaced by "intermediary sensitizing concepts" (Blumer) or "grounded concepts" (Glaser and Strauss).

A comparable significant result was also found when the impact scores of projects which followed the formal methodological rules about which there exists a reasonable consensus (Kaplan, 1964; Lim, 1976) were compared with projects that did not follow these rules in a strict sense. (A "methodology score" was correlated with the impact score.) The latter projects had more impact than the former. It also appeared that the organizational context of the research project was important, in the sense that,

> ... Internal social researchers are superior to external consultants as agents of planned social intervention and policy-making (van de Vall *et al.*, 1976, p. 165) and ... The more external the organisational context of applied social research, the lower its impact upon the diagnosis, design and development of organisational policy measures. (p. 166)

Van de Vall draws two conclusions out of this impressive research material:

(1) that the priority of nomothetic social science, highly valued in the academic tradition, needs to be reconsidered in the case of applied social research;

(2) that the priority of methodological rules in academic research is no guarantee for the applicability of such research.

Van de Vall concluded that new theoretical and methodological routes will have to be followed in order to develop an independent paradigm for applied research.

I gave abundant attention to van de Vall's research because it is to me the best known and most elaborate empirical research project on this topic. Nevertheless, I do not agree with his conclusions. The amount of impact a study has on policy-makers should not be confused with the quality of a research project. It should not even be confused with the usefulness of a study. What van de Vall demonstrates is that a certain type of applied research is more influential than other approaches. It does not compel the need for a different methodology.

In fact, I think that the application of social psychological or sociological theory in policy research and policy-making is basically comparable to the application of "natural science" in engineering. Here, too, a thorough analysis of the situational context is conditional for the successful application of the laws of natural science. Here, too, the application of knowledge may lead to a complicated research design, depending on the concrete problems on hand. There is, however, one important difference. This difference is not fundamental, but only relative. That is, the "situational context" of natural science-based problems in engineering is more or less fixed in most situations (e.g. being different on high altitudes, in deep sea waters, on the moon, in space craft, in low temperature situations, etc.). They probably differ much more in applied social science. When this is indeed the case, it is evident that the detection and demonstration of "nomothetic laws" is much more complicated in the social sciences because it is difficult to decide what variables are essential and in what respect. It is also possible, however, that "nomothetic laws" as known in the natural sciences do not exist in the social sciences.

Are individuals subject to "nomothetic laws", or should they be treated as "behavioural universes"?

In his book, "Behavioural Worlds: The Study of Single Cases", Herbst (1970) takes the view that during the hundred years of empirical study of human behaviour remarkably little progress has been made in the way of finding generally accepted "laws of behaviour". Herbst mentions three possibilities as to why this is the case:

(1) As far as human behaviour is concerned no universal principles of any kind can be formulated. Herbst considers it premature to adopt this conclusion.

(2) The second possibility is that the laws of behaviour are of a different type from those we have been looking for up to now.

(3) It is also possible that the methods of research, as presently in use, are not adequate for discovering behavioural laws.

Herbst explains that the second possibility deserves attention. The possible kinds of law in any science are definable in terms of their "invariance properties". (He states that the essential concern of science is the search for invariance in phenomena as they are conceptually represented.) Three such types of law are distinguished by Herbst:

(a) Both the functional form of a relationship between conceptually based variables as well as parametric values are universal constants. An example would be the gas law in physics, where

$$\frac{PV}{T} = R$$

This law states that if we multiply the pressure P by the volume V of a given mass of gas and divide by the absolute temperature T, then we will always obtain the same value R, which is the gas constant. Here both the functional relationship between variables as well as the parameter R are constants.

Perhaps there are no such type A laws in the social sciences.

(b) Type B laws are laws in which the functional form of the relationship is a universal constant, but the parameters are specific. An example would be the fact that a metal rod varies in length with temperature, but that each metal has its specific expansion rate parameter. Here the functional form of the relationship is the same for all metals, but the rate of expansion differs for different metals. Behavioural laws of this type are a real possibility. Herbst states:

> The law would have the same form in each case but the parameters would have different values for different persons and groups. (p. 6)

The possible existence of behavioural laws of type B implies that we may not detect such a law by studying populations or population samples. Given the behavioural law, $Y = pX$, where p is a specific parameter, we may see that p may be positive, zero, or negative without altering the (in this case) linear relationship between Y and X. When, in this case, random samples of a population are studied, it may well be that no relationship can be demonstrated: some results will suggest a positive, others a negative, and still others no relationship at all.

Instead of studying populations or samples the study of individual cases seems to be preferable when type B laws are to be expected. An

example of such a law would be a certain relationship between evoked fear and the amount of attitude change. Danger information in a message (for example with respect to the consequences of smoking) may start an emotional fear-reaction leading to drive-producing states which would be higher the more the fear is aroused. The performance of certain behavioural recommendations would reduce or stop the emotional activity. It is possible that this principle is always present, but that the fear-producing effects of a certain message, or the drive-producing effects of fear, differ between individuals. In such a case we may find positive, zero, or perhaps even negative relationships between such a message and attitude change (which is indeed the case) without having to develop a complex "parallel response model" as Leventhal did.
(c) Herbst describes another possibility which he terms "type C laws": Here

> Both the functional relationship and parameters are specific, but the generating rules for possible functional relationships are a universal constant.

The existence of type C laws

> . . . implies that each person and each group constitutes a behavioural universe which operates on the basis of its own laws.

In this case it is still possible that a set of generating rules for the possible range of behaviour principles can be detected. The consequential regularities for behaviour in certain conditions would then be due to a type C law.

Again, the research dealing with attendance at the Leiden breast-cancer screening programme may illustrate this point. As was mentioned above, a little over 30% of the relevant population failed to respond to the screening. Now it is possible that a type B law operated, and that individuals were quite differently affected by a fear-producing message. In that case, we probably would find an even distribution of "refusers" across the city. This was not the case, however. The study revealed, instead, that the percentage of the relevant population that failed to respond varied between 10% in certain parts of the town and 50% in other parts. These results strongly suggest the operation of message reappraising—factors of a social-contextual nature (e.g. family or neighbours). The fear-arousing message (the letter containing the information about the screening) was not taken at its face-value, but was discussed and probably reinterpreted in a concrete social context.

As far as I can see, social psychological research (especially theoretical social psychological research) is inclined to neglect the full operation of "social contextual" factors. By doing this it disqualifies personal and social historical factors as well.

Perhaps it is worthwhile to look at individuals as "behavioural universes" and to find out under what conditions these universes affect each other. After all, Allport defined social psychology as "an attempt to understand and explain how the thought, feeling and behaviour of individuals are influenced by the actual, imagined or implied presence of others" (1968, p. 3). Perhaps we should think along those lines. It would lead to a better understanding of individual cases, particular situations (as van de Vall demonstrates to be important), and nevertheless allow a search for emerging regularities under specific conditions as type C laws suggest.

References

Allport, G. W. (1968). The historical background of modern social psychology. In "The Handbook of Social Psychology", 2nd ed. Vol. I. Addison Wesley, Reading, Massachusetts.

Berkowitz, L. (1975). "A Survey of Social Psychology". The Dryden Press, Illinois.

Coleman, J. S. (1972). "Policy Research in the Social Sciences". General Learning Press, Morristown, N.J.

Coleman, J. S. (1975). Problems of conceptualisation and measurement in studying policy-impacts. In "Public Policy Evaluation, Sage Yearbooks in Politics and Public Policy" (K. M. Dolbaere, ed.), Vol. II, pp. 19–40. Sage Publications, Beverley Hills.

Doerbecker, G. L. and Vos, J. T. F. (1976). Taakgroepen in een bedreigende situatie. Amsterdam dissertation.

Fiedler, F. E. (1964). A contingency model of leadership effectiveness. In "Advances in Experimental Social Psychology" (L. Berkowitz, ed.), Vol. 1. Academic Press, New York/London.

Fiedler, F. E. (1967). "A Theory of Leadership Effectiveness". McGraw-Hill, New York.

Glaser, B. G. and Strauss, A. (1967). "The Discovery of Grounded Theory". Aldine, Chicago.

Herbst, P. G. (1970). "Behavioural Worlds; The Study of Single Cases". Tavistock Publications, London.

Kaplan, A, (1964). "The Conduct of Inquiry: Methodology for Behavioural Science". Chandler, San Francisco.

Lazarsfeld, P. F., Sewell, W. H. and Wilensky, H. L. (1967). "The Uses of Sociology". Basic Books, New York.

Leventhal, H (1970). Findings and theory in the study of fear communications. *In* "Advances in Experimental Social Psychology" (L. Berkowitz, ed.), Vol. 5. Academic Press, New York and London.

Lim, N. (1976). "Foundations of Social Research". McGraw-Hill, New York.

Oswalt, R. M. and Hoff, T. E. (1975). The motivations of blood donors and nondonors: a community survey. *Transfusion*, **15**, pp. 68–72.

Spruit, J. P., van Kampen-Donker, M. *et al.* (1976). Deelname aan een screeningsonderzoek op borst-kanker. *Intermediair*, **12**, No. 53.

Stammeyer, R. and Staallekker, L. (1977). Van goeden bloede; een sociaalpsychologisch onderzoek naar de faktoren die van invloed zijn op het donorschap. Leiden.

Tannenbaum, A. S. (1961). Control and effectiveness in a voluntary organization. *Am. J. Sociol.*, **67**, 33–46.

van de Vall, M. (1978). Het paradigma van sociaal beleidsonderzoek. Universitaire Pers, Leiden.

van de Vall, M. and Bolas, C. (1977). Policy research as an agent of planned social intervention: an evaluation of methods, standards, data and analytic techniques. *Sociological Practice*, **2**, No. 2. Human Sciences Press, New York.

van de Vall, M., Bolas, C. and Kang, T. S. (1976). Applied research in industrial organization: an evaluation of functions, theory and methods. *J. Appl. Behav. Sci.*, **12**, No. 2.

van der Vlist, R. (1970). Verschillen in groepsprestaties in de Nederlandse Zeevisserij. Wolters-Noordhoff N.V., Groningen. Dissertation.

Vos, K. (1979). Contingente voorwaarden van effectief leiderschap, een veldonderzoek onder volleybal-teams. *In* Sociale Psychologie in Nederland (J. M. F. Jaspars, and R. van der Vlist, eds.), deel II. Van Loghum Slaterus Deventer.

2

"... Nothing so Practical as a Good Theory." The Problematic Application of Social Psychology.[1]

J. Potter

Science is both a social activity and a social institution and as such it embodies an ideology which reflects its own values and interests (Layton, 1977). One function of this ideology is to present science as socially useful, as the origin of many of the things that improve our lives. If we are going to examine the realities of application we will need to map a path through this ideology and this will involve addressing four interrelated questions[2]:

(1) In what *sense* might a social psychological theory be applied?

(2) To what *extent* is social psychology ever applied?

(3) In what way are the fields of application and theorizing *separated* and what sort of *interchange* takes place between them?

(4) In what ways are theories *transformed* in the process of application?

There is a traditional notion of how science is applied which is also prevalent in social psychology. It can be viewed as a kind of ideology of application. The notion of science and application embodied in this ideology is false, or at least grossly inaccurate. Evidence to support this argument can be drawn from both the social studies of science literature and from research specifically on social science. The latter research is illustrated here in a social psychological context with a detailed case study of the utilization of theories by a practitioner in the field of social skills training. Of course one case study is not sufficient to conclusively demonstrate the falsity of a broad and in some respects diffuse notion of how social psychology is applied. However, it is hoped that it will help to stimulate further the more decisive research that is necessary.

What is meant by an "ideology of application"? This notion is intended to suggest the intimate relation held in scientific cultures to exist between science and technology; a relation between balding bespectacled men in white coats standing in front of blackboards covered with indecipherable hieroglyphics and vaccination jabs, silicon chips and Saturn Five rockets racing skywards. The very language for talking about science encourages these assumptions about the supposed connection between science and utility (Mulkay, 1979a). What scientists do is said to "have application in the real world"; bridges and non-stick frying pans are seen to be the "products" of science. Structurally this ideology suggests a continuum of research from "pure" to "applied", with knowledge "flowing" from one end to the other. The term "ideology of application" will be used interchangably with the "traditional view of application" throughout the chapter.

This ideology may seem far from disturbing. However it can be shown to penetrate much philosophy and sociology of science, certain marxist perspectives on science and it deeply infuses discussion of the application of social psychology. It is precisely this pervasiveness which makes it difficult to transcend; it is constantly liable to systematically distort attempts to study the reality of application.

Philosophers of science have generally been unconcerned with its application (Cartwrite, 1974). However, the notion that science has "products" (for which science was a necessary condition) has been used as a resource in certain debates. For example, Shapere (1971) has criticized that strongly relativistic reading of Kuhn (1962, 1970) which suggests progress in any scientific discipline to be simply a sequence of incommensurable conceptual world views. Shapere argues that science's "products" and "increased control over the world" amply demonstrate progress.

Similarly sociologists have, until recently, taken an intimacy between scientific knowledge and utility for granted (Mulkay, 1979a). In fact it has sometimes been assumed as grounds for the elimination of a full sociology of science. The rationale for this is that sociological explanation would be superfluous for any "true" belief system like science, and the truth of the system is demonstrated by its utility. Johnston (1977) has argued in this fashion:

> When we say that science "works", what we mean is that it provides us with the capacity to manipulate and control nature . . . the enormous attain-

ments of modern natural sciences . . . represent a fairly conclusive proof of their superiority over other systems invented by man . . . (pp. 23–4)

It has been held in certain traditions of Marxism that scientific knowledge should be tested in practical application and, when it is correct, would enable new forms of practice. Lenin (1976) claimed that a leap forward in knowledge is necessary for the realization of any radically new practice. These traditions have thus taken a view very like the philosophers and sociologists discussed above. Cornford (1963) is explicit on this relation between science and utilization:

> . . . up to modern times people had only *superficial knowledge* of chemical processes, *and so* there could be little effectively planned use of the processes in production. But modern chemistry *enables* us to break substances down . . . split atoms . . . even create new man-made elements. (p. 175, my emphasis)

The social psychology journals do not abound with articles discussing application. None the less this issue has been discussed and where such discussion has taken place it is possible to map the influence of the ideology of application. I will use an article by Helmreich (1975) as an example because it generated a large secondary literature (Gross, 1976) and represents a recent trend which takes Kurt Lewin as its figure-head.

Helmreich diagnoses a number of problems which beset applied social psychology: simplistic statistics, student subjects, aimless experiments; but he sees as crucial a "pernicious schism" between theoretical and applied social psychology. There are two camps of researchers:

> . . . those whose applied interests focus on theory validation in natural settings, demonstrating replicability of theoretically important findings, and making data available for application and those social psychologists who feel that the dominant concern of the profession should be social engineering and improvement of society. (p. 553)

Both, argues Helmreich, contribute to application. The former camp's work has potential for application, can be translated into practice. The latter are engaged in that practice in various ways. Awareness of this line between inquiry and implementation should, Helmreich claims, ameliorate some of the criticism of applied social psychology:

... if the line ... were drawn somewhat as I have suggested, it seems that social psychologists could work on both theoretical and applied problems in the laboratory and the field without perceiving a difference in orientation. (p. 554)

Helmreich can thus be seen as perceiving a dislocation of the "natural" continuum between theory and application and suggesting the repair of this continuum as a cure for the putative lack of social psychological application. His conclusion appears to be more a product of the ideology of application than any data he has produced to demonstrate the potential applicability of theory in social psychology.

In fact Helmreich's article is striking in the paucity of its data base, at least any data directly concerned with application. What he does present are tables of figures concerning the quantity of laboratory *vs* field studies and observational *vs* experimental methodology. He interprets the vast skew in this data towards laboratory experiments as being bad for application. However, it is hard to see how he could conclude this without some information on what forms of social psychology do lead to successful application. Turner (1981), for example, arguing in a similar indirect fashion, has come to an almost diametrically opposed conclusion with regards to laboratory experiments.

The social study of application

Chiding Helmreich for his lack of data is not meant to suggest that simply collecting data on application will drop the correct answers into our laps. Indeed deciding what kind of data would be pertinent is an extremely difficult problem. It is not sufficient to simply judge an attempted application by its results, for it is also necessary to make sure that the results are in fact a product of that application. For a long time it was assumed that the decrease in deaths from infectious diseases in this country was mainly due to innoculation programmes. Recent research, in contrast, suggests that innoculation has been only a minor factor in the disappearance of these diseases (McKeown, 1976). Also, when assessing the results of any utilization we must make sure that any breakdown is really in the context of application and not in the context of assessment.

Scientific disciplines are, of course, extremely complicated social and intellectual institutions with their own structure, communication systems and histories. To collect data "innocently" about some aspect of their functioning is to constantly risk being tainted with their institutional ideology. In the last ten or so years a group of European social scientists have outlined a broad perspective on the study of science which attempts to look more sceptically at the scientists espoused theory of their behaviour and hence examine scientific practice more closely (Barnes, 1974; Bloor, 1976; Collins, 1974; Latour and Woolgar, 1979; Mulkay, 1979b). This is often called the "social studies of science perspective".

This perspective must be distinguished from the customary meta-discussion in social psychology. Such discussion is often semi-philosophical, criticizing or defending a particular method or perspective with the aid of an implicit or outdated theory of scientific development.[3] Where this discussion is historical it often attempts to divide the history of ideas from its social context and present scientific progress as a steady accumulation of knowledge and techniques (Samelson, 1974; Weimer, 1974). The social studies of science perspective in contrast emphasizes the relevance of various sorts of empirical data and the importance of interpreting these data in the context of a theory of scientific development. It is less willing to countenance a view of scientific history as a rational and orderly development of ideas, insulated against the ravages of social forces (Barnes and Shapin, 1979).

This chapter on the application of social psychology is part of a larger project to use this social studies of science perspective to examine the present state and recent history of British social psychology. Issues concerning persuasion, consensus and theoretical change in the discipline will be addressed with the aid of a variety of data bases—journal articles, textbooks, interview transcripts, transcripts of semi-formal interaction at conferences—coupled with the theoretical orientation of the social studies of science perspective. The adoption of this standpoint will mean that, for example, there will not be much concern with questions of "truth" or "external validity". Whilst the examination of these issues and how they might in theory be related to application is important, such an approach still makes many possibly unwarranted assumptions about scientific practice and the nature of application (Law, 1975).

Separation and interchange between theory and application

The social studies of science literature on the separation and interchange between science and technology is contradictory (Layton, 1977). However it is clear that the traditional model of application, which portrays technology as simply applied science, has a very poor fit to the evidence. For example, Sherwin and Isenson (1967) tried to pinpoint the site of innovation in U.S. weapons systems (for which there had been an expenditure of ten billion dollars on science research). Their findings suggested that 91% of innovations originated from inside technology itself and only 9% came from scientific research events"; and of these scientific "events" only 0·3% were in basic or pure science. There was no suggestion that the 0·3% of innovations that came from pure science were any different in quality from the 91% from outside science.

Mulkay (1979a) argues that the fields of knowledge and utility are separated in important ways and that interchange has in the past been greatly overestimated:

> . . . the "literatures" of science and technology tend to remain distinctly separate, with little cross-referencing and with significantly different patterns of internal citation. As far as we can tell from citation analysis, science seems to accumulate mainly on the basis of past science, and technology primarily on the basis of past technology. (p. 69)

Blume and Sinclair (1973), in a case study of British university chemists, produce evidence which is in line with this conclusion. Chemists who work closely with industry and the problems of industrial science were found to be relatively unproductive. They also received poor evaluations from their peers. They comment that:

> British industry seems to have the attention of a minority of academic chemists whose committment to the scientific community is at the same time reduced. (p. 131)

How true is this situation of social psychology? If we take the "Journal of Applied Social Psychology" and the Deutsch and Hornstein (1975) collection of papers on application it is possible to see a range of different degrees of separation between the social "problem issue" and the attempt to confront it in research. At one extreme a study by Walton (1975) describes the implementation of a scheme to "attack boredom and alienation" in a dog food plant by a "radical structuring" of its work-force. He uses social theory in an extremely diffuse manner with a pragmatic emphasis:

> Why groups? My early exposure to the ideas of Mayo, Roethlinsberger, and Homans at Harvard, my knowledge of the work of Lewin and others in the group dynamics field, and more importantly, my direct experience with T-groups has impressed me with the power of groups—to provide their members with social satisfaction and individual identification, to develop goals, norms, and the capacities for self management. (p. 142)

The other extreme may be represented by Page and Moss's (1976) study of the influence of lighting on aggression. Here student subjects took part in a laboratory experiment using a traditional aggression paradigm ("teacher", "learner" and Buss aggression machine). The relationship between three variables: proximity, lighting and aggression was studied and they claimed their data to be "suggestive of the possibility" that better street lighting "may" reduce crime.

It is important to be reminded here of the distinction between applied social psychology and social psychology which is potentially applicable introduced by Helmreich (1975). Walton's intervention can be seen to be applied psychology and Page and Moss' paper to be potentially applicable social psychology. In the "Journal of Applied Social Psychology" the vast majority of studies fall into the category of applicable rather than applied research. If we look at this in terms of the most simple of models of application (Fig. 1) nearly all the studies ter-

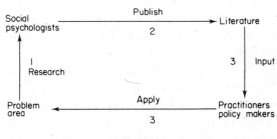

Fig. 1

minate after stage 2; stages 3 and 4 are presumably taken as unproblematic.[4] In the Deutsch and Hornstein volume there were more examples which were actually followed through the cycle, but there was still a majority which terminated after stage 2. Helmreich argues that the basic role of social psychologists is to impartially produce findings which are applicable, not necessarily applied, and thus can be seen to implicitly condone this situation. In a sense this is almost tautological and beyond reproach. However the choice of which research to call potentially applicable is, it will now be suggested, problematic.

There are various reasons why we should look critically at any claim that the social relevance of social psychology is demonstrated by the quantity of potentially applicable research. Clearly to call any research potentially applicable assumes that it could, given the right conditions, be put into effective practice. If the traditional view of scientific application is accepted then potential applicability is seen as unproblematic;

research will produce "truthful" statements with "external validity" about "entities" or "processes" of some kind. These truthful statements—laws or theories—will be utilized by practitioners, perhaps with the aid of an examination of the social context within which they will be used. However, this picture of science has not fared well under the serious empirical examination it has undergone in the last few years. It can no longer stand simply as a taken-for-granted legitimation of the social relevance of social psychological research described as applicable.

The traditional view of science does not provide criteria for deciding which research will be potentially applicable. It is not possible to clearly specify a particular body of applicable research from the mass of social psychological research. What appears to happen in practice is that certain areas of research are seen to be concerned with certain social problems. This allows them to be labeled potentially applicable. For example, to label a piece of work "prejudice research" may give an aura of applicability denied "decision making" research. Without research on the process of application and its social consequences such claims of applicability are insufficiently grounded.

A related argument for the significance of applicable research, which is also derived from the traditional view of science, claims that truth or validity is a necessary (but not sufficient) condition for successful application (Turner, 1981). It is not difficult, however, to produce counter examples, cases where a theory now universally considered to be false is successfully utilized. Mulkay (1979a) notes that medieval alchemists and Babylonian mythological astronomers successfully implemented theories which would now be considered false, if not hare-brained. Bloor (1981) gives a more specific example:

> In 1804 the Cornish engineer Arthur Woolf patented a new form of steam engine. The basis of the patent was a law of steam expansion that would appear to be completely wrong. By 1814 after some trial and error Woolf's engine was producing performances that one modern authority says "represented something like a 100 per cent improvement on the best performance of the Watt low pressure engine."

In the case study later in this chapter we find an example of a theory which is seen both as false, or at least an insufficient explanation of the phenomenon and effective in practice (see p. 41 below).

Finally there is a much more prosaic reason to doubt the social importance of a body of research which is potentially rather than actually applicable. Social psychologists frequently lament that members of their discipline ignore work which is more than a few years old (e.g. Steiner, 1974). If this is correct then any piece of research which is not quickly used is destined for perpetual obscurity along with the one in two journal articles which are never cited or even read (Cole and Cole, 1973). Perhaps much of the hard work of social psychology is wasted.

A case study of applied social psychology

The examination of the four questions which introduced this chapter will involve literature from both the social studies of science and the social study of social science. Central to the analysis, however, will be a case study of how one practitioner, in the field of social skills training, utilizes theories in his work.

Social skills training has been arguably the area of most growth in applied social psychology in recent years. The number of practitioners at present doing this work in Britain is in the hundreds. A range of social skills are taught in a variety of different settings. It is probably most commonly associated with clinical work where people who are socially inadequate in various ways are taught basic skills such as shopping, dating, opening conversations and posture. At the other extreme business men may be trained in handling clients and subordinates. Social skills training is also used in the penal services, by councillors of all kinds, and in women's groups as "assertion training".

Social skills training involves a variety of techniques. One of the most common is "role play" where the client is taught a skill or a set of skills by acting out a particular role. For example, a client may act out the role of buying groceries from the supermarket. This may involve the trainer emphasizing that the client adopts normal posture whilst shopping, makes appropriate conversation whilst paying for the groceries, accompanied by eye contact which is neither staring nor furtive.

Typically it is theories of non-verbal communication and non-verbal behaviour which are associated with social skills; there is not the same amount of theoretical development in the area of verbal skills. To give a commonplace example, Hall (1966) suggests that there are various normal distances for standing apart from others. These depend on the interactants' degree of intimacy, the number of people present and the public or private nature of the situation. It is only a small step from talking about correct distances for interaction to attempting to train people with problems how to stand at the correct distances.

There are a number of reasons why social skills training should serve as a particularly apposite case study of the application of social psychology. First, as noted above, there is a relatively clearly defined set of theoretical work associated with the area. It thus seems, *a priori*, to be an area where the traditional model of scientific application should hold true. Secondly it is a clearly social psychological area of application. It can be argued that social psychological attempts to deal with prejudice, for example, or unemployment may be ineffective because they try to deal with essentially political or economic problems as if they were social psychological. No utilization is fully immune from such criticisms, but they seem less relevant to social skills training. Thirdly, as a relatively new field it might be easier to trace the theoretical involvement in its origins and practice. Also, compared to say advertising or organizational interventions, the impact of interventions might be more clearly assessed.

The particular respondent was chosen because of his respected position within the community of social skills trainers. He was legitimized by having a university and a hospital based position—which involved him in both teaching and clinical practice—and by contributing to conferences and the literature of social skills training.

It is important, if this case study is to be persuasive, that the respondent's practice was not deviant in any ways related to his use of theory. Of course only a full scale empirical analysis of social skills trainers could make certain that this was the case. However, no reason was found to doubt that his practice was considered anything but top rate amongst social skills trainers. There was no hint from the interview that the respondent's practice was unusual in any way.

The study was carried out by constructing a fairly simple theoretical model of the relationship between theory and application with the aid of the social studies of science literature. This was used to construct a detailed interview schedule built around 32 basic questions. The respondent was assured anonymity and was interviewed for about $1^3/4$ hours, covering the questions on the schedule. Subsequently the recording of the interview was fully transcribed. The transcript was content analysed according to the various topics picked out by the model. Then the statements under each topic were sorted into those that corroborated and those that detracted from the model.

Clearly this case study is not an empirical survey of the use of theory in social skills training; nor is it intended to be. It is hoped that it will illustrate the complex processes hidden behind the notion of "applying a theory of social psychology". Many readers will be able to compare the responses with their own experience of applying social psychology and will thus be well equipped to assess the validity of the conclusions.

SYNCHRONIC INTERCHANGE BETWEEN THEORY AND APPLICATION

A marked separation between theory and practice was apparent in the respondent's account of his work in social skills training. It was possible for the respondent to describe some interchange but it did not conform to the traditional model of application, where knowledge is simply implemented with certain adjustments for the context.

The following section from the interview shows the point at which the interviewer first broached the question of theory in social skills training:

1. (a) *Interviewer*. What would you say were the important theories that you use in social skills training?
   (b) (pause).
   (c) *Respondent*. Important *theories*?
   (d) *Interviewer*. Yes.
   (e) *Respondent*. I suppose it's a learning theory model really, or what I consider learning theory to be. I see social skills training very much, really, as based on an educational model. It is *skills* training. And one can relate it much more to an education type viewpoint, which is based on learning theory.
   (f) *Interviewer*. And how about the particular theories of Argyle and Dean on gaze and Ekman and Birdwhistell on kinesics and so on?
   (g) *Respondent*. I don't take much notice of those I must admit. I mean, obviously their stuff is very useful in providing information, and in terms of instructing clients one usually gives a talk on, say eye gaze, and that may draw on the work of Argyle to just indicate the way in which eye gaze is used.

How are we to disentangle what is going on in this interchange? To do this we must go back to the notion of an ideology of application and introduce the idea of scientists using more than one conceptual system for accounting for their activity.

Gilbert and Mulkay (1980) have looked at the ways in which biochemists, from a particular subfield of their discipline, give accounts of their activity. More specifically they compared the formal accounts given in the biochemists' published work with informal accounts given in letters and interviews. Striking dissimilarities between the two accounts were found to be the rule. For example, in formal accounts experimental data were always given *both* logical and chronological priority, whilst informally this same data might be described as *following* from some theory or speculation. The authors go on to give other examples demonstrating a systematic difference between the formal and informal accounts. This difference, they argue, is significant in that it corresponds to a difference between concepts of scientific knowledge. The formal account follows a traditional empiricism, whilst the informal account intimately involves social and particularistic events in the process of arriving at data.

Coming back to the social skills transcript, we can see the influence of two accounting systems at work here also. One corresponds roughly to what has been called the ideology of application; the other to what Gilbert and Mulkay call the informal account.

At the start of the interaction [1. (a), (b) and (c)] the respondent is non-plussed by the interviewer's question which *assumes* the idea that theories are employed in social skills training. The respondent then, somewhat tentatively, proposed an example: "I *suppose* it's a learning theory model *really*" [1. (e), my emphasis]. However, this proposal is then qualified as only the respondent's interpretation of the theory: "what *I consider* learning theory to be" [1. (e), my emphasis]. Social skills training is then distanced from learning theory by proposing an intermediate model: "I see social skills training as based on an educational model" [1. (e)]. The initial proposition has now been twice qualified. Then the respondent emphasizes that it is "*skills* training" [1. (e)], which seems intended to suggest that it, therefore, must involve learning theory. This final point can hardly be viewed as a reply from experience, it seems almost philosophical in nature.

In the next interchange the respondent is questioned about more directly social psychological theories. He produces an apparently contradictory reply: "I don't take much notice of those" and "obviously their stuff is very useful" [both in 1. (g)]. However it is possible to see these comments not as straightforward contradictions but as products of different accounting systems. One system, the ideology of application, embodies the notion that relevant theories are "obviously . . . very useful"; whilst the respondent's informal account suggests that this is not the case, that theories were not found useful.

The initial interchange can also be looked at in this way. On the one hand the ideology of application (which was already embodied in the interviewer's question) suggests that an answer should be provided. On the other, the respondent is not happy with this, in the context of an informal account, and qualifies the reply in the ways discussed.

The pattern analysed above is not unique to the interview. For example a similar analysis may be performed on the following interaction:

2. *Interviewer.* Have changes in theory, or improvements in those theories inputed into your practice in any way at all?
(pause)
Respondent. I think they have. They inevitably have. But I don't think I have consciously applied them. Certainly in terms of one's reading and correcting one's knowledge. That obviously is used in terms of what you do, when you are working, in fact. But I can't say that I have consciously taken them and applied them.

Here we see that the input of theory into practice is "certain", "inevitable" and "obvious". And yet within the space of a few seconds the respondent twice notes that there was no conscious application. Again the apparent contradiction can be resolved by seeing these utterances as products of two different accounting systems. In suggesting that the respondent uses two systems to answer questions there is intended no implication that he is reasoning poorly or contradicting himself. He is simply drawing upon two commonplace resources for answering the questions; experience of application and a taken-for-granted theoretical understanding of application.

Later in the interview the respondent was more explicit about the problem of talking about the use of theories:

3. *Respondent.* I think why I find it difficult to think about the theories is that I am not familiar with the field from a theoretical point of view.

The respondent here straightforwardly describes his knowledge of theories in a way very difficult to reconcile with the ideology of application. It seems difficult to believe that the respondent could be both applying certain theories *and* be unfamiliar with those theories.

The analysis of this section illustrates that the apparently contradictory statements by the respondent can be made intelligible by viewing them as a product of two inconsistent accounting systems. The traditional view of application is consistent with those statements described as the ideology of application. This is hardly surprising if we see the traditional view as generating these statements. The informal account on the other hand does not fit well with the traditional view. The respondent found it hard to give specific instances of theories which he had utilized. This point will be elaborated in the next section.

DIACHRONIC INTERCHANGE BETWEEN THEORY AND APPLICATION

It was suggested above that theory and application should be considered as different social contexts. Both of these contexts seem to accumulate separately, each building primarily on its own history. The traditional view, however, implies that continual interchange between the different social contexts is the characteristic feature of applied science. Not only that but the direction of interchange is predominantly from science to technology; problems are solved in the context of science and then the answer is used in the context of application. Information about these longitudinal features of interchange is unfortunately scant. The social skills case study, however, proved to be a rich source of data relevant to this question.

The respondent and an associate had developed a package for social skills training:

> 4. *Interviewer.* You say you use a package. Is this something that you developed yourself in practice?
> *Respondent.* This is something we have developed ourselves . . . the package we have worked out over the years, and we use the same basic format for each session and we just use different exercises; change the exercises but the format of most of the sessions is exactly the same.
> *Interviewer.* Now, you say you have modified your procedure in various ways. Has this modification come mainly from your own experience of trying to do it or through the changing literature of social skills?
> *Respondent.* Through our own experience, that's all. Because the basic material and the basic techniques that we use are the same really. It's just that with a group you have got the added dimension of having a group and, you know, all that that involves. And one has to introduce things other than strictly speaking social skills methods to make it function as a group [inaudible]. So we have really modified things from our own experience.

The interviewer's questions in this interaction were quite broad, referring not just to utilization of social psychological theory but also to the general literature on social skills training. Even so it is clearly experience that is seen to be the crucial or possibly the sole factor in the development of the respondent's practice. If we look more closely at this passage, and note the nature of the exercises referred to, we can see that social psychological theory could only have indirect relevance. The exercises comprise the clients, for example, reporting a good thing that had happened to them recently, or role playing an every-day encounter for the group to give feedback. Teaching such exercises is as much a craft skill as the product of a theory and it seems unlikely that the ability to teach these exercises could be fully communicated in a completely formalized literature. In fact the respondent suggested that those who attempted to set up social skills groups with only knowledge of the literature, without any training and experience of the "behavioural approach", often ran very poor training sessions:

> 5. *Respondent.* Some of them are already doing it [running social skills groups without experience or training]. They have read Argyle and Trower's book and they have started. . . .
>
> *Interviewer.* And you think it would be very difficult for someone who has just taken a part of the literature—or something like Argyle and Trower's book—rather than talked to people who have been in clinical practice, to be very successful at it?
>
> *Respondent.* What happens you see is that—I will give you a typical example. We are in a day hospital setting and we have got all these patients; why not social skills training? And so they take anybody indiscriminately into the group. They don't assess. They just take them into the group. And they look at a couple of Argyle exercises. They may look at so and so's feeling about so and so. And that's the way they operate . . . they may well do some good, somewhere, but you don't really know what the hell they are doing. And they may do some harm.

The fact that the knowledge needed to carry out social skills training is not fully available from literary sources does not imply that such knowledge is not tacit in the literature. It may be that practitioners who already possess certain skills and knowledge may read the literature in a different way. The important point is that this knowledge is not completely formalized; the literature on both the theory of social skills and practice of social skills training seems to be insufficient on its own for carrying out social skills training.

With regard to the feedback into theory of knowledge acquired through the practice of social skills training the respondent said that British trainers "are not interested in theory as such". However, he did suggest that a contribution to the theoretical literature was a possibility:

> 6. *Interviewer.* Do you think that the results of clinical practice like yours could have an important role in evaluating theories, I mean, if you were interested in it?
>
> *Respondent.* Yes, I am almost sure it could. Yes of course it could. If one were prepared to do a lot of painstaking work. I mean, just thinking

about eye gaze, if one really looked at that in the context of social skills
work I am sure you could get an enormous amount of data to feed back.
And it would challenge most of the ideas, because most of the experimental work has been done out of context. It would be very nice to replicate
that. Not that social skills is a very real context, but it is a different context that one might use.

The respondent here describes an inadequacy in what he sees as a central area of the theoretical literature of social skills. This again supports
the claim that these ideas are not *straightforwardly* applied by the respondent. The explanation given by the respondent for the inadequacy of
the theoretical work on gaze is also significant for the argument of this
chapter. This explanation is in terms of the "reality" of the context in
which research is undertaken. The argument seems to be that the more
real the context the more correct the results. Thus the respondent himself has a notion of the context dependence of research. Unfortunately
the transcript does not contain enough information to decide how
elaborated the respondent's ideas are.

In one place in the interview the respondent discussed a theoretical
issue which they had "directly addressed":

> 7. *Respondent.* In the early days we were very much interested in the differ-
> ence between social anxiety and social behaviour. And we assumed that
> social skills was much more suitable for people who have social skills de-
> ficits, behavioural deficits, and it wasn't particularly suitable, say, for
> social phobics whose fear of social situations was based on anxiety rather
> than lack of skills. And so our assessment in the early days was really
> geared to looking at that. And we used to give them measures of social
> anxiety as well as social skills to see if there was any difference between the
> two. And what we tended to find was that social anxiety reduced as social
> behaviour improved [both laugh]. Even in our early groups. And as we
> proceeded it became increasingly clear that the two hold together. And
> now we don't worry about distinguishing between the two.

Here the respondent had assumed that the theoretical distinction between social behaviour and social anxiety would be important for practice. This was not found to be the case.

On the whole the case study material is in line with the general research on scientific disciplines. Interchange in either direction, between the contexts of basic research and of utilization, was not easily
demonstrable. Modification in social skills training procedures was
seen to come from experience in practice rather than the literature of
social skills. The fact that people attempting to do social skills work
solely from the literature run into problems suggests a certain amount of

tacit knowledge or craft skill is involved. This implies that experience of a *tradition* of social skills work is important. The evaluation of theories in practice was mooted as a possibility but not done by the respondent.

Transformation of fact and theory in the process of application

Philosophers of science in the tradition of Kuhn (1962, 1970) and Hanson (1965) have been less willing than their predecessors to talk of facts and theories as stable, unnegotiable, objects. For example Ravetz (1971) suggests that facts and theories undergo radical reinterpretation when they pass from the contexts of pure science to those of practical application:

> ... it can be seen that a version of a standardised fact which is good enough for one function can be quite inadequate for another ... (p. 202)

Social studies of science researchers have examined this argument about the contextualization of facts and theories empirically (Gilbert, 1976; Collins and Pinch, 1981; Latour and Woolgar, 1979). Mulkay (1979a) concludes that:

> ... the formulations of basic science ... undergo major transformations of meaning as they come nearer to the realm of application. (p. 71)

Some theories, of course, explicitly predict contextual changes: acceleration is not expected to be constant in different gravitational fields; cognitive dissonance is only expected to result where experimental subjects have a choice of different responses (Linder *et al.*, 1976). The transformations referred to by Mulkay, however, are not of this kind; they are changes in the theories themselves.

If major transformations such as this were a ubiquitous feature of social psychological application it might suggest a need for re-thinking the role of pure research in applied settings. Van der Vlist (this volume) discusses some research which suggests that pure social psychological research is relatively unsuccessful—when compared to less formalized research—in terms of impact on policy. He suggests that the central problem concerns translation between "scientific concepts" and "dependent variables", and he proffers a solution of his own.

A striking example of such contextualization of theories is provided by Wood (1980). He has looked at the application of four contrasting theories of child development, those of Piaget, Chomsky, Bernstein and

Vygotsky, and has found that when those theories were actually utilized in the teaching process there was a "marked degree" of agreement. Thus, despite the very large theoretical divergence, in the context of application these differences were obscured in practice.

The transformation of theories cannot be straightforwardly demonstrated with the social skills case study because there is no instance where the respondent is unambiguously claiming to use a particular theory. None the less there is information relating to this phenomenon in the case study.

Perhaps the most direct example of social psychological theory in use is illustrated in the following quote:

> 8. *Respondent.* If we are working on posture or eye gaze we would use an explanation—or the theory if you like—the instructions about posture and why it is important.

First of all we must note that it is not clear in this quote whether the respondent was referring to theory in the sense of a theory in the literature. He may be referring to a more pragmatic understanding or "theory in practice"; the "explanation" is perhaps being redescribed as a theory *for the interviewer*. The respondent does, however, imply that formal social psychological theories are related to this task in quote 1 (g) above. We perhaps clarify this ambiguity by noting that the respondent thought that there were problems with the work on gaze—see quote 6 above. Taking these three quotes together does seem to indicate that there is some modification of the theories when they are used for explanation and instructions to clients. This cannot be conclusively demonstrated in the interview.

At a more general, and less theoretical level it is possible to see the phenomenon of translation more clearly. The respondent referred to the Argyle approach, sometimes as a body of literature, sometimes as a set of practices. Whilst the respondent clearly felt that he was using, at least to some extent, an Argyle type approach he considered the emphasis to be different in significant ways:

> 9. *Respondent.* I don't accept the idea that there are basic social skills and that we all have them, that we can then teach if they seem to be deficient in some way. I don't believe in teaching people particular ways of behaving. I believe in providing people with enough practice so that they can *use* their skills in whatever way *they* feel is useful to them in order to achieve their needs; which I think is a different emphasis really from the Argyle approach.

The distinction the respondent is making between his approach and Argyle's seems to be between, on the one hand, giving clients practice in using a *variety* of skills which can then be used in any way they please and, on the other, teaching them a *universal* set of skills appropriate for each particular situation. Unfortunately it is not clear from the interview whether the respondent has taken something like an Argyle approach and then transformed it in his own practice, or whether he is simply describing a difference between their respective approaches.

Another candidate for the role of a classically applied theory in the respondent's practice—as illustrated in quote 1 (e)—is learning theory. The respondent suggested that this might be a prerequisite for doing efficient social skills training:

> 10. *Respondent.* The problem that we have in training non-psychologists is that they don't know what the behavioural approach is, they have never actually assessed problems in the sort of detail that is necessary. They are not used to even looking at behaviour as such.

However, when elaborating on this point later in the interview the respondent suggested some problems with the behavioural approach:

> 11. *Respondent.* I think I see a lot of problems myself with things like conversational skills. O.K., you might teach someone a set of skills of how one might go about having a conversation. The assumed goal is that there is some end point, but, in fact, half the pleasure of having a conversation is just having the conversation with someone . . . I suppose what I am saying, in a very confused way, is that the behavioural model isn't a sufficient explanation of social behaviour. Social skills training is really based on learning theory. I think it works, but at a theoretical level it is not a sufficient explanation for what is happening.

It seems, then, that the behavioural approach is not simply a theory put into practice; certain craft skills are hinted at—detailed assessment, looking at patients' problems in a certain way—whilst *as a theory* the approach was seen as insufficient.

The respondent was aware of one sort of transformation that took place in practice. This is where methods are interpreted differently from different general perspectives:

> 12. *Respondent.* Because it is such a bandwaggon using social skills, quite a lot of people, are misusing it . . . To give you an example; they might get somebody to role play being assertive and they will get them to do the

> role play and then they will start asking them how they felt about it and
> go into the feeling, the dynamics . . . That is using a different sort of
> model to get at it.
> *Interviewer*. Would someone from an analytic perspective—a
> psychoanalytic perspective—interpret the theories on gaze and body
> positions, and so on, in terms of a different kind of framework?
> *Respondent*. Yes. You see there is a lot of overlap with other sorts of
> activity-type therapies. I mean drama, psychodrama, there is an awful
> lot of it going on . . . you might get people doing very similar sorts of
> exercises, but they will use them in an interpretative way. They will not
> be trying to teach the client behaviours.

Despite the formulation of the question in terms of theories of gaze and
body positions the reply is concerned with practical social skills exercises. It is these that are seen to have different meanings depending on
the perspective within which they are used.

The lack of any clear-cut utilization of theory by the respondent
makes it difficult to talk in specific terms about his transformation of
theories in application. However, as I have illustrated, there are a
number of sections of the interview which are indirectly relevant. The
respondent mentioned the theory of gaze as one which would be found
wanting in the practical context of social skills groups. In contrast he
mentioned learning theory as a theory that worked in practice but was,
as a theory, insufficient for explaining what was happening. This indicates that the respondent did not necessarily hold that something which
is sufficient in one context must be sufficient for the other; which
suggests that translation may be necessary when theories are moved between contexts.

The societal context of theory and application

Up to now I have looked at problems of the relation between theory and
utilization arising from social processes *within* science. The literature
which has been reviewed on science and social science, and the social
skills case study, suggest that many problems with the application of
social psychology arise from interchange between the different social
contexts of scientific theorizing and application. It was traditionally argued that the social processes within science are important only so far
as they sustain the conditions for the production of truthful scientific
knowledge and explain false scientific beliefs (Merton, 1957). The last

decade of social research on science has, however, been able to demonstrate social processes at work in what were previously considered to be the most mechanical, routinized aspects of the hardest of sciences (Gilbert and Mulkay, 1980).

It is also possible to chart the input of extra-scientific social processes into the scientific field. In case studies of research findings and theories which are relevant to broader societal issues the pervasiveness of different social interests has been clearly demonstrated. To give just one recent example, Kopp (1979) has studied the American debate over fall-out hazard conducted between scientists with interests in the Atomic Energy Commission (either economic or official) and scientists who were critical of the AEC. Kopp emphasizes the complexity of the political and institutional interests involved and notes how the AEC scientists chose to characterize risk in terms of percentage *increase* in risk. Their critics, on the other hand, used a measure of likely number of deaths resulting from the increase in the radioactive background. The AEC scientists can be seen to have chosen a measure or risk that made it appear minimal. Their critics chose an alternative measure which was far more psychologically salient.

As far as social psychology is concerned the quantity of work illustrating the impact of societal interests on theorizing is steadily growing (Buss, 1979). For example, Lubek (1979) has attempted to make explicit some of the assumptions tacit in North American aggression research. In particular he notes a tendency to look for sources of violence within individuals, as opposed to seeing them as products of particular institutional structures:

> . . . it would appear that whatever aggressive acts an individual may commit, they are never performed against a societal backdrop devoid of violent elements. Yet few theories of violence, especially in social psychology, actually begin with an examination of the societal milieu; rather they focus on the assumption that the causes of aggression can be sought within the individual. (p. 270)

Thus he is arguing that there is a congruence between U.S. aggression research and the individualistic ideology predominant in the U.S.

At a slightly different level, Platt (1976) has interviewed British social researchers working for businesses or agencies. She found a number of instances where researchers have been asked to change the tone of a concluding paragraph, or have had their results reinterpreted.

On some occasions their research has been "buried" forever because the results were in conflict with the funding bodies' goals.

The role of the broader societal context in social skills training can be seen in the various sections of the interview concerned with the popularity of social skills training. The respondent's explanation indicates that the burgeoning popularity of the field does not arise from purely scientific considerations.

Social skills training is seen to fit with a growing trend in the social services towards community-based treatment:

> 13. *Respondent*. I would think that people are, in most of the services, becoming much more community orientated. In other words getting away from some sort of institutional model of dealing with problems, punishing for crime and so on. And they are moving much more into the ideal of working with the community in trying to rehabilitate them. And that assumes that you have got to teach these people how they are going to fit into society, into their community. And I suppose the idea of then improving on social skills is one way of making it fit the model you use.

The respondent points out that there is a move away from punishment towards rehabilitation. The propriety of this trend is not decided by scientific factors for it is a moral and political issue. At another level of analysis it might be desirable to study the influence of economic factors on this trend towards community care. For example the relative thrift of community care, in contrast to institutional care, may make it a much more attractive alternative in times of economic recession. As with the Kopp example, social interests may be seen as selecting and encouraging certain orientations from the available possibilities.

The attention shown by the Women's Movement in social skills training was seen as another factor influencing growth:

> 14. *Respondent*. One of the areas in which it is widely used is in assertion training for women. That is very much the thing in the Women's Movement. And assertion training in Britain has almost become synonymous with women's groups.

Thus any attempt to fully explain the increase in the popularity of social skills training in this country might have to take into account the particular interests of the Women's Movement.

The respondent also suggested that the social skills trainer's stance towards their clients might aid its popularity because of its emphasis on internal locus of control:

15. *Respondent.* . . . they see it as a less mechanical process than the other approach, and they see it as a way of people getting or achieving goals for themselves. I suppose that there is the implication that it is moving towards a more internally locus of control type behaviour therapy, in the sense that the individuals tend to have goals and are given the skills with which to achieve those goals.

This was not, however, seen as a feature of Argyle's approach. Here again it is some extra-scientific factor rather than any breakthrough in theory that is seen as leading to the popularity of social skills training.

It is not easy to make explicit the role of diffuse social interests in the scientific field. They are rarely so clear cut as in the Kopp example. Despite this it is plain that broad social factors are at work in the recent popularity of social skills. A larger scale study than the present one would be needed to clarify the influence at work and to assess whether they have had any impact on the content of the practice and theory rather than just its popularity.

To talk of the role of societal interests in research is not necessarily to talk of bias and hidden influence. It is possible to formally explicate the relativity of research goals and procedures to particular social interests. For example, Stringer (1979) clarifies the complex relation between political and social analyses of crowding and the way these are related to the formulation of the problem and desirability of certain solutions. However, such explication is rare and many social psychologists take the research process and results to be neutral with regard to interventions.

Conclusions

Up to now the emphasis of this chapter has been on the nature of utilization as actually practiced; there has been no intention to claim that this is necessarily the most effective form social psychological utilization may take. The social skills case study certainly suggests effective practice can be compatible with a style of application of theories which is very far removed from the traditional model. However it is possible that, in other cases, a more stringent enforcement of the traditional model would result in more effective practice. What is needed is more empirical work to explore this possibility.

Any empirical study of application will have to face up to the complexity of its subject. The traditional notion that theories are decontextualized entities has been uprooted. They must instead be looked at as fully situated; first within the institutional context of science, and all that entails, and secondly, within more diffuse social, political and economic contexts. The interests of the participants cannot be properly ignored (the disinterested scientist is an ideological veneer). It is not hard to conceive of theories being used as a gloss on application which has been undertaken for quite different reasons. At the same time we want to be sure that it makes sense to identify the theory as applied with the theory as described in the scientific literature. It may be found that theories, when they are involved in utilization, are transformed so much in the process that it is no longer sensible to make this identification. It is also important to remember that a "false" or scientifically discredited theory might lead to effective practice.

There are a number of tentative conclusions which can be derived from the literature on the social studies of science and which have been illustrated here in relation to social psychology by reference to social skills training:

(1) Interchange between theory and application is less common than might be expected from traditional models of application.

(2) Utilization tends to be grounded in previous practice rather than theory.

(3) Changes in applied social psychology tend to originate in practice rather than any change in theory.

(4) The idea that applicable—as opposed to applied—research could be used to justify the social relevance of social psycholology should be examined more closely.

(5) Where theories are utilized the social context of application leads to a transformation of those theories.

(6) Broad social interests have an impact on theory application.

Whilst being non-prescriptive in themselves these conclusions support the claim that debates about the application of social psychology have not done justice to the complicated realities of application. They also imply that statements like Lewin's, used as the title of this chapter, are surely in need of justification and explication. The ambiguous nature of "a good theory" and the term "practical" allow Lewin's aphorism to be pinned to virtually any modern psychology. There is, as yet, no empirical justification for viewing an increase in the use of theories by social psychologists (Potter, forthcoming) as unproblematically good for applied social psychology.

The study of the application of social psychology may eventually enable us to properly address many of the unanswered questions about applied social psychology. Answering these questions may then help us to decide whether our discipline is really the positive and critical social force that many would like.

Notes

1. I am deeply indebted to Margaret Wetherell, Peter Stringer and Mike Mulkay whose ideas appear in the paper at various different levels. All three have put considerable time into ironing out some of the confusions. Dick Eiser and John Lockwood have also made helpful comments. I am also very grateful to my respondent who gave up valuable time to discuss his work. This research has been supported by the UK Social Science Research Council.
2. Throughout the paper I assume that social psychology is a science.
3. To talk, for example, of a new paradigm for viewing social phenomena, or the importance of theory in the development of the discipline, is to make implicit assumptions about the nature of science. Often these assumptions are so widely taken-for-granted as to be invisible.
4. This model is a gross oversimplification of an extremely complicated system and should not be taken as anything more than a clarificatory device. Clearly social psychologists do not research the problem area, as the arrow might suggest, but work with various representations of it.

References

Barnes, B. (1974). "Scientific Knowledge and Sociological Theory". Routledge, London.

Barnes, B. and Shapin, S. (1979). "Natural Order: Historical Studies of Scientific Culture". Sage, London and Beverly Hills, California.

Bloor, D. (1976). "Knowledge and Social Imagery". Routledge and Kegan Paul, London.

Bloor, D. (1981). Durkheim and Mauss revisited; classification and the sociology of knowledge. In "The Language of Sociology" (J. Law, ed.). Sociological Review Monographs, University of Keele.

Blume, S. and Sinclair, R. (1973). Chemists in British universities. Am. Sociol. Rev. 38, 126–38.

Buss, A. R. (1979). "Psychology in Social Context". Irvington, New York.

Cartwrite, N. D. (1974). How do we apply science? In "Boston Studies", Vol. 32 (R. S. Cohen, C. A. Hooker, A. C. Michalos and J. W. van Evra, eds). Reidel, Boston.

Cole, S. and Cole, J. (1973). "Social Stratification in Science". University of Chicago Press, London and Chicago.

Collins, H. M. (1974). The TEA set; tacit knowledge and scientific networks. *Sci. Studies* **4**, 165–85.

Collins, H. M. and Pinch (1980). "Science and the Spoon Benders: Frames of Meaning and Extraordinary Science" (in preparation).

Cornford, M. (1963). "Theory of Knowledge". Lawrence and Wishart, London.

Deutsch, M. and Hornstein, H. A. (1975). "Applying Social Psychology". Lawrence Erlbaum, Hillsdale, N.J.

Gilbert, G. N. (1976). The transformation of research findings into scientific knowledge. *Soc. Studies Sci.* **8**, 281–306.

Gilbert, G. N. and Mulkay, M. (1980). Contexts of scientific discourse: Social accounting in experimental papers. *In* "The Social Process of Scientific Investigation" (K. D. Knorr, R. Krohn and R. Whitley, eds). Reidel, Dordrecht.

Gross, A. E. (1976). Applied social psychology—problems and prospects; some responses to Helmreich. *Person. Soc. Psychol. Bull.* **2**, 114–5.

Hall, E. (1966). "The Hidden Dimension". Doubleday, New York.

Hanson, N. R. (1965). "Patterns of Discovery". Cambridge University Press, Cambridge.

Helmreich, R. (1975). Applied social psychology: the unfulfilled promise. *Person. Soc. Psychol. Bull.* **1**, 548–60.

Johnston, R. (1977). "Science and Rationality", Pt. 2. SISCON, Manchester.

Kopp, C. (1979). The origins of the American scientific debate over fallout hazards. *Soc. Studies Sci.* **9**, 403–22.

Kuhn, T. S. (1962, 1970). "The Structure of Scientific Revolutions". University of Chicago Press, Chicago and London.

Law, J. (1975). Is epistemology redundant? A sociological view. *Phil. Soc. Sci.* **5**, 317–37.

Latour, B. and Woolgar, S. (1979). "Laboratory Life: The Social Construction of Scientific Facts". Sage, London and Beverly Hills, California.

Layton, E. (1977). Conditions for technological development. *In* "Science, Technology and Society" (I. Spiegel-Rosing and D. J. de Solla Price, eds). Sage, London and Beverly Hills, California.

Lenin, V. I. (1976). "Materialism and Empirico-criticism". Foreign Languages Press, Peking.

Linder, D. E., Cooper, J. and Jones, E. E. (1976). Decision freedom as a determinant of the role of incentive magnitude in attitude change. *J. Person. Soc. Psychol.* **6**, 245–54.

Lubek, I. (1979). A brief psychological analysis of research on aggression in social psychology. *In* "Psychology in Social Context" (A. P. Buss, ed.). Irvington, New York.

McKeown, T. (1976). "The Modern Rise of Population". Arnold, London.

Merton, R. K. (1957). "Social Theory and Social Structure". The Free Press, New York.

Mulkay, M. (1979a). Knowledge and utility; implications for the sociology of knowledge. *Soc. Studies Sci.* **9**, 63–80.

Mulkay, M. (1979b). "Science and the Sociology of Knowledge". Allen and Unwin, London.

Page, R. A. and Moss, M. K. (1976). Environmental influences on aggression; the effects of darkness and proximity on violence. *J. Appl.. Soc. Psychol.* **6**, 126–33.

Platt, J. (1976). "Realities of Social Research: An Empirical Study of British Sociologists". Sussex University Press, Brighton.

Potter, J. (forthcoming). The development of social psychology: Consensus, theory and methodology in the British Journal of Social and Clinical Psychology. *Brit. J. Soc. Psychol.*

Ravetz, J. (1971). "Scientific Knowledge and Its Social Problems". Clarendon Press, Oxford.

Samelson, F. (1974). History, origin myth and ideology; Comte's "discovery" of social psychology. *J. Theory Soc. Behav.* **4**, 217–31.

Shapere, D. (1971). The paradigm concept: a review of the "Structure of Scientific Revolutions" by Thomas S. Kuhn and "Criticism and the Growth of Knowledge" by I. Lakatos and A. Musgrave, eds. *Science* **172**, 706–9.

Sherwin, C. W. and Isenson, R. S. (1967). Project hindsight. *Science* **156**, 1571–1577.

Steiner, I. (1974). What happened to the group in social psychology? *J. Exp. Soc. Psychol.* **10**, 93–109.

Stringer, P. (1979). A politico-psychological perspective on crowding. *In* "Human Consequences of Crowding" (M. R. Gurkaynak and W. A. Lecompte, eds). Plenum, New York.

Turner, J. (1981). Some considerations in generalising experimental social psychology. *In* "Progress in Applied Social Psychology" (G. M. Stephenson and J. H. Davis, eds), Vol. I. Wiley, New York.

Walton, R. E. (1975). Using social psychology to create a new plant culture. *In* "Applying Social Psychology" (M. Deutsch and H. A. Hornstein, eds). Lawrence Erlbaum, Hillsdale, N.J.

Weimer, W. B. (1974). The history of psychology and its retrieval from historiography: I. the problematic nature of history. *Sci. Studies* **4**, 235–58.

Wood, D. J. (1980). Models of childhood. *In* "Models of Man" (T. Chapman and D. Jones, eds). British Psychological Society, Leicester.

3

Models in Action: The Use of Theories by Practitioners

G. M. Breakwell

Rudyard Kipling, when asked by Sir Henry Montagu how native Indians would react when the newly invented aeroplane appeared in their sky, said that "they will be as profoundly incurious as a metaphysian or a psychologist once he has labelled a phenomenon". Kipling may have been wrong about the natives, but his intuition that psychologists assume that they understand a phenomenon that they have merely classified or described is too near the truth to be comfortable. However, psychological theorists are not alone in their naïvety over the value of labels. Practitioners in many disparate professional settings now employ psychological theories, and their derivatives, to inform, direct and rationalize their activities. Social workers, probation officers, teachers, doctors, health visitors and various para-medical and para-psychiatric services are among the many groups who, most frequently without direct training in psychology, seek to utilize psychological theory. Obviously, professionals who are recognized to be "applied psychologists"—the clinical, occupational and educational psychologists—will also be seeking to garner from existing paradigms of human behaviour insights and a framework for action which will enable them to deal most profitably for their clients.

The real problem for practitioners of all sorts is to know how to choose the right theory to use. It is the contention of this chapter that many myths have grown up around this issue of choosing a theory and in order to overcome them it is necessary to look at the nature of theories and the ways in which they can be evaluated. The ultimate objective is to dissuade practitioners from investing all their allegiance in one theory which then encourages a profound distrust of other formulations and an equally profound lack of curiosity about the real nature of the phenomenon. A theory can be just as effective as what Kipling called a "label" in engendering an illusory sense of security.

Before continuing to the main body of the argument, it is only fair to lay bare two assumptions made here when referring to practitioners. First, it is assumed that the practitioners are those who work with people: educating them, restoring them to physical or mental well-being; or providing them with the means to survive and become effective in complex social contexts. It is not intended that the argument should be extended to practitioners applying theoretical principles to asocial material problems. Though parts will still apply, the essential difference lies in the fact that the theories they use tend not, by their mere existence, to change the phenomena they seek to elucidate. So, the argument is limited for the sake of simplicity to those who might be called primarily "social practitioners". Although it must be admitted that many such "social practitioners" may also deal with asocial problems as part of their job. In many cases, whether a problem is seen as social or asocial depends on the level of analysis adopted and the level of explanation sought. Without getting into the question of the relativism of the social and the physical world, it is enough to say that what follows concentrates on theories about and practice in the social world.

The second assumption underlying the argument is a little more contentious: it will be taken as a given that all practitioners use theory. This is really an assumption fraught with hazards. Many "social practitioners" argue that theory is of no value to them. They argue that their approach is *atheoretical*; that it is purely pragmatic. Such practitioners will argue that any attempt to teach practitioners how to evaluate theory is truly pointless since a superordinate evaluation of all theory has been made and this has led them to abandon all theory.

There are two replies to this argument. The first response must be to the illogical nature of the argument. Even the superordinate evaluation has to be made at some point, which means that practitioners need to know what they are doing when they appraise theory. Of course, the atheoretical practitioner may counter by arguing that the rejection of theory is based not on an abstract appraisal but on knowledge that it fails in the field. This would be merely to admit the use of one form of theory-evaluation: appraisal in relation to results. If any evaluation is to be made, it should be made consciously rather than in this relatively covert and implicit way in order that artefact and bias may be considered and, if feasible, eliminated. Simply acknowledging that the process is taking place may promote its efficiency.

The second sort of response to the practitioner who claims to have abandoned all theory is not based on logic but on experience: it is not possible to eliminate all of the effects of having once understood a theory. This contention is based on the way in which training is structured. Training the "social practitioner" entails communicating how to analyse and solve problems. These analyses and solutions are shaped, no matter how distantly, by theories of social behaviour and social structure. These theories embody and transmit ways of conceptualizing the social world: how to break it into bits and how these bits should look and how they are related to each other. Theories encapsulate within themselves "world views"; they carry assumptions about the right and wrong ways to see the world. Theories, through training, become ways of thinking: constraining and moulding the pattern of perception and analysis. They can evolve into the mental blocks which barricade one alleyway to push the thinker into the next. The interesting thing is that the after effects of theories can be seen in the thinker long after they have been publicly recanted. Their exorcism is never complete because they channel, even in the moment that they are expunged, future ways of thinking. Abhorrence of an old theoretical enthusiasm can lead to the most dogmatic adherence to its antithesis. The imprint of a theory, whether good or bad, planted during training is difficult to remove even if initial conversion was incomplete. Those who reject theories and rail at their irrelevance are not free of theory. In fact, they are at considerable risk because they seek to deny a very real part of their way of thinking.

To restate the second assumption which underlies the argument: all practitioners use theory, even when they are unaware that they do so. It might be even more accurate to say that theory uses the practitioner. Obviously, this is why it is considered so important here to be able to choose an appropriate theory and, where no appropriate theory exists, to know where the weaknesses lie. There is certainly some value in any real effort to identify which theories exist covertly in one's way of conceptualizing the world—particularly if this brings the subjective and inconsistent process of evaluating these theories under control.

Some aspects of the nature of theoretical models

No attempt will be made here to provide a philosophical definition of a "theory" or a "model". Each writer employing the term "theory" means something different from every other writer and the same is true of the way in which the notion of a "model" is used. Both are used to label attempts to causally or rationally (Hollis, 1977) explain a phenomenon. Some differentiate between a theory and a model in terms of the greater complexity of the former. Models are seen as simpler, heuristic devices which elucidate one part of the phenomenon which will ultimately be totally explained by a theory which subsumes, perhaps, several models. To gain the status of a theory an explanation, ideally, has to have been validated empirically. Of course, there is no consensus that these are the features which differentiate a theory from a model. Perhaps more importantly, there is no consistency in the way in which the terms are used. Many notions are called theories when they are yet to receive verification; many explanations are labelled models when they have been supported by considerable empirical testing. For instance, Festinger (1957) was said to have produced a "theory of cognitive dissonance" whereas Argyle (1967) was said to have produced a "model of social skills". Yet Festinger has found unambiguous support for his "theory" an elusive thing and Argyle has found nothing to falsify his "model". Perhaps the label attached to a set of explanatory or descriptive constructs has more to do with the personality of the originator than any intrinsic merit they possess. Whether the explanation is a theory or a model depends on the perspective of the labeller.

Of course, there is a difference between the problems involved in the pragmatic labelling of a specific explanation as a "theory" or a "model" and the problems faced by philosophers who seek to differentiate "theory" from "model" in abstract terms. However, it is possible to take a pragmatic stance. For the present purposes, it is meaningless to differentiate model from theory for two reasons. First, social practitioners tend to use the terms as if they were interchangeable. Secondly, the same problems face the practitioner whether he calls what he wishes to evaluate a model or a theory. As a consequence, the distinction between the terms will be ignored in what follows. Where the term "model" is used it should be understood that "theory" might have been used just as validly. Of course, this is merely to sweep the abstract distinction under a pragmatic carpet; it does not go away, but it does not intrude irrelevantly.

In order to keep the argument brief and its line relatively lucid, it will be phrased in terms of a series of ten propositions which are illustrated

by examples. Propositions are numbered; qualifications to propositions
are lettered.

1. MODELS DO NOT TOTALLY DESCRIBE THE PHENOMENA
WHICH THEY SEEK TO EXPLAIN OR PREDICT

As Horton (1967) said:

> "Theory places things in a causal context wider than that provided by com-
> mon sense" and "The quest for explanatory theory is basically the quest for
> unity underlying apparent diversity; for simplicity underlying apparent
> complexity; for order underlying apparent disorder; for regularity underly-
> ing apparent anomaly".

The main purpose of theory or model building is to establish the relationship between one phenomenon and others and to ascribe reasons
and causes. Normally, a model operates in terms of general principles.
The specific is explained in relation to the fact that it is similar to a
group of other specifics. Grouped together such specifics can be labelled; they can be construed in the same way and a theoretical construct
can be attached to them and can be said to characterize them.
Similarities between specifics may be in terms of structure or function
and may only become apparent after the theoretical construct has been
superimposed upon them: theoretical constructs can alter the conceptualization of a specific in retrospect. Learning theory applies such
superordinate constructs. For the behaviourist all phenomena are
either stimuli or responses and can be simultaneously both. The mul-
titudinous social world is suddenly broken into two sorts of phenomena,
responses and stimuli, and it is the relationship between these which is
to be explained. A model is comprised of those constructs or abstrac-
tions which make feasible the derivation of generalized principles about
the relationship between phenomena.

Thus, the detailed description of a single set of relationships between
phenomena does not become a model unless general principles about
the relationships of similar phenomena are formulated. To say, even if
the description is accurate, that: "Janet hit John on the head after he
had pushed her over and John was not known to push her over again" is
merely a description of a pattern of events. It is not a model. But if one
were to say: "Janet punished John's aggression and he was less likely to
be aggressive with her in the future" only one further step has to be

made before a model comes into being. This step is a further move towards generalization: "Punishment of a response leads to the diminution of that response". The result, of course, is a fundamental tenet of
learning theory which is modified by qualifications about the frequency
of punishment and its temporal relation to the response. The point is
that in model building the description of the phenomenon is merely a
precursor to the prime activity of producing theoretical constructs
which reflect generalizable characteristics of phenomena.

Since models impose order and simplicity through abstracting themselves from the phenomena which they discuss, they are often considered to be analogues. They run parallel to the phenomenal relationships which they describe; replicating them in abstract concepts. The
model builder does not say "I show you what is there", but rather "I
show you something which is like what is there". A model is related to
the phenomena in something like the way in which a landscape paint-
ing is related to the landscape. Of course, theoretical models should be
more dynamic analogues than paintings can be. Yet it remains the case
that they are similar in that neither is produced of the substance of the
phenomena which they seek to represent.

2. MODELS ARE CONNECTED TO PHENOMENA THROUGH
A SET OF PREMISES WHICH SERVE TO HOLD THE
RELATIONSHIP BETWEEN THE TWO CONSTANT

In purely formal terms, the premises are the suppositions upon which
the model rests. They are the substructure of the model and may be
explicitly stated or remain implicit. Normally, they become explicit
when a model is critically evaluated. Such premises have two aspects:
the stipulative and the definitional. These two aspects normally con-
found each other and to distinguish between them in practice may be
difficult and unproductive. In analytical terms they can be distinguished. The stipulative aspect of a premise is similar to what Israel
(1972) called a "stipulative statement":

> At least three types of stipulative statements can be distinguished in these
> (social science) theories. They are: assumptions concerning (1) the nature of
> Man, including the nature of knowledge which Man has, (2) the nature of
> society, and (3) the nature of the relationship between Man and society. . . .
>   These statements may often be interrelated in a theoretical system. In ad-
> dition, such statements enter into empirical theories and are not usually

clearly differentiated from descriptive statements. In fact, they are usually formulated as descriptive statements, thus veiling their true nature which is that of normative statements. These statements have a regulative function. They determine the content of empirical theories and together with formal methodological rules, influence the procedures of scientific research, which themselves affect theory. They can be relatively "freely" chosen from among alternative sets of stipulative systems. Different sets of stipulative systems will give rise to different empirical theories. The choice of stipulative systems is in turn influenced by value-statements.

Israel uses an example of the stipulative assumptions concerning Man which are often used in economics. Economic Man is stipulated to be rational: choosing to behave in a way which will "maximize utility". Such a choice entails a further stipulation that he has complete knowledge of alternative courses of action and their utility. Economic models of behaviour rest on this assumption that, within the limits of his information, Man is rational. If that assumption were ill-founded, economic models of behaviour would be meaningless. There are fundamental stipulations of this sort underlying all models. Psychological theories abound in these assumptions: Piagetian cognitive developmental theory assumes a self-generated active and interacting organism; behaviourism assumes a passive, if responsive, organism without the power of self-motivation. Such assumptions are one aspect of the premises which relate the model to the phenomena.

The second aspect of premises is the definitional. This is in some ways simpler than the stipulative. The theoretical constructs which make up a model are tied to the phenomena through operational definitions. An operational definition takes part of the phenomena and aligns it with a theoretical construct. This translation process is the second way of relating the model to the phenomena. Obviously, with many theoretical concepts the translation process is not altogether obvious. The same construct may be given several different operational definitions and the choice between these different definitions will control how the construct may be used later in the model. In this sense, the operational definition is a premise supporting the model: it will shape the model's development through interaction with other aspects of the model; it will direct the way in which the model is tested; and it acts to reduce the number of alternative ways in which the model can be related to the phenomena.

This can be exemplified in the case of theories which try to explain conflict between groups. These theories rely upon the notion that there are things which can be labelled "groups". However, they differ considerably in what they believe to be a "group". Cartwright and Zander (1968, pp. 46–48) list eight different types of definition of "group". Definitions range from those which argue that a number of people can be considered to be a group only if, as Sherif (1966, p. 62) puts it, they:

> stand in status and role relationships with one another, stabilized in some degree, and (2) possess, explicitly or implicitly, a set of norms or values regulating the behaviour of individual members, at least in matters of consequence to the group

to those who claim, with Tajfel (1978), that a group is a "body of people who feel they are a group". The definition chosen will precondition those factors which are considered salient in the explanation of relations between groups. Starting from such different definitions of "group", it is hardly surprising that Sherif and Tajfel provide very different theories of intergroup relations.

Obviously, in the production of a model, the stipulative and definitional aspects of premises interact. Sherif (1966) stipulates that the behaviour of individuals acting as group members has to be interpreted differently from when they act as autonomous agents. He goes on to say that explanations centring on the psychodynamics of the individual can never predict group behaviour. Moreover, it is insufficient to deal merely with intragroup dynamics, Sherif (1966, p. 12) states:

> the characteristics of functional relations between groups cannot be deduced or extrapolated solely from the properties of relations that prevail among members within the group itself.

These stipulations are entirely congruent with a definition of group in objective, structural terms; they virtually necessitate such a definition. In the same way, the cognitive-emotional definition of group proposed by Tajfel is a fundamental offshoot of his stipulation that individuals gain their social identity from their group memberships. Both sorts of premise produce an explanation of intergroup behaviour: in Sherif's case it is intimately tied to the goals of the group; in Tajfel's case it is intimately tied to the needs of the individual. In both of these examples, the interaction of stipulative and definitional premise can be seen to be complex. Drawing a hard and fast line between the two sorts of premise becomes an analytic rather than a practical exercise.

The nature of premises is further complicated because they can be lifted wholesale from other models. For instance attempts to explain interpersonal attraction in terms of exchange theory borrow all of the assumptions associated with the economic model of "rational" Man discussed earlier (Duck, 1977). Exchange theory, in all its guises, represents a model built on the back of another. Models are frequently related to the phenomena through a hierarchy of other models and the premises that they each employ tend to get enmeshed. This is most likely to occur when a model evolves to explain a small part of the entire range of phenomena, if more global models already exist to explain that range. A hierarchy of models builds around the fulcrum of increasing specialization: more specialized models sit on the backs of generalists, pyramid-fashion. Specialized models tend to make less assumptions of their own because they align themselves with global models that have committed themselves to a certain set of premises. Such specialized models, since they make less overt assumptions and thus appear "closer" to the phenomena they explain, are less open to challenge.

The social skills model of interpersonal interaction might be an example of such a specialized model. According to Argyle (1967) interaction between two people (A and B) has five characteristics: A has *goals* for B; A *perceives* B and uses this information to *translate* his goal into appropriate *social techniques* in order to *influence B's actions*. It is assumed that B is doing the same thing to A. Each of the five aspects in this model is readily mapped on to phenomena and the model is successful in elucidating all sorts of social interaction. However, its apparent simplicity belies the fact that it rests on a pile of other theories: theories about motivation, perception, problem-solving and cognition, not to mention models of motor skills. Each of these theories in the pile underneath the social skills model has its own set of premises; to the extent that these theories support the social skills model, their premises infiltrate the model. If the premises of the theory on the bottom of the pile have generated false understandings then the model on the top must be inadequate. Though there is no suggestion here that the social skills model is inadequate for this reason.

2a. *Premises are Unfalsifiable*
They can, of course, be challenged, but their nature makes them impervious to any test. They are stipulative and definitional and fundamentally *arbitrary*. Obviously, the predictions and the relationships derived from them may be tested empirically and this may mean that a premise

is abandoned. In such a case, the premise would have been shown to be sterile rather than false.

Effectively, this means that any number of sets of premises related to any number of models may be erected to explain or predict the "same" phenomena. So frustration-aggression (Berkowitz, 1962; Gurr, 1974), social identity (Tajfel, 1978) and goal-conflict (Sherif, 1966) models may all seek to explain the same phenomenon—intergroup conflict— but they are each related to that phenomenon through very different and unique premises. The interesting thing is that the nature of the premises will determine how the phenomena are construed and structured. The premises act as a force for selective perception and attention—having determined what will be perceived they frequently then go on to determine how it will be conceived.

In this it is evident that premises are not purely derived from the phenomena; phenomena may be derivative of premises. At least, phenomena may be derivative in the sense of being chosen for examination because a certain premise would indicate their relevance. The transition which phenomena make from being data to being social facts is mediated by these premises. As a consequence, models may claim to address the same phenomena but be actually "seeing" through their restricted construal very different faces of those phenomena. It is unfortunate that there are no oculists who deal with theoretical tunnel-vision. If we had such wonder-workers it might be that we would avoid the cardinal sins of only looking for evidence to support our basic assumptions and of ignoring or misunderstanding data which does vitiate those assumptions.

3. SINCE MODELS OF SOCIAL PHENOMENA EXIST IN THE SOCIAL WORLD THEIR EXISTENCE MAY CHANGE THAT WORLD IN SUCH A WAY THAT THEY INVALIDATE THEMSELVES

Since models exist within the social world that they seek to explain or predict or interpret, they will also act to change that world merely by their presence. The model may, in fact, come to exert such an influence that it can alter the very phenomena which it sought to explain and come, in time, to invalidate itself. This becomes especially true when a model attaches to itself a technology designed to initiate change.

Psychoanalytic theory must represent a prime example here on both

counts: it has altered the conceptualization of sexual mores and has promoted therapies to change the experiences of those who suffer. At the
most superficial level, Freudian language has permeated the culture of
the Western world. For instance, "the Freudian slip" is a well-known
concept: it is that apparently innocent statement which is distorted in
some way to reveal repressed desires or impulses. Such slips were said
to relieve inner conflicts by admitting repressed desires without admitting them to consciousness. Of course, the very act of identifying such
"slips" attacks their usefulness: if one knows the reason for the slip, the
repressed desire has to be, in some sense, confronted; conscious confrontation of the repressed desires was the eventuality which the slip
was designed to avoid. The "slip" explicated is made redundant. Once
people are made consciously aware of the "slip" it is unlikely, even if it
continues to occur, to serve the same ends. The theory of
psychoanalysis, through its own success, invalidates its predictions. In
fact, the more a model is apparently valid and the more it permeates a
society, the more likely it is to set into motion a chain-reaction which attacks its validity.

In such situations, models will change to accommodate the changes
that they instigate in the phenomena. In so far as it remains necessary
to explain a set of phenomena, models will be reflexive: responding to
changes in the phenomena (as long as tunnel-vision does not strike). As
models influence phenomena, their abstraction from them wanes; the
premises which served to relate model and phenomena become redundant and should change. Premises should change but this does not
mean that they always do. The point is that both the model and the premises which co-ordinate its relation to the phenomena may change in
order to cope with the need to be reflexive.

The problem of evaluating a model

To discuss the formal properties of theoretical models may seem rather
pointless to a practitioner who wants answers to immediate practical
problems. Yet is has relevance since the formal parameters of a model
set the limits within which it can be meaningfully evaluated. Much time
can be wasted in making inappropriate attempts to evaluate a model
and much damage can be caused by acting as if such attempts generate
evidence on which decisions may be used. The prime inappropriate

strategy of evaluation to avoid is one which seeks to evaluate a model through direct comparison with others—a strategy employed extensively by social policy, social administration and social work theorists and practitioners.

4. SINCE PREMISES ARE NOT AMENABLE TO COMPARATIVE EVALUATION, IT IS ILLOGICAL TO EVALUATE MODELS IN RELATION TO EACH OTHER

Premises establish the rules within which explanations are made. They lay the boundaries and act normatively. Where explanations are founded on different premises, as they are in different models, the rules surrounding them differ and it is illogical to evaluate them in relation to each other. It would be like saying that a man playing cricket was offside or a footballer should be sent off for being run out. Perhaps an even more apposite analogy would be the bowler who was dismissed for handling the ball. The rules of a game are specific to that game in their application; they are what make it unique. The same is true of models: the premises which make them unique annul comparative evaluation. This may seem obvious, but the error of direct comparative evaluation is repeatedly made by practitioners when they become embedded in one theory which then becomes the criterion against which all others are measured.

5. MODELS SHOULD BE EVALUATED IN TERMS OF THEIR OWN PREMISES AND AS IF NO OTHER COMPETING MODEL EXISTED

A model may be evaluated on several dimensions:
i. In terms of *internal consistency*—if propositions and constructs used in the model are contradictory then it is said to lack internal consistency.
ii. In terms of its *responsiveness to new evidence*—a moribund model has little value in a changing social world.
iii. In terms of *parsimony*—a model should be uncluttered by propositions which do not serve to promote the explanation of the phenomena.
iv. In terms of its *ease of communication* and the *stimulus* for further insights which it provides.
v. In terms of *external validity*—its capacity to predict phenomena or its ability to interpret them may be a model's prime value.

Some models perform well in relation to some of these dimensions, other models perform well in relation to the others.

6. PRACTITIONERS NEED TO CHOOSE BETWEEN AVAILABLE MODELS IN ORDER TO GUIDE THEIR ACTIONS

They must, therefore, in some sense, compare models. If Propositions 4 and 5 hold, the only route available to practitioners is to evaluate models in comparison to each other not in logical but in pragmatic terms.

6a. *Pragmatic Comparative Evaluation of Models Begins with Deciding Upon an Objective*

The practitioner needs to decide what s/he wants to achieve and the models available can be measured against this objective. Again, the practitioner will not be comparing models in the abstract but comparing them in relation to their contribution to achieving the objective. The result is a purely utilitarian strategy: whatever achieves the objective is evaluated most highly.

6b. *As Objectives Vary Across Time, Models Which Were Once Considered Most Useful Will Lose Their Attraction*

Different models will be adopted. So, one might see a pattern such as this:

Objective 1 at Time 1 leads to Model A being preferred = Option 1;
Objective 1 at Time 2 leads to Model B being preferred = Option 2;
Objective 2 at Time 3 leads to Model C being preferred = Option 3.

The existence of Option 2 is predicated upon the assumption that the objective may stay the same but the conditions under which it is sought may change so radically that a new model is more productive in achieving the objective. The third option is self-evident.

The options illuminate the importance not merely of time but of the inhabitations of time which are social phenomena. It is logically impossible to have the fourth option (Objective 2 at Time 1) unless Objective 1 and Objective 2 are compatible. It is assumed above that the objectives are mutually exclusive.

6c. *A Model Has No Constant Value*

The value of a model is conditional upon the objective of the evaluator and the social time and social space which is the context of its evaluation. Dogmatic adherence to a model because it once served an end is an error which it is easy to make. Practitioners need to remain flexible if they are to get maximum help in achieving their objectives from theoretical models. The advice here is to be ever-critical, even of old allies.

7. THE MEANS OF EVALUATING A MODEL IN RELATION TO AN OBJECTIVE ARE A FUNCTION OF THE AVAILABILITY OF INFORMATION ABOUT THE POSSIBLE IMPLICATIONS OF THE MODEL

Such information may not be available to all who might wish to use it. The flow of such information, in fact, can be controlled in order to bias the evaluative process as conducted by individuals.

7a. *As Long As Knowledge About the Implications of a Model is Imperfect, There is Room for Propagandists of a Model to Manoeuvre*

Propaganda movements can explain in large part the tendency for models to come into vogue and then disappear for a while only to reappear later attached to a new name or discipline. Of course, the reasons for the existence of certain types of propaganda at certain times needs to be explained. There are several models in existence which would serve to explain these propagandist movements. Choosing between them would be a matter of deciding which satisfied the objective in hand and this would be influenced by currently dominant propagandas! Discussing the nature of theory building and evaluation is founded upon so many prior evaluations that the exercise can enter realms of relativism rarely visited.

7b. *Theories May Even be Offshoots of Propaganda*

Models can be vacuous forms of rhetoric evolved to support adherence to a particular stance. The relationship betwen propaganda for models and models for propaganda is vague and begs specification. An example of a model wavering on this line between propaganda and theorizing must lie in Szasz's (1961, 1970) model of mental illness. Szasz has the fundamental idea that mental illness is "created" through the stigmatization and incarceration of "mental patients". His argument is that mental illness is a matter of labels: being involuntarily labelled ill and being treated as if you were ill. According to Szasz mental patients are created just like witches were created by persecution, imprisonment and torture. Mental illness is as much of a myth as witchcraft. This model is interesting in two respects: it acts as a propaganda agent against institutionalization of the so-called mentally ill, but it also pinpoints the extent of propaganda and vested interests involved in other models of mental illness (like the medical, psychodynamic and behaviourist models).

Szasz has a lesson to teach any practitioner seeking models to help with social problems: propaganda influences on model building and evaluation are important. This is particularly true where the practitioner is dealing with social problems that are in the limelight of public concern—for instance, a social worker dealing with child-battering. Social problems of this sort exist within a matrix of power relations. Power involves vested interests and power gives the means to control the presentation and credibility given to models. Vested interests may, therefore, result in information being withheld or distorted and thus prevent any accurate evaluation of the model. Thus, for instance, it may be that child-battering can be explained in terms other than those which rely on the medical model of puerperal depression. Battering may be understood as a result of the socialization of the batterer (people who were mistreated as children tend to mistreat their own children) and a psychological model can be employed. Alternatively, a sociological model could be invoked: battering being the result of economic or social frustrations. At any one time, attention will be channelled onto one of these models rather than the others. An emphasis on individual rather than societal malfunctioning as the origin of battering may come when those capable of directing the practitioners' attention wish individual rather than social change to be the order of the day. Understanding what processes can channel attention not only makes for effective model evaluation, it may also aid the practitioner to avoid becoming the scapegoat when things go wrong. Recognition that the popularity of any particular model may be in large part determined by factors quite independent of the objective value of the model in achieving a specific goal is protection against naïve involvement.

Of course, the impact of vested interest and propaganda lies not only in control and distortion of information about the implications of a model. Vested interests may influence each of those dimensions (listed in Proposition 5) on which a model can be evaluated. Propaganda can establish the degrees of freedom to be regarded as permissible around notions of consistency, responsiveness, parsimony, communicability and validity. No aspect of model evaluation is free of the impact of sociological demands; any abstract criterion of evaluation loses its pristine purity the instant that it makes contact with the real world.

8. WHERE MODEL A AND MODEL B ARE EVALUATED IN RELATION TO THE SAME OBJECTIVE, THERE IS STILL NO FORM OF COMMENSURABILITY BETWEEN THE TWO EVALUATIONS

This proposition arises from the fact that it is unlikely that they can be evaluated in relation to the same objective upon an identical scale or, at least, not unless a mutually applicable set of criteria of value can be established.

8a. *Establishing a Set of Criteria of Value Will Involve Subjective Judgements About What is Good in Relation to the Objective: What Constitutes Success*

The criteria might comprise standards against which outcomes could be appraised and graded. There could be a duly acknowledged gradient of consequences ranging from total success to total failure (where failure and success are arbitrarily decreed). The models could then be compared in terms of their effectiveness related to these criteria. Of course, this would only be important if neither of the models were totally successful in achieving the objective. The criteria come into play where we want to establish the extent of non-total success. Achieving consensus about what constituted adequate criteria of success would necessitate as much power politics as is involved in control of knowledge about models. This is especially true since adherents to a theoretical system normally seek to claim that the outcome of their theorizing is substantively different from that of other models. This would mean that many would actively withstand any attempt to institute a standardized measure of success.

For instance, one can only imagine with difficulty a psychoanalyst and a behaviourist agreeing upon what constituted success in the treatment of a neurotic. The behaviourist might be content to remove the neurotic symptom arguing that certain levels of conditionability and the neuroses they cause are functions of the nervous system and are, as such, immutable. The psychoanalyst would regard the removal of the neurotic symptom a mere respite if the repressions and complexes which caused the symptom were not analysed. For one, success is the removal of the symptom; for the other, success is the removal of the cause of the symptom. The philosophy which determines their methods determines what they consider to be success. There is, therefore, little chance of establishing a common criterion for the measurement of their success.

9. PRACTITIONERS ARE FACED WITH A FURTHER PROBLEM IN THAT THEORISTS SEEK TO EXPLAIN AND INTERPRET WITH THEIR MODELS; MODELS DO NOT NORMALLY HAVE BUILT-IN PRESCRIPTIONS FOR ACTION

Once the model is evaluated, the practitioner still has to decide what it means in terms of action. It is the practitioner, in the last resort, who decides how to act—a simplistic statement which ignores the immense structural constraints which are laid on any practitioner. One can imagine a psychiatrist who acted to release all her patients because she had been convinced by Szasz, she would not retain her job too long. Of course, such a converted psychiatrist would not wish to keep her job. But the job itself would be maintained within a structure that sees the value of psychiatric institutions. The individual practitioner who acts against the structural constraints is likely to find there is no second opportunity to do so. So, the practitioner decides how a theory will be translated into action, but that action is severely constrained by the professional and institutional demands.

9a. *The Practitioner May Turn Theorist*
So far the argument has been put as though there is a cut and dried distinction between a "theorist" and a "practitioner". This is, of course, not so. Practitioners may become theorists for their own colleagues producing notions which tend to be derivative of other models. Where theory-builders are themselves practitioners, objectives and actions will be vital influences on premises and on what are taken to be basal phenomena. The cybernetic nature of this process can be schematized, as below.

Of course, at each stage in this cycle, the impact of the power structure will be seen to operate. Theory-building, whether by practitioners or not, does not take place in a vacuum of social time or social space; nor does its interpretation.

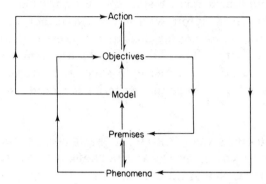

10. PRACTITIONERS DO NOT ALWAYS USE MODELS FOR THEIR EFFECTIVENESS IN ELUCIDATING PROBLEMS OR DIRECTING ACTION

Models can act in a totally illogical way as supports for practitioners who never seek to evaluate them at all. Models can too easily serve an anti-intellectual function: they can be props for the rationalization of habit or inactivity. Genetic models of intelligence, which argue that differences in I.Q. are in large part inherited, support those who would not act to provide equal educational opportunities for everyone. An environmental (nurture) or interactionist explanation for differences in intelligence would promote the need to make attempts to ameliorate the effects of disadvantaging environments. On the whole, the genetic model entails less work.

Models can also provide a jargon which cloaks ignorance. When a thing is difficult to understand or deal with, one of the easiest routes to take is to dismiss it by wrapping it in jargon. The jargon serves a second purpose, this is to identify the user as part of a group of like-minded people who adhere to that model. Identification with a group of like-minded people may be more important than the principles around which the group originally coalesced. Models which use propaganda and rhetoric to encourage support are likely to make use of the affiliative tendencies of practitioners.

When models are used for reasons of habit or for purposes of group allegiance the principles of evaluation considered above become irrelevant, at least to the individual involved. The skill lies in knowing when a practitioner is pursuing a particular theoretical line because of unlogical reasons and when it is a consequence of objectified comparative evaluation. This can be important if it is a colleague's motives which have to be judged before you work together. A trick which provides a safety net in this situation is to always assume the worst until proven wrong.

References

Argyle, M. (1967). "The Psychology of Interpersonal Behaviour". Penguin, Harmondsworth.

Berkowitz, L. (1962). "Aggression". McGraw-Hall, New York.

Cartwright, D. and Zander, A. (1968). "Group Dynamics" (3rd ed). Harper and Row, New York.

Duck, S. (1977). (ed.) "Theory and Practice in Interpersonal Attraction". Academic Press, London.

Festinger, L. (1957). "A Theory of Cognitive Dissonance". Row Peterson, New York.

Gurr, T. (1974). "Why Men Rebel". Princeton, New Jersey.

Hollis, M. (1977). "Models of Man". Cambridge University Press, Cambridge.

Horton, R. (1967). African traditional thought and Western science. *Africa* **37**, 50–71.

Israel, J. (1972). Stipulations and construction in the social sciences. *In* "The Context of Social Psychology" (J. Israel and H. Tajfel, eds). Academic Press, London.

Sherif, M. (1966). "Group Conflict and Co-operation". Routledge and Kegan Paul, London.

Szasz, T. (1961). "The Myth of Mental Illness". Hoeber-Harper, New York.

Szasz, T. (1970). "The Manufacture of Madness". Harper and Row, New York.

Tajfel, H. (1978). (ed.) "Differentiation Between Social Groups". Academic Press, London.

II

Empirical Research:
Energy, Housing, Mass Media

Introduction

This part differs from the rest of the volume in being less discursive. The five chapters deal directly and almost entirely with empirical research projects conducted by the authors. They cover topics such as attitudes towards energy production and conservation, vandalism and the effects of viewing films of violence.

Although they contribute to a book on applied social psychology the authors are wary about claiming that their work is "applied". In chapters seven and eight there is an outright denial—though it is hoped that the research sponsor or some other institution will nevertheless choose to apply the research. Other authors claim that their work is interpretative or a re-definition of concepts prior to application. It is interesting to contrast the two stances. Certainly application is in the background. For example, the energy conservation research was funded by a national research council in specific response to widespread concern about problems of supplying plentiful and cheap energy. Another chapter examines residents' concepts of their housing estates, as a result of architects' worry over the causes of and cures for vandalism.

There is an apparent paradox when authors disclaim the applied nature of their work and yet insist that there is not a sharp distinction between "pure" and "applied" research. If there is a schism between the development of theoretical models and a concern for the understanding and amelioration of social problems, they see themselves as bridging it. The paradox can be resolved if one accepts the lack of distinction. Presumably then the research is distinguished by being about real problems. As one author writes: "We all want to study 'real problems'". One has also to accept that research on real problems is more likely to be used or applied, but that the manner of use is not the concern of the researcher.

Behind the paradox is an understandable desire to have one's feet in two camps, or to kill two birds with one stone. The intellectual roots of social psychology now rest on the pre-eminence of theory and rigorous theory testing. At the same time, we have a conscience, more or less recently awakened, which says that we ought to investigate "relevant" topics, by field-oriented methods, in the hope of contributing positively to the wider society in which we live and which is our paymaster. One way to satisfy both sets of demands is to deny the difference between them. If social psychology were social in the fullest sense of the word, of course there would be no distinction to overcome: research could not help but reflect the problems of society at large.

But what those problems may be is not at all simple to determine. Energy conservation, anti-nuclear attitudes, a concern for vandalism and for violence in the media may be taken as self-evidently social problems. If a research council or government department embarks on a particular topic, it must be assumed that it is of some importance. The client will be reflecting or anticipating a current of concern in society. The temptation, however, is to accept the salience of the topic at face-value rather than subject it to a critical examination. An assumed social issue becomes a fashionable topic for study for a few years.

The reason why social psychologists have done virtually no research on health questions until very recently and need astronomical un-employment statistics to suggest that that is now a possible field of re-search is partly because they do not include among their tasks the active analysis and criticism of societal processes. (There are also more cyni-cal reasons.) They are reacting to gross, external forces in selecting issues for research. Any refinement of the problem is guided by un-acknowledged, hidden value positions and by theoretical and methodological considerations which are peculiar to the discipline. For example, why should energy conservation research assume that cheap energy will not be available, that the proper goal of energy policy is the efficient and economic use of energy, or that conservation should be particularly encouraged on the part of individual consumers in the home? Is smoking really the single most important problem in preven-tive medicine? On what basis are people afraid of being the victim of violent crime? Indeed, in what sense are they *afraid*? In all three areas how far is it a matter of convenience to assume that the "problem" re-sides with individuals rather than society and its institutions?

One of the most pervasive internal factors influencing the specifica-tion of problems is the individualism of most social psychology. The domestic consumer is easier to handle methodologically than the much heavier commercial and industrial user; and he is more conveniently treated as an individual than a household. Most of the literature on smoking and addiction focuses essentially on individual, cognitive pro-cesses rather than on relations, group processes or social representa-tions. Research on the effects of watching violent pictures has taken on a number of social variables, but the effects examined are still analysed at the level of what happens to the individual rather than intrinsically to the dyad, family or social group which is more usually the audience.

"Real problems" are taken as given; perhaps because they seem so real. If they are treated interpretatively, it is usually at the dictate of considerations internal to social psychology. A critical analysis is very rarely undertaken of, for example, dominant and non-dominant problem definitions (such as whether or not addiction is pathological). Even a critical scientific analysis of whether one's chosen problem is susceptible to research at all is sometimes neglected. There are "impossible" pieces of research in the literature. The scale at which a problem is presented may be misleading. Nearly always a course needs to be steered between over-specific case-studies of local variants of the problem and grandiose attempts to deal with the "whole phenomenon". The researcher should scrutinize his own motives for accepting a problem in the form in which it is most usually presented. What are his moral and social responsibilities in selecting to study a particular problem?

Despite this rather bitter portrayal of social psychology attempting to confront real problems, it is possible for the experience to throw up some lessons. There are two points at least which emerge from several of the next five chapters. A multi-disciplinary approach is required when approaching topics such as energy conservation. All the topics discussed here have certainly been studied by more than one discipline. But what one misses is an indication of how the contributions of many disciplines might be melded, or of their relative impact on policy and decision-making. Psychology has been slower than other social sciences in grappling with many social issues. In the first instance, it is understandable if undue attention is paid to demonstrating that social psychology has a contribution to make. Hopefully the second generation of studies will take that for granted and move towards a more integrated multi-disciplinary strategy.

A second lesson from the accounts here is that looking at applied problems may demand of the psychologist fundamental redefinitions or reorientations. The example of movie violence and aggressiveness is again relevant. As soon as one deals with real audiences, it is apparent that the previous individually-based experimental paradigm is inappropriate. But at the same time we have to reiterate that the reorientation in this case could have been more radical. Chapter Four is based on an argument for the redevelopment of our concept of attitude. Without it attitudes towards nuclear energy provision or smoking are difficult to understand. Yet a thoroughgoing re-examination of the concept would have included the possibility of people having no attitudes to speak of on these topics and the consequences of that cognitive state; or an investigation of *how* attitudes are used wherever they operate in social life. Attitudes in social psychology are still intervening variables rather than a demonstrable part of the experience of social beings.

The dominant approach to applied social psychology rests on the belief that if research is "addressed to social problems" or is "relevant to practical issues" then, provided that practitioners get to hear of it, it has a reasonable chance of being used. Unfortunately this is an article of faith. There is very little empirical evidence of direct application of the results of research which was done under this assumption. Cases of *apparent* application may be misleading: there are always alternative routes by which the practitioner may have come to his decision. The most reliable instances are those in which the researcher has himself intervened in the problem area: as, for example, in action research or when he sets up training courses.

The arguments and results reported in these five chapters may or may not be potentially applicable. Are they qualified for the label "applied"? The problems of laying claim to the label are plainly visible. For example, Ellis undertook his research while working for an architectural practice. Yet that in no way guaranteed architects' attention to his results. Although the research originated from design evaluation work carried out for architects, which showed that children's play was a nuisance on housing estates, the results are not laid out so as to directly clarify that issue for designers. Instead they throw light on competing theoretical views. (Though one suspects that Newman, being himself an architect, has and will have the greater influence.) The phenomenalist approach in particular is intended to help the designer gain insight into the outcome of his work. But the conventions of reporting in academic psychology conceal, both here and in the original dissertation, any of the basic substance of that approach.

Gaskell and Ellis and Leyens and his colleagues are straightforward examples of researchers who would hope that their results would be applied because of the manifest significance of the topic. The researchers bear no special relationship to potential practitioners, nor do they suggest that making their results more likely of application is any part of their research agenda. Gaskell and Ellis do devote energy in attempting to demonstrate that there are irreducibly psychological components in their multi-disciplinary field. Their stated goal is to understand social issues rather than directly to seek application.

Whether the research results on energy conservation and on housing estates are ever put into practice might depend on a number of underlying assumptions. For example, although the researchers are explicit about their model of Man, they do not offer any evidence as to whether their subjects or potential practitioners share that model. The tendency in recent social psychology to replace passive by active models of Man has been bolstered by a rhetorical insistence that the latter is more appropriate and representative. An allied assumption is that qualitative phenomenological reports can be economically communicated to decision-makers and are the kind of information which they are looking for. Or again, it is assumed that multi-disciplinary topics can be investigated by any one discipline independently of the others and still come up with practicable results. It is possible that assumptions of this type are inevitable in research which is funded by an academically oriented research council.

Who pays for the research is, or should be, a major influence on the research. There are different types of client and different relationships are possible between client and researcher. Some of the difficulties which the researcher may confront are the differing presuppositions of himself and his client; the client's reluctance to define the problem at all tightly; and his preference for technical solutions as opposed to conceptual or problem analysis. If the researcher wishes his research results to have a concrete effect on policy, he obviously needs a client who is looking towards change. But the largely "gestural" funding of some policy-related research, especially by government bodies, can be deceptive in this respect. Even if the client is sincere, making knowledge available to and usable by him is not necessarily straightforward. On a moral rather than practical note, the researcher may find difficulties when the interests of the client differ from those of the subjects of the research.

The research discussed in these five chapters was funded by research councils, with the exception of that of Doob, which was set up by a Royal Commission on Violence in the Communications Industry. In this case the researchers' assumption seems to have been that research is worthwhile if it helps us to understand something important. This is a stance frequently taken by academics to justify doing work which they believe to be more important than the brief which a client may have given them. Here, the research contract followed on a decision by the Royal Commission "that some aspects of media effects might be specific to the culture in which the media were available". Interestingly, the research did show that results from the United States could not be replicated in Canada. But that seems to have been due to inadequate research design in the former case. In any event, cultural variables which may differentially influence media effects are not investigated.

One of the principal items on the agenda of the workshops which discussed these papers was just this question of cultural specificity; and in particular the question of whether North American applied social psychology could be relevant at any level in European societies. But the question was hardly taken up at all. The only references here are Doob's caution about generalizing his findings outside of Canada, and a suggestion by Leyens that his work is characteristic neither of Europe nor any other part of the world.

The unwillingness to confront this question is a part of a wider reluctance to accept that the social and historical context is a critical part of an analysis for applied purposes and that it has to be determined rather than left shadowy and implicit. Leyens does point out that more decriptive data are needed if research is to have societal implications; but he apparently believes that its collection can be an operation independent of the research experiments. Gaskell and Ellis subordinate description or ethnography to theoretical considerations, on the grounds that a description of how matters stand today gives no indication of how they may be changed in future. Only a theoretically based account enables us to move forward from the present state. In their chapter there is no explicit evidence that social, political or economic contexts of energy use and conservation have a bearing on theory development. And yet the birth of any theory is contextually bound. How can we apply it in another context if we do not understand the original parameters?

Eiser's chapter suggests a similar position, though within a different approach to applied social psychology. The discussion of energy-related questions is an example of the analysis of social issues by extrapolation from psychology rather than by direct empirical investigation. It is assumed that attitudes are an appropriate and crucial variable in understanding energy use or smoking behaviour. Attitudinal differences are primarily to be explained by individual factors, and not at all, apparently, by the individual's social and historical position. The value of an applied orientation seems to be that it leads to an increase in conceptual sophistication: the concept of attitude is sharpened by confronting practical questions. But although a considerable reexamination of "attitude" is carried out, the goals of so much attitude research in the past—persuasion and attitude change—are accepted at face-value.

Leyens and his colleagues point out that a lot of field research has been no more than running a conventional laboratory experiment in a non-laboratory setting. In this way vaguely stated demands for "relevance" are thought to be satisfied. But the problems of reductionism, generalizability and external validity, which plague laboratory experiments, are carried into the field. There are discussions of applied social psychology which appear to equate laboratory studies with a theoretical emphasis and field studies with an applied. This is obviously bogus—not least because a laboratory experiment could be the best way to tackle certain applied questions. Furthermore, Leyens sees the field as a useful context for testing out propositions which have developed elsewhere. The characteristics of the field which differentiate it from the laboratory should be exploited. Shuttling between the two contexts is a means of developing theory and construct validity rather than of doing a more relevant psychology.

4

Attitudes and Applied Research

J. R. Eiser

The position of the concept of attitude within social psychology has become rather like that of a constitutional monarchy—it is there, and is too much effort to get rid of, even if one could think of a better alternative, the rituals associated with it may be a bit costly, but they impress foreigners and probably help our balance of payments. It adds style to the inauguration of many otherwise uninspiring undertakings, it serves as a reminder of a more expansionist yet more chauvinist past, it is absolutely respectable, but it does not actually do anything. I shall nonetheless argue that some concept of attitude is vital to applied research in social psychology, and shall outline a number of considerations to be taken into account in the redevelopment of applied attitude research.

I say "redevelopment" because the concept of attitude, as at present institutionalized, is unlikely, in my view, to provide a sufficiently fertile source of hypotheses and creative ideas for applied research. I make this assertion in spite of the fact that the questionnaire is the single most important instrument of the applied social psychologist, that questionnaire design and attitude scale construction together constitute probably the best worked-out part of the social psychologist's methodological repertoire of techniques, and that there have been numerous applications of established attitude theories to "real-world" contexts. However, I am suggesting that we will not be able to proceed much further without a reexamination of the basic concept, and of the tasks we require of it.

The concept of attitude

DECISIONS AND DIMENSIONALITY

The first consideration to be borne in mind in such a reexamination is that attitudes involve categorization and decisions which vary in complexity, both between issues and between individuals. This may seem an unremarkable assertion, until one considers that conventional techniques of attitude measurement (with a few exceptions) do not vary in complexity, but instead impose a dimensionality on the issue in question. One can see this most clearly in the procedures for construction of unidimensional attitude scales, such as Thurstone equal-appearing interval scales. For such scales to provide reliable discriminations, it is not enough to select statements which have good face validity in terms of their apparent relevance to the issue. One needs statements which intercorrelate with each other so that agreement with any given statement is a simple function of overall attitude favourability. For this reason any statement which does not so intercorrelate, either because almost everyone agreees with it, or because almost everyone disagrees with it, or, more interestingly, because it produces a spread of agreement and disagreement which is unrelated to that on other items, is supposed to be discarded from the final scale on grounds of "irrelevance".

The point that needs making is that this assumption of a unidimensional continuum of attitude favourability is not tested by this technique—it is reified by it. The scale therefore may or may not provide a good index of those attitudinal differences on the issue that are of most importance to one's subjects, or which, perhaps, have the most direct implications for behaviour. This may not matter too much for laboratory experiments where the issue as such is unimportant, and all one needs is some attitude on which to measure change as a function of some manipulation. On the other hand, in applied social psychological research, the issue itself is of paramount importance, and so our measures must reflect the issue as it is and as it is seen, and not impose a conception in the aim of mathematical simplicity alone.

The situation is not necessarily improved through the use of multidimensional scaling or factor-analytic techniques. Although researchers who use these techniques may start from a position of actual or professed innocence concerning the dimensionality of an issue, a number of arbitrary decisions and assumptions still need to be made. One of these is the need to restrict the number of items in the scale below a certain proportion (20% or so) of the number of subjects in one's sample. If this restriction is ignored less reliance can be placed on the factor solution obtained. No such restriction applies if one is simply averaging or adding responses to a unidimensional (e.g. Thurstone or Likert) scale. Such restriction inevitably involves the researcher in making arbitrary or intuitive selections of items for inclusion in the scale and/or the analysis. Again, this selectivity is not tested by one's scaling technique, and one's factor solution or description of underlying dimensions may reflect merely the dimensionality of one's selection, and not the dimensionality of the issue as such. There is also the danger of extrapolating from any such solution or description to the responses of different individuals or groups, that is, of assuming that one's factors or dimensions are "basic", even universal. However, overall solutions may disguise important individual differences, both within and outside one's sample, in terms of which aspects of an issue are most salient. These dangers are apparent, for instance, in Eysenck's (1971) attempts to describe the "structure of social attitudes", and to identify social class differences, on the basis of a mere 28-item questionnaire (see Eiser and Roiser, 1972).

These dangers are not completely avoided by the use of repertory grid techniques, in view of the practice of using "supplied" constructs, and of scaling assumptions which need to be made before numerical analysis. Comparing the grids of different individuals may be a valuable way of discerning differences in attitude structure between different individuals. Another way is to conduct factor or multidimensional scaling analyses of the responses of contrasting groups. However, the further one goes down this methodological road, the more complex one's analyses become and the less is retained of the simplificatory power which first attracted researchers to these techniques.

ATTITUDE CONTENT

The next major consideration is that attitudes have content: obvious as this might seem, it is something which is regularly ignored in approaches which look only at the valence of a person's expressive behaviour, and ignore its meaning. Thus, once an attitude scale is constructed, no more attention is typically paid by the researcher to the content of the individual items. The same neglect of content is apparent in many of the best known attitude theories. For instance, Osgood and Tannenbaum (1955), in their congruity theory, conceptualize the relationship between a communicator (source) and the topic of communication (concept) in terms of a simple dichotomy of approval/disapproval (associative/disassociative link). How strongly, or even more simply *how*, such approval/disapproval is expressed, is just not something which the model considers.

Another example of neglect of content is provided, paradoxically, by the Fishbein and Ajzen (1975) model of attitude and behavioural intention. I say "paradoxically" because, if one had to pick a single social psychological model of attitudes which has been seized upon and used with profit by applied researchers, this would be it. The utility of the model rests squarely upon its predictive success, which in turn rests squarely upon the emphasis it places on matching the specificity of one's attitudinal and behavioural criteria. All this is considerably to the model's credit. However, although Fishbein and Ajzen are very careful in defining the "attitude towards the act" (A_{act}) which precedes behavioural intention in their model, they pay much less attention to the specific evaluative and normative beliefs which are summed to predict A_{act}, beyond a consideration of their valence. Again, whilst another point in the model's favour is the recommendation that researchers should elicit "salient" beliefs on an issue, and base their prediction on these beliefs alone, those using the model move quickly to the convenience of "modal salient beliefs" (beliefs assumed to be most salient to one's sample as a whole), without looking for differences in the salience of specific beliefs to different individuals.

The limitation of both these approaches is once again, that they impose, or at least assume, a dimensionality without putting such an assumption to the test. A unidimensional preference space is assumed, and it is further assumed that this space is comparable over different individuals. This assumption requires that one attends only to the valence or favourability of different statements made or endorsed by the same or different individuals, and ignores all other aspects of the meaning of such statements. To regard attitude statements in this way, that is, simply as evaluations, is to waste a great deal of valuable information. In particular, it means that one resigns oneself to learning little if anything, by this methodology, concerning people's intuitive theories, the elucidation of which should be one of the major aims of applied social psychology.

COMMUNICATION OF ATTITUDES

From the fact that attitudes have content, i.e. that expressive behaviour has meaning, it follows that *attitudes are communicated*. By this I mean that statements of attitude convey more than mere positive or negative evaluation—they convey the perception and interpretation of events of which such evaluation is just a part. It is not that attitudes are intervening variables *inferred* from expressive behaviour—rather, they are the *meaning of* such expressive behaviour, and so are *directly* communicated by it. The relationship between attitudes and expression is logical, not causal, corresponding to that between meaning and utterance, not that between stimulus and response.

This has important implications for how one views persuasion, and also the resistance of individuals to persuasion. If, as in the Osgood and Tannenbaum model, one deals with persuasive communications simply as expressions of positive or negative evaluation, one is hard put to explain why some messages persuade and others do not. Granted such a conception, it is understandable that so much attention should have been paid by researchers to attributes of the communicator (e.g. credibility, likeability, status) or to those of the audience (e.g. individual differences in persuasibility, or involvement), but so little to attributes of the message itself.

This would matter less in practical terms if attitude change was solely, or even mostly, the product of the expression of positive or negative evaluation by a communicator. However, in group decision making, the mere exchange by participants of their preferences, without discussion or communication of their reasons for their preferences, does *not* reliably produce shifts to risk or caution, or group polarization (e.g. Moscovici *et al.*, 1972; Tegar and Pruitt, 1967).

There also seem limitations to a simple "didactic" model of attitude change, as assumed by the Yale studies of the 1950's, according to which attitude change is principally a function of the information conveyed. Such a model may work for issues where the individual has no strong preconceptions or commitments, but on controversial issues, the problem is often not so much what the facts are, but how they are to be interpreted, and what implications they have for behaviour or policy. I am therefore suggesting that a large part of what goes on in persuasion is in fact the communication of interpretative frameworks, into which available and hopefully future facts can be fitted, and which provide a possible basis for preference and choice. I am further suggesting that a typical feature of such interpretative frameworks is that they attach salience and value to certain aspects of an issue at the expense of others.

In support of this contention, let me briefly mention three strands of research. The first is Abelson's (1976) theory of cognitive scripts. According to Abelson, the notion of cognitive consistency should be liberated from its reliance on formal, abstract conceptions of balance and imbalance, and instead be conceived of in terms of the perceived correspondence of situations to a wider variety of rules, expressed in ordinary language, which he refers to as "implicational molecules" or "scripts". Different forms of expression can suggest the applicability of different "scripts". This was supported in two field experiments by Langer and Abelson (1972) which showed that the willingness of bystanders to help a person who asked them a favour depended on simple cues contained in the person's appeal which characterized it as "legitimate" or "illegitimate" and "victims" or "target-oriented".

Another piece of supportive evidence comes from a Prisoner's Dilemma study by Alexander and Weil (1968), who had subjects rate players in a (supposedly genuine) previous game, where one person had behaved consistently cooperatively and the other consistently exploitatively. In one condition, ratings were required in terms of traits chosen to enhance the salience of "good person" criteria for comparison (e.g. friendly, generous *vs* treacherous, vicious), whereas in another condition the terms emphasized "good player" qualities (e.g. clever, enterprising *vs* gullible, spineless). When then required to play the game themselves, subjects in the first condition behaved more cooperatively than those in the second.

Comparable conclusions, though without the benefit of a behavioural index of attitude change, are suggested by two studies in which subjects were required to incorporate evaluatively biased language in essays on a controversial topic, but were completely free to choose which side of the issue to support (unlike in forced compliance research). Eiser and Ross (1977) observed that the self-reported attitudes of a group of Canadian students towards capital punishment became more abolitionist after having to incorporate words implying a clear negative evaluation of capital punishment in their essays (e.g. callous, sadistic), but less abolitionist after using words with opposite connotations (e.g. wishy-washy, spineless). Eiser and Pancer (1979) found similar results with British school students, using the issue of attitudes towards adult authority. These two studies were an extension of previous social judgement research (Eiser and Mower White, 1974, 1975) showing that individuals discriminate more markedly between attitude statements in terms of judgemental language which is evaluatively congruent with their own positions on an issue.

The common implication of these very different strands of research is that changes can be produced through the use of attitudinal language which is interpretative rather than strictly informative. It is interpretative in that it is selective in those aspects of the situation or issue which it emphasizes as most relevant, and it also assigns clear positive or negative value connotations to those aspects. In particular, it provides the individual with reasons for adopting a particular viewpoint, or choosing a particular course of behaviour—but reasons which are not easily analysed in terms of logical consistency or decision-making rationality. The "reasoning" is of the form "This is the way to categorize what is going on here, and so this is what is right and this is what is wrong".

SHARING OF ATTITUDES

The fourth point to be considered is that attitudes are shared. In saying this I am not espousing any mythology of collective mental processes, nor am I denying that individuals have privileged access to their own attitudes and may often choose to keep their opinions private. What I am saying is that attitudes in many circumstances provide the basis for a shared social reality and require consensual validation for their stability. If attitudes were mere affect, the question of validation would not arise. It is because attitudes are selective and intepretative in the ways described that it becomes important for the individual to feel that they are valid and justifiable. The more a person's attitudes are shared by comparable others, the more he will regard his attitudes as having external validity.

In applied social psychological research, the attitudes with which one is dealing (with the possible exception of attitudes towards new commercial products) are held not simply by individuals, but also by groups. In other words, although there will almost always be a degree of within-group variation in attitude, there will also often be a non-random distribution of attitudes over different social groups. Thus, particular attitudes may become a differentiating feature of particular social groups. The point is not just that members of a given group are likely to be exposed only to certain kinds of information and influence, and acquire certain attitudes as a consequence. It is rather that certain attitudes themselves can become a valued aspect of membership of a given group, and hence contribute to what Tajfel (1978) calls a person's "positive social identity".

Attitudes are thus embedded in a wider social context not just in the sense that membership of different societal groups, demographic status, etc. may be related to differential experiences and access to information, which may produce attitudinal differences. Rather, it is that the holding of a particular attitude is functional for both group cohesiveness and group distinctiveness. Indeed, there are many groups within society (e.g. political or religious) where public commitment to a particular system of attitudes or beliefs, however acquired, is the primary criterion of membership.

There are, however, attitudes which may take on the function of a badge of membership of a particular group without being a defining criterion of that group. A person can be defined as a member of a particular age, sex, social class, professional, national or ethnic group without any consideration of the attitudes he or she might hold on any given issue. For many people, many of the group classifications which might be applied to them may have little impact on their self-concepts or social relationships. On the other hand, some group classifications may sometimes matter very much, and in such circumstances, it is assumed that individuals will look for dimensions of comparison between their own group and others which will enable them to maintain a sense of positive social identity. Attitudes can provide such a basis for comparison, both in the case of social stereotypes which are held concerning outgroup members (Tajfel, 1981) and in the case of attitudes on some (possibly) distantly related issue.

As an example of the latter, it seems implausible to consider the move towards legalization of marijuana (particularly in North America) over the last two decades, merely as some kind of learning process, based on weighing up the pros and cons of woolly experience and woolly evidence. Such a view fails to explain the strength of the opinions held on either side of the issue. The point about the youth culture of the 1960's was that it was a youth culture which deliberately sought to differentiate itself from establishment values. Marijuana use became a part and a symbol of that differentiation.

Similarly, it is difficult to explain how a "lobby" can be translated into a "movement", sometimes seemingly overnight, without an appreciation of group affiliations and differentiations within society. A contemporary example is the anti-nuclear movement. Is it mere coincidence that this movement has inherited so much of the organizational structure of the peace movement at the time of the Vietnam War? Why should an episode like the Three Mile Island fiasco have triggered so much protest compared with other nuclear accidents, or other ecological disasters related to energy, such as oil tanker collisions? To suggest that large numbers of individuals have simultaneously and independently weighed up the pros and cons of the issue and come to the same conclusion, seems less plausible than to suggest that the sides have become drawn, and the issue has crystallized into one where many people feel that a commitment is now required of them, and that this is a cause to which they should rally, or else disown their right to self-definition as politically involved citizens. None of these remarks should be taken to denigrate the reasonableness of either side's position. All I am saying is that "factual information", by itself cannot explain the social context in which such attitudes are now held. The search for interpretations of events in which individuals are engaged is to a great extent a search for socially validated interpretations shared by comparable others, and what counts as "actual" is also dependent on social validation.

Energy policy and conservation

In spite of its far-reaching political and social importance, energy policy has been surprisingly neglected by social psychologists. Decisions between alternative energy policies have typically concerned themselves with the technical feasibility of the exploitation of different energy resources, and have depended on assumptions concerning supply and demand and on predictions of industrial and social consequences viewed from the perspective of economics. The problem of social acceptability, as distinct from technical and economic feasibility, has only recently become a matter of concern for researchers in this field. Indeed, it is the very fact that economic optimality and social acceptability are *not* always synonymous that provides an exciting challenge to social psychology.

Part of this challenge can be met by considering how individuals, who are not in the position of "experts", may make decisions in this area. Let us start with the apparent ineffectiveness of President Carter's energy policy, and his failure to persuade the American public voluntarily to use less energy, particularly oil and gasoline. The message that he has attempted to get across is essentially "Unless you reduce energy consumption, dire consequences will follow for the nation's economy". One could imagine some societies at some periods of their history where such a statement from a head of state would be unquestioningly accepted and acted upon. Suffice it to say that neither the United States nor Europe are currently that kind of society. Instead, ordinary people are likely to check out the validity of such public pronouncements on the basis of their own experience.

This checking out might take on the following structure:

(1) "What is the *observable* relationship between my controlling or not controlling my energy consumption and the occurrence of dire consequences to the nation's economy?"

The answer to this seems to be essentially none. Wall Street will not rejoice if I sell my Cadillac and buy a Toyota—indeed the contrary might happen if too many people did so. More importantly, the most dramatic effects ("dire consequences") on the nation's oil supply in recent memory have been, and continue to be, the outcome of decisions by OPEC ministers, over which I have no control, rather than of any personal self-indulgence. Such consequences, moreover, are not my fault or my responsibility.

(2) "What *would* I expect to happen if I reduced my energy consumption?"

The answer is, probably, nothing drastic, but it could be inconvenient and unenjoyable, especially when I suspect that not many of my friends would be that keen on using either smaller cars or public transport, or keeping their houses less cool in the summer and less hot in the winter. In short, I would be punishing myself, and making myself different from my friends, and no observable benefits would result.

Such reasoning would, and no doubt does, appal economists, but it contains many features which are familiar to social psychologists. Causal relationships are inferred essentially on the basis of covariation (cf. Kelley, 1971), concrete instances have more influence than abstract statistics (cf. Kahneman and Tversky, 1973; Nisbett *et al.*, 1976), and there is a dependence on short-range rather than long-range thinking in comparing immediate personal interest with longer-term consequences both to oneself and others (cf. Pruitt and Kimmel, 1977). From a simple reinforcement point of view, the contingencies (at least in the short term) all militate against a change in behaviour.

Furthermore, the "consistency" which such reasoning reveals, whilst not the consistency of logical or statistical induction, is very much the kind of consistency shown by many attitude structures—it is selective, evaluative, self-defensive and intuitively interpretative. The answers to questions 1 and 2 above imply rules perhaps related to what Abelson (1976) calls "cognitive scripts", which could be summarized as "Nothing I can do makes any real difference" and "Why should I have to put myself out?" It is not just that people might *say* such things, it is that they might *use* such "scripts" as organizing principles in interpreting a very complex situation, in discussing the issues with friends and family, so consensually validating their interpretations, and in deciding on appropriate action (or inaction). It is for such reasons that a *purely* "informational" view of attitudes is unlikely to prove the most usefully applicable to issues of this kind.

The importance of intuitive interpretations can be seen even more clearly in research which has examined the probabilistic judgements which individuals make under conditions of uncertainty. One might suppose that research procedures which required numerical estimates of probabilities should induce a set for rationality and objective precision. Research by Tversky and Kahneman (1974), however, has shown that people will frequently ignore statistically valid information (concerning base-rate probabilities), and rely instead upon a number of simplificatory cognitive biases or "heuristics". These heuristics include those of "representativeness", according to which an event or stimulus will be categorized as belonging to a particular class on the basis of its resemblance to "typical" examples of that class, "availability", according to which events are judged as more probable, the more easily they can be pictured or recalled; and "anchoring", which refers to people's failure to revise their estimates adequately when new information is presented. Ajzen (1977) has identified a further heuristic, which he terms that of "causality" according to which, individuals take statistical information into account only insofar as it appears relevant in terms of their intuitive causal theories.

Nuclear energy and risk

Such research speaks directly to the problematic nature of people's perceptions of risk. Risk, actual or perceived, is an extremely important aspect of energy decisions. The most obvious example is that of nuclear power. It is by no means obvious why this is the example which springs so immediately to mind as a high-risk energy source. Proponents of nuclear power claim a high industrial safety record, albeit with international variation, whilst pointing out the actual deaths incurred in coalmining or oil-drilling, the dangers of pollution from chemical explosions and tanker groundings and collisions, and even the estimated fatalities from falls during the installation of solar energy panels (Beckmann, 1976)! Yet still nuclear power is seen by many as intrinsically more dangerous—why should this be?

Slovic *et al.* (1976, 1979) have explored the relevance of such cognitive biases and heuristics to perceptions of risk in relation to nuclear energy and in other contexts. Slovik and Lichtenstein (1968) have suggested that individuals rely on different cognitive strategies when considering possible costs on the one hand and benefits on the other (e.g. "always minimize the maximum loss" as opposed to "always maximize the probability of winning"). This may imply that they will be more likely to reject energy options which are seen to contain any risk, however remote, of a major catastrophe. The difficulty of stating a convincing upper limit (particularly after Three Mile Island) to the scale of a "maximal credible" nuclear disaster is probably the weakest part of the pro-nuclear case. Even if such an upper limit could be defined, however, it does not follow that a policy which involves a one-in-a-million chance of a 100 000 death disaster would be seen as safer than a policy which regularly led to deaths of 100 persons per year. In a study sponsored by the U.S. Atomic Energy Commission, Rasmussen (1974) estimated the risks of loss of coolant accident in a nuclear reactor as 10^{-5} for a 10-death accident, and 10^{-9} for a 1000-death accident, per reactor year.

Intuitive heuristics may influence both lay and technological estimates of probabilities. Faced with the question "What would happen in the event of a nuclear accident?", it is scarcely to be wondered at that people outside the nuclear industry and nuclear research will search their memory for "available" information on the destructive potential of nuclear energy, and they will find Nagasaki. Assurances that "No reactor can explode with the force of an atomic bomb", provide scant comfort by comparison, particularly if one knows little of the technical processes involved in the working of bombs on the one hand and reactors on the other.

Even the more technical estimates of risks, however, may not be free from the influence of intuitive biases. Statistical risk estimates (as in "fault tree analysis") require the assignment of mathematical values to large numbers of low probability events, including the malfunctioning of mechanical components which have never been known to go wrong in the past. Many of these mathematical values may reflect the subjective estimates of experts rather than the conclusions of empirical experimentation. Moreover, one wonders how any fault tree could successfully anticipate, or assign a realistic probability, to extraneous mishaps, such as a small light bulb being accidentally dropped into the workings of an instrument console and making danger signals unreliable.

Even if completely accurate fault trees could be devised, it is still possible that their interpretation might be open to bias. The sheer number of possible pathways to disaster might make a disaster seem more probable, and the amount of detail within any one pathway might make that pathway seem more important (Fischhoff et al., 1978). Furthermore, Slovic et al. (1976) suggest that individuals do not combine probabilities in multi-link scenarios according to the normative multiplicative rule, but are more likely to form an evaluation of probability based upon an average impression of the likelihood of the different links—a processed highly suggestive of the notion of "cognitive algebra". What is more, "scenarios which tell a 'good story' by burying weak links in masses of coherent detail may be accorded much more credibility than they deserve" (p. 178). For "good story", perhaps, one might wish to read "good script".

Another example of the selectivity of people's conceptions of nuclear energy can be seen by directly examining which aspects of the issue are seen as most salient by those with different attitudes on the issue. In a study by Eiser and van der Pligt (1979) a group of supporters and opponents of nuclear energy completed a questionnaire dealing with possible consequences of the proposed reprocessing plant for spent nuclear fuel at Windscale. The study took place 12 days after the publication of the Parker Report of the public inquiry and four days before a debate on the report in the House of Commons in March 1978. The results showed clear differences between the pro- and anti-nuclear subjects in terms of their estimates of different possible consequences of the Windscale Plant (increases or decreases in, e.g. the strength of the U.K. economy, restrictions on individual civil liberties in the U.K.), with, as one would expect, pro-nuclear subjects predicting that these consequences would be beneficial, and anti-nuclear subjects believing they would be detrimental.

More interestingly, subjects were also asked to select those possible consequences which they personally regarded as most important. Here we see a clear differentiation of "salience" with the pro-nuclear subjects choosing consequences such as: the U.K.'s ability to meet future energy demands, the strength of the U.K. economy, total environmental damage produced by the U.K. nuclear, coal, oil and gas industries combined, and total health hazards to members of the public from routine pollution by the U.K. nuclear, coal, oil and gas industries combined. In contrast, the anti-nuclear subjects chose as most important: restrictions on individual civil liberties in the U.K., the risk of nuclear terrorism, the risk of nuclear proliferation, and the risk of a serious nuclear accident in the U.K.

A similar differentiation was observed when subjects were asked to choose factors contributing most, in their view, to the overall "quality of life". Both sides regarded "conservation of the natural environment" as very important, but thereafter they diverged, with the pros choosing advances in science and technology, security of employment and industrial modernization, and the antis choosing decreased emphasis on materialistic values, reduction in scale of industrial, commercial and governmental units, and improved social welfare.

All subjects were also asked to choose, from a list of 16, any adjectives they thought to be applicable to the "pro-nuclear" and "anti-nuclear lobby". In terms of the most frequent choices, the pros decribed the pro lobby as realistic, rational and responsible, and the anti lobby as emotional, alarmist and ill-informed. In contrast, the antis decribed the pro lobby as materialistic, complacent and elitist, but the anti lobby as far-sighted, humanitarian and responsible.

Any analysis, which attempts to understand attitudes towards different energy sources in terms of some bland unidimensional continuum of approval/disapproval, is unlikely to be able to account for the selective and interpretative nature of these attitudes as revealed by a study of their content, and of the language in terms of which they are expressed, communicated and consensually validated.

Health and addiction

As with energy, health is an area which has, until recently, been largely neglected by social psychologists. It has instead been left largely to clinical psychologists to explore the relevance of psychology to medical problems, and their achievements have tended to be in the context of psychiatric illness, rather than that of physical illness and its prevention. Social psychologists, however, could have a particularly important part to play in such fields as preventive medicine, health education and rehabilitation. The further a person is from an operating theatre or hospital pharmacy, the more his health is likely to depend on his *own* decisions, attitudes and behaviour, and it is in helping to understand such decisions that social psychology can make a major contribution.

Let us consider the single most important problem in preventive medicine in the developed world: cigarette smoking and the diseases which it causes. The paradox is that so many millions of people continue to do something which they "know" is damaging to their health. The easy answer to this paradox is to say that smokers continue to smoke because they are "addicted", but this is almost totally uninformative unless one specifies what it means to be addicted. The position taken here is that the question of whether or not a given substance or behaviour is addictive is *not* independent of the attitudes a person holds and the decisions he makes concerning his behaviour.

Let us concentrate on the apparent paradox—people "know" they are risking their health but they carry on doing it. I would suggest that the kind of "knowing" that is involved here is very much the same as that involved when people say they "know" that they should conserve energy. In each case, it is often little more than an acceptance of a general form of words, which remains relatively insulated from concrete decisions. Although it may be accepted at an abstract level, its validity at the level of immediate personal decision involves much the same kind of checking out as that involved in energy conservation decisions. For instance:

(1) "What is the *observable* relationship between my stopping or continuing to smoke and the occurrences of dire consequences to my health?"

The answer to this seems to be very little. Maybe my cough is worse when I have been smoking heavily, and I get a bit short of breath, but I cannot ever really say, this cigarette's the one that's going to kill me. I cannot say, if I smoke this cigarette, it is going to make me less healthy than if I do not smoke it. What is more, I could get all kinds of diseases, or get knocked down by a car, whether I smoke or not. Diseases can happen to me anyway, without me being able to do anything about it.

(2) "What *would* I expect to happen if I tried to stop smoking?"
The answer is again, nothing very drastic, but it would be pretty unpleasant, and it would make me feel irritable, unable to concentrate and uncomfortable generally. If I kept it up for a while, I might feel a bit fitter, but I might also put on more weight, and would not expect to receive too much support from my friends. If I really managed to stop for good, I might live a bit longer, but right now I would be punishing myself, and giving up something I enjoy. Anyway, I would be very likely to fail if I tried to give up, so there is no point in trying.

Once again the reasoning shows departures from logical "rationality" in the direction of reliance on intuitive theories and heuristics. As with the energy conservation example, there is the same use of the covariation principle, the same emphasis on concrete rather than abstract instances, and the same dependence on short-range rather than long-range thinking, and again, in the short term, the reinforcement contingencies operate in favour of the smoker smoking another cigarette.

Where there is a difference is that one is dealing, it is generally acknowledged, with dependence on a pharmacologically addictive substance (Russell, 1976). But what does this mean in cognitive or attitudinal terms? In one sense, to say that a substance is addictive is to do little, if anything, more than make a statement about the reinforcement contingencies associated with consumption of that substance and the physiological processes associated with those contingencies. One is saying, typically, that the smoker finds the immediate experience of smoking very reinforcing, and finds it very unpleasant to go without cigarettes for any length of time. To say that a smoker "can't help" smoking is, from this point of view, as true and as false as it is to say that people "can't help" behaving in accordance with strong reinforcement contingencies.

A special difference does arise, however, when one considers people's intuitive theories about "addiction" and the social context in which the concept is used. The smoker is not simply someone in a reinforcement trap—there is something wrong with him, an addiction, a dependence, even a "mental disorder" (Jaffe, 1977) which he has, and of which he needs to be cured. I have argued elsewhere (Eiser, 1978; Eiser *et al.*,

1977, 1978) that non-smokers may be more likely than smokers themselves to make this kind of internal attribution, in a manner reminiscent
of actor-observer differences; smokers may nonetheless be relatively willing to define themselves as "addicts" and thereby, granted the prevalent
"sick role" conception of what an addict is, absolve themselves from
personal responsibility for "curing" themselves of smoking without outside help. In decision terms, this will mean that they will attach a very low
probability to their chances of success in any attempt to give up.

Another important example of the ascendancy of intuitive heuristics
over normative principles comes from smokers' perceptions of the
health risk itself. It is one thing to say that smoking is "very dangerous";
it is another thing to have an accurate picture of the relative dangers of
smoking and other avoidable and unavoidable threats to life. Slovic *et
al.* (1976, 1979) compared subjective frequency estimates of various
possible causes of death, and concluded that frequencies of dramatic
and sensational causes of death, which attract heavy media coverage,
tend to be overestimated, whereas people tend to underestimate the frequency of silent, undramatic killers of one person at a time or of lethal
events which are also common in non-fatal forms.

In a recent study (Eiser *et al.*, 1979) we asked smokers and non-smokers the question "Which do you think kills more people in Britain today;
smoking or road accidents?" the response alternatives being "smoking", "road accidents", and "both about equal". Under a quarter of the
sample gave the correct answer ("smoking") and the percentage of
smokers doing so (14%) was significantly lower than that of non-smokers. These results reduce one's confidence in the assertion that smokers
fully appreciate the risks of smoking, particularly when comparisons
with other risks such as accidents appear a frequent source of rationali-
zations, and when we know that statistical information about risks is
anyway difficult to process. Smoking therefore provides another example of an issue where attitudes and behaviour cannot be understood
without a consideration of the simplificatory strategies which individuals will use to cope with complex attitude-relevant information and
communications.

Furthermore, we can again expect such simplificatory strategies to
lead to people with different attitudes (and behaviour) viewing different aspects of the issue as more salient, and organizing their attitudes in
terms of different "scripts". An analysis now being conducted of un-
structured discussions about smoking held by groups of teenagers (two

smokers and two non-smokers per group) has revealed clear differences between the themes introduced into the discussion by the smokers on the one hand and the non-smokers on the other. For example, smokers were more likely to introduce themes such as relaxation, enjoyment, sociability, and comparisons between smoking and drinking and other habits, whereas non-smokers introduced themes such as general health, cancer, the smell and dirt of smoking, monetary cost and parental opinions.

It has become almost a truism that smoking in childhood and adolescence is largely determined by "social factors" and "peer group influence". With a few important exceptions, however, such as work on modelling and deterrence by Evans (1976), such "social factors" have received little social psychological analysis. Just as the activity of smoking may itself be a means by which teenage smokers can find a differentiated social identity, so also there is an attitudinal differentiation in the contrastingly selective views held by groups of smokers and non-smokers. Peer group influence is also peer group validation of such selectivity.

Conclusions

The primary contribution which attitude research can make to applied social psychology is that of illuminating the judgements and behavioural decisions made by groups and individuals. The potential role of the attitude researcher as an agent of change—as a persuader or propagandist—can raise ethical issues which I have made no attempt to deal with here. Even when it is deemed ethical for the attitude researcher to seek to persuade, however, the role of persuader is still premised on the antecedent role of analyst. Without an analysis of the intuitive theories and categorizations implicit in any attitude, any attempt at persuasion must at best be an undifferentiated, hit-or-miss endeavour. When such attempts fail, we are likely to hear the familiar refrains of "Attitudes can't be changed" or "Attitudes don't predict behaviour" or "Why bother with attitudes anyway?" I have tried to argue that any such failures of application stem, in the first place, from failures of theory, and that a more applied social psychology requires a more sensitive and differentiated concept of attitude.

In one sense, the role of change agent need entail fewer misgivings. The definition of a problem as a "problem" itself is rarely attitudinally neutral, and often involves preconceptions about the motives, abilities and perceptions of the individuals involved. To analyse the social psychological context of social problems may often involve directly challenging such preconceptions. For such a challenge to be successful, however, one cannot simply accept unquestioningly the preconceptions which much social psychology itself has held concerning the nature of attitudes and their relation to social behaviour. Without a re-examination of theory, one can barely even start explaining the most obvious, but in some ways also the most mysterious, fact about attitudes, namely that honest, relatively well informed individuals can hold diametrically opposed views about the same issue, and hold them strongly.

To explain attitudinal differences, one must explain and identify differences in the *content* of such attitudes, in the intuitive interpretations and selective judgements implicit in such content, in the language in which such interpretations and judgements are communicated, and in the social process and distinctions which may both maintain and be maintained by such differences. There are few issues, if any, where there is *no* room for choice over the aspects to which most salience should be attached, or for different selective interpretations which may each achieve apparent internal consistency, or for different social groups to adopt and defend different conceptions of the "truth". Where there is room for choice, there will also be room for conflict, and where there is conflict, there will be work to be done.

References

Abelson, R. P. (1976). Script processing in attitude formation and decision making. *In* "Cognition and Social Behavior" (J. S. Carroll and J. W. Payne, eds.). Erlbaum, Hillsdale, New Jersey.

Ajzen, I. (1977). Intuitive theories of events and the effects of base-rate information on prediction. *J. Person. Soc. Psychol.* **35**, 303–314.

Alexander, C. N. Jr. and Weil, H. C. (1969). Players, persons, and purposes: situational meaning and the Prisoner's Dilemma game. *Sociometry* **32**, 121–144.

Beckmann, P. (1976). "The Health Hazards of Not Going Nuclear". Golem Press, Boulder, Col.

Eiser, J. R. (1978). Discrepancy, dissonance and the "dissonant" smoker. *Int. J. Addictions* **13**, 1295–1305.

Eiser, J. R. and Mower White, C. J. (1974). Evaluative consistency and social judgment. *J. Person. Soc. Psychol.* **30**, 349–359.

Eiser, J. R. and Mower White, C. J. (1975). Categorization and congruity in attitudinal judgment. *J. Person. Soc. Psychol.* **31**, 769–775.

Eiser, J. R. and Pancer, S. M. (1979). Attitudinal effects of the use of evaluative biased language. *Eur. J. Soc. Psychol.* **9**, 39–47.

Eiser, J. R. and Roiser, M. J. (1972). The sampling of social attitudes: A comment on Eysenck's "Social Attitudes and Social Class". *Brit. J. Soc. Clin. Psychol.* **11**, 397–401.

Eiser, J. R. and Ross, M. (1977). Partisan language, immediacy, and attitude change. *Eur. J. Soc. Psychol.* **7**, 477–489.

Eiser, J. R. and van der Pligt, J. (1979). Beliefs and values in the nuclear debate. *J. Appl. Soc. Psychol.* **9**, 524–536.

Eiser, J. R., Sutton, S. R. and Wober, M. (1977). Smokers, non-smokers, and the attribution of addiction. *Brit. J. Soc. Clin. Psychol.* **16**, 329–336.

Eiser, J. R., Sutton, S. R. and Wober, M. (1978). Smokers' and non-smokers' attributions about smoking: a case of actor-observer differences? *Brit. J. Soc. Clin. Psychol.* **17**, 189–190.

Eiser, J. R., Sutton, S. R. and Wober, M. (1979). Smoking, seat-belts, and beliefs about health. *Additive Behav.* **4**, 331–338.

Evans, R. I. (1976). Smoking in children: developing a social psychological strategy of deterrence. *Preventive Med.* **5**, 122–127.

Eysenck, H. J. (1971). Social attitudes and social class. *Brit. J. Soc. Clin. Psychol.* **10**, 201–212.

Fischhoff, B., Slovic, P. and Lichtenstein, S. (1978). Fault trees: sensitivity of estimated failure probabilities to problem representation. *J. Exp. Psychol.: Hum. Percept. Perform.* **4**, 330–344.

Fishbein, M. and Ajzen, I. (1975). "Belief, Attitude, Intention and Behaviour: An Introduction to Theory and Research". Addison-Wesley, Reading, Mass.

Jaffe, J. H. (1977). Tobacco use as a mental disorder: the rediscovery of a medical problem. *In* "Research on Smoking Behaviour", (M. E. Jarvik, J. W. Cullen, E. R. Gritz, T. M. Vogt and L. J. West, eds). Department of Health Education, and Welfare: National Institute on Drug Abuse, Rockville, Md.

Kahnemann, D. and Tversky, A. (1973). On the psychology of prediction. *Psychol. Rev.* **80**, 237–251.

Kelley, H. H. (1971). Causal schemata and the attribution process. *In* "Attribution: Perceiving the Causes of Behavior" (E. E. Jones, D. E. Kanouse, H. H. Kelley, R. E. Nisbett, S. Valins and B. Weiner, eds). General Learning Press, Morristown, N.J.

Langer, E. J. and Abelson, R. P. (1972). The semantics of asking a favor: how to succeed in getting help without really dying. *J. Person. Soc. Psychol.* **24**, 26–32.

Moscovici, S., Doise, W. and Dulong, R (1972). Studies in group decisions, II: differences of positions, differences of opinion and group polarization. *Eur. J. Soc. Psychol.* **2**, 385–399.

Nisbett, R. E., Borgida, E., Crandall, R. and Reed, H. (1976). Popular induction: information is not always informative. *In* "Cognition and Social Behavior" (J. S. Carroll and J. W. Payne, eds). Erlbaum, Hillsdale, New Jersey.

Osgood, C. E. and Tannenbaum, P. H. (1955). The principle of congruity in the prediction of attitude change. *Psychol. Rev.* **62**, 42–55.

Pruitt, D. G. and Kimmell, M. J. (1977). Twenty years of experimental gaming: critique, synthesis, and suggestions for the future. *Ann. Rev. Psychol.* **28**, 363–392.

Rasmussen, N. C. (1974). "An Assessment of Accident Risks in U.S. Commercial Nuclear Power Plants". (WASH-1400) U.S. Atomic Energy Commission, Washington, D.C.

Russell, M. A. H. (1976). Tobacco smoking and nicotine dependence. *In*, "Research Advances in Alcohol and Drug Problems" (R. J. Gibbins *et al.*, eds), Vol. 3. Wiley, New York.

Slovic, P. and Lichtenstein, S. (1968). Relative importance of probabilities and pay offs in risk taking. *J. Exp. Psychol. Monogr.* **78**, 3(pt. 2) 1–18.

Slovic, P., Fishchoff, B. and Lichtenstein, S. (1976). Cognitive processes and societal risk taking. *In* "Cognition and Social Behavior" (J. S. Carroll and J. W. Payne, eds). Erlbaum, Hillsdale, New Jersey.

Slovic, P., Fishchoff, B. and Lichtenstein, S. (1979). Perceived risk: psychological research and public policy implications. American Psychological Association 87th Annual Convention, New York.

Tajfel, H. (ed.) (1978). "Differentiation Between Social Groups: Studies in the Social Psychology of Intergroup Relations". Academic Press, London.

Tajfel, H. (1981). Social stereotypes and social groups. *In* "Intergroup Behaviour" (J. C. Turner and H. Giles, eds). Blackwell, Oxford.

Teger, A. I. and Pruitt, D. G. (1967). Components of group risk taking. *J. Exp. Soc. Psychol.* **3**, 189–205.

Tversky, A. and Kahneman, D. (1974). Judgment under uncertainty: heuristics and biases. *Science* **185**, 1124–1131.

5

Energy Conservation:
A Psychological Perspective
on a Multidisciplinary
Phenomenon

G. Gaskell and P. Ellis

Conservation of energy is now an important ingredient in the energy policy of most Western countries. While there is a major impetus to develop renewable energy resources such as solar, wind and geothermal power, equal efforts are directed toward the conservation on nonrenewable reserves. It is the latter that have made an impact on consumers through government campaigns, the price and availability of energy and in the design of both dwellings and energy consuming appliances. In the past sometimes profligate consumption was legitimated by the assumption of cheap and almost unlimited energy and life styles reflected an unappreciated good fortune. Today, however, as most people must be aware, the era of plentiful cheap energy is over, bringing both domestic and international repercussions. More efficient and economical use of energy must become part of everyday life with individual contributions bringing personal benefits in terms of lower costs, or at least in reducing the impact of inevitable price rises, and collectively in lower levels of national consumption.

Social scientists in many countries have joined the legion of experts attempting to promote conservation in the domestic sector, a major contributor to total energy consumption: in the U.K. some 30%. The scope for conservation in this sector is debatable, but even the lower estimates represent a substantial saving. With no change in patterns of use other than certain good housekeeping measures, it is estimated that

This chapter is part of a continuing programme of research on Energy Conservation supported by the Social Science Research Council Grant No. RB 18-12-3.

savings of 15% could be achieved (Morris, 1974). Further savings would accrue from changes in preferred temperature levels, changes in the insulation of current and future housing, and the introduction of new technology. A recent influential analysis estimated that by 2025, U.K. domestic consumption could fall by 50% if a range of measures were to be adopted (Leach *et al.*, 1979).

Since 1978 the authors have been conducting a programme of research into energy use and conservation focussing particularly on the energy consumer rather than the purely technical or physical aspects of energy use. There is merit in giving priority to the understanding of consumer behaviour in the context of the domestic household sector. In the home there is considerable scope for personal control of energy use, it is where people are most likely to be motivated by price and exposed to new technology, and it is where people can learn new behaviours and assimilate energy related attitudes and values in a social setting. Given appropriate encouragement, consumers who use energy efficiency at home may generalize that behaviour to their place of work and to other situations where incentives may be less apparent. The general objectives of our research were two-fold: first to make a practical contribution to energy conservation policy using a social scientific perspective and secondly to approach this practical problem from a sound theoretical position so that the research might directly comment on contemporary social psychological theory.

In the course of this work which has involved liason with architects, economists and sociologists, and in terms of methodology with surveys, interviews and field experiments, frequent questions about the nature of social research have arisen. This paper is concerned with two interrelated aspects of this work. It begins by discussing a number of theoretical and methodological issues which have influenced our approach to applied research and then illustrates these issues by describing our social psychological analysis of energy conservation.

Theoretical and methodological considerations

With the benefit of hindsight, the creation, within the social sciences, of a variety of almost mutually exclusive disciplines may have limited the extent to which social scientific theory can contribute to general societal concerns. Probably the division of the social sciences was fostered partly by academic imperialism and partly by its convenience within university establishments. One of the costs of this has been the retreat away from broader social issues to small scale theories which fit more comfortably into the defined subject matter of a particular discipline; another cost is the extent to which researchers in the various disciplines work in relative isolation, ignorant for the most part of developments elsewhere in the social sciences which might have an important bearing on their work. Genuine multidisciplinary research is hampered by ignorance, mutual suspicion and the arcane languages of the various disciplines.

Perhaps uniquely among the social sciences, psychology sought to emulate the natural sciences in its pursuit of academic respectability. In some respects the paradigm of the natural sciences was and still is appropriate: the virtues of the experimental method in its most general sense for the evaluation of theory must be almost a *sine qua non* of an empirical science. Popper (1963) has shown how central to the development of scientific theory is the testing and refutation of the scientist's conjectures. But in other ways adherence to certain ideas and practices which are integral to the natural sciences has led psychology astray.

In this respect three related issues will be discussed, each of which has a bearing on the research reported; for convenience they will be discussed separately.

PASSIVE *VS* ACTIVE MODELS OF MAN

Popper (1972) makes a useful distinction between "passivist" and "activist" theories of knowledge in his broader discussion of epistemology and the philosophy of science. Classical empiricism, the model implicitly adopted by many psychologists is par excellence a passivist theory of knowledge. Providing the scientist can rid himself of biases, inhibitions and other confounding factors, the truths of nature will be revealed. Hence the hypothesis—free inquiry and the reliance on induction. Man, the focus of study, is seen as a passive object responding to the changing environmental contingencies as a function of past experience. In contrast to this passivist model is the activist approach advocated by Popper, in the tradition of the rationalist philosophers. Here mental activity is seen as a prerequisite for any observation, true for scientist and layman alike. Mental activity may be an hypothesis or a conceptual framework through which the world is viewed, interpreted and understood. Thus understanding of the world is a reflection of mental activity rather than of the true state of nature. Since mental activity preceeds understanding, man becomes an active, anticipatory agent. In this way actions and responses must be understood in the context of the actor's interpretation of his experience. In social psychology the provocative research on experimenter effects and artefacts [c.f. Orne (1962), Rosenthal (1966)] should have no-one unconvinced of the need to conceptualize man's behaviour in the light of activist models and to move away from narrowly deterministic models.

The effects of this change in fundamental epistemology are still reverberating in social psychology and confusion is rife. Some confuse epistemological and methodological considerations and wrongly claim that an "activist" psychology is *ipso facto* non-experimental because experiments necessarily imply a passivist approach. They fail to appreciate that choice of methods and of models of man are relatively independent and in their haste to purge psychology of all the attributes of the "ancien régime" run the risk of losing an important and powerful technique for the testing of theories of human behaviour. Given an activist epistemology the goal of science is not absolute, value free truths, but better understanding and explanation. Progress in science is the goal, the process by which new theories replace the old thereby expanding knowledge and experimentation is one means to that end.

PURE *VS* APPLIED RESEARCH

Another unfortunate hangover from the natural sciences is the notion that a useful distinction can be drawn between pure and applied social psychology. In the natural sciences such a view may be valid although it is difficult to see how any knowledge can eschew application. Pure science is the pursuit of theory, knowledge for knowledge's sake and as such thought to be free of value bias. Applied science merely takes the results of pure research to produce solutions to particular problems and makes no contribution to theoretical development. Thus pure science is accorded greater academic respectablity and prestige since, the argument goes, it alone leads to the growth of knowledge. Such a view is commonplace in social psychology notwithstanding the pioneering work of Lewin (1952) who saw the role of the social psychologist as that of contributing simultaneously to the understanding and amelioration of current social problems and to the development of theories about the processes involved: consider for example Lewin's work on group decision making and social change (Lewin, 1958). But after Lewin there was a retreat away from action research to the less contentious haven of "pure research"—the psychological laboratory. The experimental testing of hypotheses and propositions became synonymous with scientific psychology and applied research came to be viewed as second rate since it was considered to be value-laden and inevitably of little or no theoretical significance. Such considerations, however, are based on a limited conception of the nature of both pure and applied research. It is our contention that the study of social issues can contribute to both society and psychological theory and should be given a more central position within academic social psychology.

Given an activist epistemology it is dubious to consider any research as value free. As Rawson (1976) comments, social science is a social system and like any other institution with its particular ideology. The ideology of science leads to a particular kind of truth, but there are arguably several different kinds of truth depending upon the questions asked in the first place and who asked them.

Given recent developments in multivariate statistics, applied research can be methodologically more ambitious but in addition, we maintain that the most effective way of understanding social issues is to do so through a theoretical analysis and related empirical research.

Of course, atheoretical research can suggest a solution to a particular social issue, but such an approach is haphazard and restricted since any change in the prevailing situation can only be countered by guessing a new solution or further research. The advantage of theoretically based applied research is that its theoretical component not only contributes to the discipline itself but allows for the specification of practical procedures to obtain desired results in both stable and changing conditions. Moreover, a theoretical framework gives rational direction to further research by identifying anomalies or problematic issues. Theory must be an integral aspect of research not an optional extra and the explanatory power of a theory assessed in contexts beyond the psychological laboratory. Exploratory fact finding is a necessary component of science and may be required in the early stages of an investigation but such work should not become an end in itself. Its goal should be that of contributing to broader scale conceptions of the processes under investigation. It is these considerations which lead us to the view that distinctions between pure and applied social psychology are somewhat meaningless and a hindrance to progress: good research leads to both theory and application.

QUANTITATIVE AND QUALITATIVE DATA

In his Kurt Lewin memorial address, Campbell (1974) calls for the inclusion of qualitative knowing as data in action research. Qualitative
knowing comes from case studies, field work, participant observation
and common-sense understanding and is rarely accepted as sufficiently
objective to merit inclusion alongside quantitative, or "scientific data".

Campbell's paper attempts to achieve what Lewin failed to do—to
make the non-experimental methods of action research more accept-
able. In a sense it is an acknowledgement that the methods typical in
anthropology and sociology for decades have a place in social
psychological research. Such qualitative styles are not without prece-
dent in social psychology. La Piere (1934) concluded the report on his
famous attitudes and behaviour study remarking that:

> it would seem far more worthwhile to make a shrewd guess regarding that
> which is essential than to accurately measure that which is likely to prove
> irrelevant.

Asch (1956) used the understanding gained from extensive interviews with his conforming subjects to interpret their behavioural responses. However, in social psychology generally, the existence of a
trade off between reliability and validity has all too often been ignored
and putting almost exclusive emphasis on the former, researchers have
restricted themselves to a narrow range of phenomena which could be
distilled into numbers. When these numbers achieve statistical significance psychological relevance is automatically assumed. In our view a
more catholic approach towards research methods should be adopted,
in which the nature of the problem directs the choice of methods to be
used and where the experiences of the participants are systematically
explored. Qualitative approaches have a particularly important role in
furnishing the researcher with an analytic description of the phenomenon in question, an understanding of the situation as it appears to those
involved. The greater the researcher's appreciation of the other's perspective the more likely is he to be guided by informed judgement rather
than trial and error in the selection of hypotheses. In the process of collecting quantitative data the researcher will inevitably gain qualitative
insights which can contribute to the interpretation of the results and
allow for cross validation from different approaches.

Given a commitment to theory, and to an activist model of man, research must be seen in a dynamic, cumulative context. No one study is likely to lead to the complete corroboration or disproof of a theory. Every piece of research raises new questions, throws up further anomalies. Thus programmes of research must be assessed over a period of time and judged on the basis of their extent of understanding and explanation; not upon the quality of data used at any particular phase of the research. A social psychology without qualitative data would be as restrictive as one without experimentation. We now turn to a discussion of our work on energy conservation and illustrate how these considerations have influenced our approach.

Approaches to energy conservation: perspectives from different disciplines

In order to promote conservation of energy in the domestic sector, three broad instruments can be distinguished:

(a) The technical solution sometimes called a "fix" with the emphasis placed on the design of buildings, appliances and control systems. In the context of buildings smaller windows, better insulation and controlled ventillation are advocated.

(b) The economic solution with emphasis on pricing policy and tariffs. According to the tenets of classical economic theory, as the availability of a resource decreases so should price increase correspondingly, thus those consuming more are penalized and in aggregate demand will be reduced. On the face of it, two desirable objectives are met, conservation and social equity.

(c) The social solution with the emphasis on the use of persuasion, information and social norms to change the consumers' attitudes, knowledge and behaviours in the context of energy. It is assumed that if people come to appreciate the problem and know how to respond, the majority will behave accordingly and make the necessary savings.

All three strategies bear upon the consumer through either his house, pocket or attitudes and cognitions and social relations respectively, but it might be thought that only in the context of the social solution can social scientists make a contribution to energy conservation. We will argue however, that any solution to energy conservation involves social elements. New technology has to be accepted and properly used by householders if it is to be effective. The price mechanism too, must be viewed in more discriminating ways than making simple assumptions about a negative correlation between price and consumption. In our view an effective conservation policy must include technical, economic and social factors. This view, however, is far from generally accepted and a case needs to be made for the analysis of the human factors in energy consumption and conservation in relation to each type of conservation strategy.

Human factors in energy conservation

THE TECHNICAL SOLUTION

The technical solution seeks to reduce the energy requirements of buildings by introducing new designs for houses, new materials for buildings and sophisticated systems for space heating and ventilation. Thus, smaller windows, increased insulation of walls, floors, roof spaces and pipes, more efficient boilers and complex controls are used. Many of these innovations have been tested in a number of experimental building developments. Typically, in a group of houses half are built to the traditional standards and compared with the others built to include the new and improved specifications.

A number of such schemes have provided corroboration of the worth of particular features and have contributed to the development of models of energy use in buildings based on the physical parameters of the building and its energy system. Amongst the parameters of such models are the volume of the house, conductivity of the walls and windows, the efficiency of the space and water heating system. However, these models make good predictions only when the dwellings are unoccupied or include a simulated occupation. But when people live in the houses the levels of consumption and effects of technical innovations are difficult to predict. The behaviour of the occupants is outside the scope of these physical models which consequently are left wanting when innovations are assessed in the context of occupied dwellings.

The effects of loft insulation are a good example. By reducing heat loss this should lead to reductions in consumption. However, given an

insulated loft, some take up the beneficial effects by increasing tempera-
tures or the extent of their space heating. Thus bedrooms which were
previously unheated are heated and the occupants enjoy greater comfort levels. Clearly this is a more efficient use of energy: greater comfort
is achieved at the same level of consumption but it is not conservation in
the sense of reducing demand.

In some cases, occupants preferences militate against the effects of
technical innovations. Instead of using thermostats and time clocks to
control temperature, some prefer fresh air and use the windows for temperature control. Thus all the effects of insulation and draught proofing
are immediately wasted.

The extent of the contribution of consumers' behaviour to levels of
energy use is well illustrated by the finding that even in identical houses
similar families show variability in consumption of up to 4 to 1 (Cornish, 1976; Minogue, 1977). High and low consumption must be seen
as resulting partially from consumers' preferences and behaviour.
While technical contributions to conservation are clearly important, it
seems unrealistic to attribute the failure to achieve potential savings to
the perversity of consumers as argued by the Advisory Council on
Energy Conservation (1977). The alternative view that energy consumption is a sociotechnical phenomenon and that innovations must be
designed and assessed in the context of an understanding of consumers'
reactions is more logical and likely to be of greater value in the longer
term.

THE ECONOMIC SOLUTION

The economic solution is based on the price mechanism and the central
concept, demand elasticity is defined as the percentage change in demand over price. Estimates of demand elasticity in relation to energy in
the domestic and other sectors vary considerably. Olsen and Goodnight
(1977) report estimates from econometric studies in the U.S. ranging
between -0.67 and -2.00 (low to high elasticity respectively) for
household fuel consumption, with elasticity for electricity being generally higher than for petrol. On the basis of these estimates the reviewers
concluded that pricing strategies should be effective in reducing demand. At first glance, pricing policy seems to be the rational and equit-
able solution to the consumption of limited resources. Without doubt
sufficient increases in price restrict consumption thereby conserving

energy and is it not reasonable that those who consume relatively more of the scarce resource should be penalized?

This common sense logic is corroborated by the findings that consumers in unmetered district heating schemes use some 25% more fuel than those with individual meters (British Gas Corporation). However, there are some problems with pricing policy from both economic and psychological perspectives.

Lancaster (1969) discusses the general analytical problems associated with the concept of demand elasticity. He argues that it cannot be assumed that elasticity is constant over the whole range of price and demand change, thus an empirical estimate of demand assessed at one point on the curve may have no application to another point. Lopreato and Merriwether (1976) found that a 40% price increase in electricity was required before substantial reductions in consumption resulted, but if this level of increase were necessary the social consequences for the low income groups would be dramatic and probably too draconian for governments to contemplate. Whether such a policy would be effective in aggregate terms is questionable. The heaviest consumers in the domestic sector are the most wealthy and whilst these are the people who should be encouraged to conserve they show the least inclination to do so. As Katona (1963) argues, demand is not purely a function of price but of the individual's ability and willingness to pay. Many consumers do not believe that they can cut back on their energy consumption and absorb price rises by cutting down on other commodities.

Futhermore, the price of energy is not a perfect signal to direct demand. In the U.K. there are complex energy tariff structures which few understand. Increases in energy costs are paralleled by general inflation in other services and commodities and these factors serve to obscure particular changes in energy prices which might *ceteris paribus* lead to conservation.

Consumers seem to adapt to increased prices in a Helsonian sense (Helson, 1958). When petrol prices increased in 1974 there was a dramatic drop in consumption but the reduction was short-lived as documented by Lowe-Watson (1975).

Adaptation theory, in this context would predict that to maintain a continued reduction in energy consumption repeated price increases would be required at regular intervals. Thus as Kelman (1961) asserted, compliance only occurs when the rewards and punishments are present to control the behaviour.

But the most important shortcoming of a purely economic strategy such as pricing is that while it may motivate people to cut back it fails to tell them how to do so. With minimal levels of knowledge of efficient energy use, people adopt ill-conceived solutions often leading to lower levels of comfort at minimal reductions in cost. Such changes in behaviour are typically short-term and not paralleled by longer-term changes in attitudes and cognitions which are necessary if more efficient energy use and consequent reductions in consumption are to be obtained. To maximize its contribution to conservation of energy the price mechanism must be seen in the light of socio-economic models which take the knowledge, attitudes and behaviours of consumers into account.

THE SOCIAL SOLUTION

Having identified the need for both socio-technical and socio-economic approaches, energy conservation becomes a multidisciplinary issue. The psychological contribution centres on the understanding of the energy consumer and on the development of instruments which lead to personal and social change by affecting the attitudes, values and behaviours of individuals. To date, much social research has been descriptive and atheoretical in nature using surveys to assess consumers' attitudes, knowledge and reported conservation behaviours with the objective of specifying the characteristics of those who are more or less likely to conserve energy. Such a categorization of consumers is central to the design of campaigns and to the understanding of reactions to the technical and economic strategies.

A number of studies have demonstrated a weak correlation between education level, attitudes to conservation and likelihood of adopting conservation measures, but the relation with income is less clear. While studies show that low income groups are less likely to conserve, there is disagreement on whether high income groups are more inclined to save, although they have the greatest scope for conservation, they may also have little economic incentive to do so. (Ellis and Gaskell, 1978). In general the relations between socio-demographic indicators and conservation are rather equivocal and as Olsen and Cluett (1979) conclude "do not provide very useful information of what kinds of people will or will not conserve energy".

Thus an alternative approach to the categorization of consumers is required. Drawing on pilot research and on evaluation of public persuasion campaigns we have found it useful to hypothesize a dimension of energy literacy in order to describe consumers' current behaviours and understand their reactions to different conservation strategies. We make no assumptions about the relations between energy literacy and social class or educational level. The person low on energy literacy is likely to have only minimal knowledge about the energy crisis and a vague feeling that something needs to be done. He may also tend to attribute the problem and its solution to the government, oil companies, Arabs, etc. and typically feel that no individual can do anything to ameliorate the situation. Energy is rather like taxation—it has to be paid for and is outside the scope of individual control. If household finances demand that economies must be made, attempts to cut back are ineffective and inefficient due to lack of understanding of energy use in the home. Many householders on limited budgets have stopped using central heating and switched to localized heat sources. But in many such cases an efficient use of that central heating would be as cheap and much more convenient.

Through greater knowledge the energy literate is in a better position to conserve. Such a person appreciates the general energy problem and is knowledgeable about his domestic energy use. He knows which appliances consume most fuel and where savings can be made. The energy literate has decisional freedom, that is more options available with which to respond to changing conditions. Our research has been directed towards promoting energy literacy rather than conservation because the knowledge about energy use, the prerequisite for energy literacy and decisional freedom, encourages people to use energy more efficiently and when circumstances demand, to cut back. Without this kind of knowledge, even the strongest motivation to conserve, derived from high prices or persuasive appeals cannot be effectively realized.

Promoting energy literacy by mass media campaigns

The value of this theoretical categorization of consumers can be seen in the evaluation of public campaigns designed to promote conservation, e.g. the "Save It" campaign in Britain. Its effectiveness was gauged by a number of "intermediate indicators" such as the rate of acquisition of certain energy saving devices like loft insulation and hot water tank lagging. No attempt was made to monitor changes in consumption but householders were asked about other conservation measures and future intentions. The evaluation of the campaign over a three year period suggested that it had been cost effective (Phillips and Nelson, 1976).

The comparative success of this campaign is contrasted with some American experiences. Olsen and Goodnight (1977) conclude that the results of general publicity on energy issues had been minimal. Information concerning the overall energy problem had increased professed willingness to conserve, but there was no evidence that this had been translated into action.

Differences between the American and British campaigns may reflect government credibility, but another factor may be the type of message communicated. The "Save It" campaign was broadly conceived, advertisements stressed that over-consumption today would lead to future shortages. So in common with the American campaigns people were exhorted to save. But the "Save It" campaign included attempts to raise energy literacy by giving specific suggestions to reduce consumption: insulating lofts, doors, windows and hot water tanks, turning down thermostats and unwanted lights. With some of these measures the financial savings were shown. It is this type of useful information which may have been absent from the early American campaigns.

The failure of general appeals to change behaviour must come as no surprise to social psychologists familiar with the low correlations between attitudes and behaviour (Wicker, 1969). However, Fishbein and Ajzen (1975) demonstrate that attitudes can be predictive of behaviour if the former are specifically related to the latter. According to their thesis, changing general attitudes about energy issues would not be expected to affect specific acts of energy conservation. The relevant attitudes which communications should be trying to change are those about specific conservation behaviours. Such attitudes are made up from a set of beliefs held by the individual and the task of the communicator is to identify those relevant or "salient" beliefs and to couch communications in terms which are likely to change them. In a factor analytic study, Seligman et al. (1979) show that attitudes to comfort are amongst these salient beliefs and are important predictors of levels of consumption, implying that one obstacle to conservation may be beliefs and attitudes about the need to preserve comfort levels.

It should not be thought, however, that more general appeals are worthless but that their effects will be limited to certain consumer types. Only those who are relatively literate will be receptive to specific conservation suggestions. Those low on energy literacy will not be since they have yet to appreciate their ability to make a personal effort to reduce consumption. But these people may be influenced by more general communications. In designing campaigns therefore, general appeals may serve to raise levels of energy awareness so that more specific communications will fall upon receptive ears. This analysis affords an interpretation of the impact of price increases. For the energy literate they are a signal to either pay up or decide how to reduce consumption from the options available. For those low on energy literacy they are an affirmation that a problem exists, which may lead to greater receptivity to specific suggestions to conserve and in turn promote the change to literacy. Similarly certain technical innovations and developments such as energy labelling will be ignored or misused by those low on literacy.

We are currently developing this model of consumer behaviour. In particular we are testing the assumption of a dimension of energy literacy. It is possible that there are several dimensions reflecting different aspects of energy related behaviour, in its widest sense. Changes on one dimension may be the antecedent to changes on another or a consequence of it. A more sophisticated model may have important implications not only for energy conservation policy but also for the understanding of issues in social psychology such as cognitive structure and the relations between attitudes and behaviour. Even though we assume that the present conceptualization is too limited it has proved to be useful in synthesizing diverse research findings and suggesting new avenues for exploration. In the next section a further illustration of the importance within social research of a coherent theoretical model is discussed and of the way in which quantitative and qualitative empirical research led to modification of a particular model.

Consumption feedback and the involvement of the consumer

Often those consumers low on energy literacy fail to appreciate that they can achieve significant savings without resorting to dramatic and unattractive actions such as doing without space heating altogether. Even if this is appreciated they often lack the confidence in their ability to turn ideas into actions. Part of our approach to the social psychological aspects of energy conservation has been to investigate a particular social strategy—that of providing the domestic consumer with feedback on his energy consumption. A discussion of the background work and of our own research serves to highlight the issues concerning applied research made earlier in this paper.

In America a number of empirical studies have converged on the utility of providing domestic consumers with regular feedback on levels of energy consumption (for a review see Ellis and Gaskell, 1978). Several methods of providing feedback have been used. The immediacy has been varied from daily to monthly intervals, and the nature of the feedback itself has included unadjusted consumption levels, consumption adjusted for outside air temperature, converted into monetary units, or against some base line. With a few exceptions, studies in this genre lead to reductions in consumption of between 10 and 15%. Savings of this magnitude bring financial benefit to the consumer and would in aggregate lead to substantial national savings. But the research has not elucidated the nature of the mechanisms leading to reduced consumption, although it was generally assumed that feedback was clearly relevant to the individual, and with the advantage of credibility provided an observable consequence showing the effectiveness of conserving behaviour. However, in the absence of a conceptual framework there was no way of interpreting the processes underlying the results or of determining the most effective method of providing feedback. Thus here was an important practical contribution to energy policy with minimal theoretical under-pinning; this is its key limitation.

In Ellis and Gaskell (1978) we proposed that the literate energy consumer should be conceptualized in the light of activist models as an information processor engaged in operating a complex man/machine system. The term "system" is used to denote aspects of the dwelling and all appliances which consume energy. Thus, use of space and water heating, lighting and electrical appliances are inputs to the system giving an output of metered level of consumption. The perspective we adopted is taken by Annett (1969) in a review of research on feedback and task performance. In contrast to the behaviouristic view, Annett favours the information processing model of man in which the individual is seen as actively engaged in making sense of the world. The individual makes plans of action and anticipates the consequences. In order to monitor these plans he must receive and process information (feedback) on the results of his actions. Following Annett's analysis our initial formulation of the effects of feedback on energy consumption was to hypothesize that it had two consequences, a motivating and a learning function. In brief, we proposed that feedback might reduce consumption either by motivating the individual to change his overall consumption levels, i.e. a change in goal requiring a new plan, or by increasing system knowledge and thereby facilitating more efficient use of that system, i.e. the learning function. Such a model has also been proposed by Becker (1977) and McClelland and Cook (1978). Given this perspective other aspects of skills learning are relevant. Feedback is not necessarily an aid to learning unless the individual knows the appropriate transformation rules by which to interpret the output (level of consumption), in relation to his inputs (behaviours leading to consumption). Feedback must also be specific and immediate for learning to occur. Quarterly accounts as issued in Britain are one form of feedback, but one which clearly lacks the immediacy and specificity required for learning. We also thought that feedback might have a differential effect depending on the consumer's level of energy literacy. The learning function may be more applicable to literate consumers, while the motivating function may influence all consumers but lead to different behavioural consequences.

For the literate, it may lead to the specification of new goals and to efforts to reduce consumption to achieve these goals. Through drawing on knowledge of the energy system, such efforts are likely to be rational. But for those low on energy literacy motivation to cut back does not necessarily lead to conservation and efficient energy use for this requires knowledge of the system which is lacking. However, the formulation of a goal to cut back may make other energy issues more salient, thereby promoting increased receptiveness to specific information on conservation. Thus motivation stimulates those with knowledge to use it and those without knowledge to obtain it.

Whilst at that time we had no means of assessing energy literacy, this formulation led us to conduct two empirical pilot projects. In the first, a field experiment, sixty houses were sampled from a large municipal estate in London and divided into four conditions. A control condition provided base-line consumption levels. The others involved information, feedback on consumption and feedback combined with information. For the information manipulation a leaflet was prepared giving specific suggestions as to how energy could be saved—a simulation of a media campaign. Householders in feedback conditions recorded their consumption levels on specially prepared charts which allowed for the conversion of fuel consumption to monetary units and for day to day and week by week comparisons to be made. In the study, which lasted for three weeks, depth interviews concerning general energy issues and specific knowledge about conservation were conducted.

The experiment partially corroborated the predictions from the theoretical analysis but raised some doubts about the nature of the processes involved. The information condition was no different from the control in terms of reported saving measures. Information by itself had little impact. Feedback and feedback and information had similar effects in significantly increasing reported saving measures. But the low level of system learning in the feedback conditions suggested that those changes had occurred in the absence of increased knowledge of the input/output relationships of the system. From the interviews it was apparent that respondents were aware only of the gross aspects of their system, but not of the contribution of specific inputs to consumption. While this was a pilot project with relatively few subjects, it was clear that either the learning function of feedback had not occurred or that the type of learning involved was not the same as that predicted in the model.

This led us to conduct a second investigation focussing particularly on the nature of learning through feedback. In this project ten householders monitored their daily consumption for a period of eight weeks. Conceptually this project drew on Brunswik's lens model and the related research on multiple cue probability learning (Brunswik, 1956; Slovic and Lichtenstein, 1973). The lens model mapping the subject/environment system is analogous to the energy system. The criterion value becomes total energy consumption, and the cues to the criterion value, the individual inputs of the system—space and water heating, appliances, etc. The extent of system learning was operationalized by the accuracy of prediction of daily consumption. Given that the subjects had control over use of the inputs, their task becomes the assessment of the ecological validity of each input, i.e. its contribution to total consumption. In this research considerable importance was given to the qualitative accounts of the participants. They were interviewed regularly, and some kept notes on aspects of the task which either facilitated or inhibited their accuracy of prediction and understanding of their changing daily consumption levels.

The results of these two studies have led us to reformulate our ideas about feedback and its consequences. Originally we had viewed the motivating and learning functions of feedback as distinct processes— the former leading to short term changes in goals while the latter to longer term behavioural change. Learning about aspects of the energy system was thought to be the *sine qua non* of conservation. We now see the motivating and learning functions as different aspects of the same process.

The intial impact of feedback is to foster an energy awareness, the knowledge that energy consumption is reasonably predictable, potentially controllable and of intrinsic interest. We were surprised to find how much people enjoyed monitoring their consumption. Certainly they wanted to help us. People were attracted and enthused by the opportunity of exercising control over a hitherto unexplored aspect of their daily lives, c.f. White's concept of personal efficacy (White, 1959).

This awareness is the first hurdle on the path to energy literacy. But this by itself does not lead to attempts to conserve unless the person sets a goal to cut back. For most people the motivation for this new goal is the financial cost attached to everyday consumption. But here augmented knowledge is important. It is estimated that 15% of domestic energy is wasted and if consumers were to recognize this and appreciate the cost involved it might have a greater motivating function than appeals to "Save It". Some consumers fail to set a goal because they are not concerned about the expense and worry lest they might live less comfortably. Publicising the waste component in domestic use could provide a salient belief to counter such opinions. Even the super rich stop short of burning money!

However, given awareness and some consumption goal, feedback has two consequences which can be characterized as learning functions. It provides immediate and readily understandable information on task performance indicating in aggregate terms whether the goal has been achieved or not. Secondly feedback may lead to the learning about the characteristics of the system. This is necessary for energy literacy but conservation does occur in its absence. System learning, relating specific inputs with output is inherently difficult. Given the complexity of a house as an energy system having many inputs, with different use patterns and consumption levels and often simultaneous use, the interpretation of the output in terms of particular inputs is problematic. Our research suggests that system learning occurs but is restricted to the major energy consumers such as heating, cooking and washing. Use of these creates obvious peaks in the daily consumption record which are correctly identified as those aspects of the system which can potentially lead to savings. Both the motivational and learning functions of feedback are complex and interact continually. In order for feedback to lead to conservation augmented knowledge encourages goal setting and in the form of specific knowledge such as energy labelling, may facilitate system learning. But without energy awareness such information is not utilized because it is not salient to the individual. Our present research is aimed at testing these hypotheses.

References

Advisory Council on Energy Conservation (1977). Report of the Working Group on Buildings, Paper 7, Department of Energy, London.

Annett, J. (1969). "Feedback and Human Behaviour". Penguin, Harmondsworth.

Asch, S. (1956). Studies in independence and conformity: a minority of one against a unanimous majority. *Psychol. Monogr.* **70**, 416.

Becker, L. J. (1977). "Reducing Residential Energy Consumption Through Feedback and Goal Setting". Report PU/CES 55, Center for Environmental Studies, Princeton University, New Jersey.

British Gas Corporation. "Energy Usage in Buildings". Research and Development Report. BGC, London.

Brunswick, E. (1956). "Perception and the Representative Design of Psychological Experiments". University of California Press, California.

Campbell, D. T. (1978). Qualitative knowing in action research. *In* "The Social Contexts of Method" (M. Brenner *et al.*, eds). Croom Helm, London.

Cornish, J. P. (1976). "The effect of thermal insulation on energy consumption in houses". *In* "Energy Conservation in the Built Environment" (R. G. Courtney, ed.). Construction Press, London.

Ellis, H. P. and Gaskell, G. (1978). "A review of social research on the individual energy consumer". Department of Social Psychology, London School of Economics.

Fishbein, M. and Ajzen, I. (1975). "Belief, Attitude, Intention and Behaviour". Addison-Wesley, London.

Helson, H. (1958). The theory of adaptation level. *In* "Readings in Perception" (O. C. Beardslee and M. Wertheimer, eds). Van Nostrand, Reading.

Katona, G. (1963). The relationship between psychology and economics. *In* "Psychology: a Study of a Science" (S. Koch, ed.), Vol. 6, 639–676. MacGraw Hill, London.

Kelman, H. (1961). Processes of opinion change. *Public Opinion Quart.* **25**, 57–78.

Lancaster, K. (1969). "Introduction to Modern Microeconomics". Rand McNally, New York.

La Piere, R. T. (1934). Attitudes v. actions. *Social Forces* **13**, 230–7.

Leach, G., Lewis, C., Romig, F., van Buren, A. and Foley, G. (1979). A low energy strategy for the U.K. *IIED Science Reviews*.

Lewin, K. (1952). Problems of research in social psychology. *In* "Field Theory in Social Science" (D. Cartwright, ed.). Tavistock Publications, London.

Lewin, K. (1958). Group decision and social change. *In* "Readings in Social Psychology" (E. E. Maccoby, M. Newcomb and E. L. Hartley, eds), 3 edn. Holt Rinehart and Winston, New York.

Lopreato, S. C. and Merriwether, M. W. (1976). "Energy attitudinal surveys: Summary, annotations, research recommendation". Final report. Office of Conservation, U.S. Energy Research and Development Administration.

Lowe-Watson, D. (1975). The British motorist and the oil crisis. Proceedings of ESOMAR conference, Montreux, 131–146.

McClelland, L. and Cook, S. W. (1978). "Energy conservation effects of continuous in-home feedback in all-electric homes". Institute of Behavioural Research, U. Colorado, Denver.

Minogue, P. J. (1977). "Symposium: Thermal performance and energy use in housing". National Institute for Physical Planning and Construction Research, Dublin.

Morris, D. N. (1974). "Effects of energy shortages on the way we live". Paper P-5377, Rand Corporation, Santa Monica, California.

Olsen, M. E. and Cluett, C. (1979). Evaluation of the Seattle City Light Neighbourhood Energy Conservation Program. Batelle Human Affairs Research Centre, Seattle, Washington.

Olsen, M. E. and Goodnight, J. A. (1977). "Social aspects of energy conservation". Northwest Energy Policy Project, Study Module 18, Final Report.

Orne, M. T. (1962). On the social psychology of the psychological experiment. *Am. Psychol.* **17**, 776–783.

Phillips, N. and Nelson, E. (1976). Energy savings in private households—an integrated research programme. *J. Market Res. Soc.* **18**(4), 180–200.

Popper, K. (1963). "Conjectures and Refutations". Routledge and Kegan Paul, London.

Popper, K. (1972). "Objective Knowledge". Oxford University Press, Oxford.

Rawson, D. (1976). "Restructing value-issue reconsiderations of social psychology". Department of Social Psychology, London School of Economics.

Rosenthal, R. (1966). "Experimenter Effects in Behavioral Research". Appleton Century-Crofts, New York.

Seligman, C., Kriss, M., Darley, J. M., Fazio, R. H., Becker, L. J. and Pryor, J. B. (1979). Predicting residential energy consumption from homeowners' attitudes. *J. Appl. Soc. Psychol.* **9**, 70–90.

Slovic, P. and Lichtenstein, S. (1973). Comparison of Bayesian and regression approaches to the study of information processing in judgment. *In* "Human Judgment and Social Interaction" (L. Rappoport and D. A. Summers, eds). Holt Rinehart and Winston, New York.

White, R. W. (1959). Motivation reconsidered: the concept of competence. *Psychol. Rev.* **66**, 297–333.

Wicker, A. W. (1969). Attitudes versus actions: the relationship of verbal and overt behavioural responses to attitude objects. *J. Soc. Issues* **25**, 41–78.

6

The Phenomenology of Defensible Space

P. Ellis

Theories in environmental psychology

In discussions on the state of theory in social psychology, an emerging theme in recent years has been the idea that all theoretical approaches are embedded in sets of values which qualify their apparent objectivity. Among such values or "stipulations", the "model of man" underlying any theory is singled out for particular attention (Israel 1972). Contrast is drawn between those approaches which are modelled on the Newtonian paradigm of the physical sciences, which views man as equivalent to a physical object whose actions are determined purely by external forces, and those which take as their starting point the intuition that man is internally motivated and actively engaged in pursuing various social goals (Harré and Secord, 1972).

Approaches of the first type focus on the study of overt behaviour. Internal states of being, i.e. states of mind, may be indirectly inferred by the researcher, but may not be directly tapped from the conscious expressions of subjects because such expressions cannot be verified through observation (Joynson, 1970).

Approaches of the second type regard people's own reports of their internal states, and descriptions and justifications of their actions, as being essential data for understanding patterns of social behaviour, since these constitute direct evidence about the antecedents of individual activity. To give the name "phenomenalist" to these latter approaches is to assert that the essence of social phenomena is to be found in direct reports of human conscious experience (Ashworth, 1976).

In those branches of the social sciences which have addressed themselves to the study of relations between man and the built environment, the contrast between these two kinds of approach is particularly clear.

Since in the original formulation of behaviourist psychology the stimuli which were supposed to evoke human responses were physical, the view of buildings as constituting independent variables whose relationship with dependent behaviour should be the focus of systematic investigation follows naturally from a behaviourist stance. Much theorizing in environmental psychology has followed this path, as is evident from any of the standard texts (e.g. Proshansky *et al.*, 1970), but in psychology there has not yet been any systematic development of a phenomenalist approach.

Such an approach might be based on the application of the ethogenic model developed by Harré and Secord (op. cit.), as suggested by Buscescu and Stringer (1979). According to this, the built environment would be defined in terms of its relevance to patterns of social events (called "episodes" by Harré and Secord) which in turn were defined by reference to the rules and roles perceived by the participants to apply to them. In other words, the starting point for such an approach would be the fact of people engaged in social transactions, the structure of which could only be ascertained by reference to their own accounts of their behaviour and its antecedents; while the physical environment, instead of being a determining force, is viewed as relevant for study insofar as it is either used to further the social goals of those involved, or gets in the way of the achievement of those goals.

The consequence for environmental psychology of stipulating that man is an agent of his own behaviour is that the built environment is viewed as a medium of communication. In the same way that language is used to aid communication between individuals, so buildings are thought to provide raw materials for non-verbal linguistic expression. Whereas the study of non-verbal communication through body language is well developed in psychology (e.g. Argyle, 1967), the study of spatial language has hardly started. The anthropologist E. T. Hall is one of the few to have systematically explored cultural differences in "proxemic space" (Hall, 1968), but this has not been extended to a study of the way in which buildings are used to communicate, apart from some work on the "semiotics" of architectural form (Broadbent *et al.*, 1979).

The use of this kind of approach to environmental psychology would have a number of advantages. First it would meet the requirement for theory in environmental psychology, on which a number of writers have laid stress (e.g. Proshansky, 1976), that it be able to cope with the evident fact that man both creates buildings, and experiences them.

Whereas behaviourism has only dealt with the latter relationship, a communications model can address itself to both, since the meanings which are carried by spatial language are a medium of communication between one who generated them and one who receives them.

The second advantage is a consequence of the first. A theoretical approach which can entertain ideas of man as both creating and experiencing his environment is able to evaluate not just the active model of man on which it is based, but the alternative passive model which is assumed by behaviourism. By excluding data on human experience, behaviourist research is forced to confine itself to testing its own model, whereas a phenomenalist approach draws on both behavioural and experiential data and is thus able to test both behaviourist and phenomenalist models.

Such an approach also challenges the distinction generally made between pure and applied research. The idea that theory can only validly be generated in the "pure" conditions of the research laboratory without the contaminating influences of the outside world derives from the same Newtonian paradigm of value-free science which underlies behaviourism. The recognition by philosophers of science that the theorist inevitably introduces certain predilections and assumptions of his own in the act of theorising implies that "pure" objectivity is impossible to achieve. According to this view, as long as the theorist makes explicit the values which underlie his propositions (Israel, op. cit.), the research context in which theory develops is unimportant. If applied research allows for the entertainment of alternative models, then it provides scope for the development of theory which is just as "scientific" as that deriving from a more "pure" context.

The remainder of this paper attempts to demonstrate this point in relation to a particular area of research—that of the relationship between the design of housing areas and associated "territorial" behaviour. A behaviourist approach which led to the "defensible space" thesis will be first described. Then the author will describe his own research related to the same problem, which took a phenomenalist approach based on an active model of man.

The "defensible space" thesis

In his book "Defensible Space" (1972), the American planner and sociologist Oscar Newman addresses the problem of designing housing areas in such a way that the residents can exercise control over their surroundings and deter criminal acts there by intruders. He presents evidence that urban crime rates are directly linked with the physical design of the buildings, and concludes that certain modifications to the design are necessary conditions for making spaces "defensible". He develops a number of principles for the achievement of defensibility, as follows:

(i) The capacity of the physical environment to create perceived zones of territorial influence, by subdivision and articulation of areas so as to assist territorial attitudes.

(ii) The capacity of the physical environment to provide opportunities for surveillance of the surrounding spaces.

(iii) The capacity of the design to influence perception of a project's uniqueness, isolation and stigma, through the use of mechanisms which neutralize the symbolic stigma which often attaches to the physical form of housing projects, in such a way as to reduce the vulnerability of the inhabitants.

(iv) The juxtaposition of residential areas with other "safe" functional facilities such as commercial, institutional and entertainment buildings.

These principles were derived from the results of case studies of housing projects in New York City. Newman's basic research method was to compare crime rates in different projects with their physical design characteristics, seeking to make inferences about how the two were related when other variables were controlled. His methodology has been criticized (Hillier, 1973; Mawby, 1977) on the grounds that in presenting his evidence he tended to select those cases which supported his thesis, but ignored others which did not; further, that he did not adequately control for differing characteristics of the populations occupying housing projects to be compared, so that differences in criminal behaviour may have been due to pre-existing social differences rather than differences in architectural design. Mawby concludes that Newman "failed to establish the specific prescriptions of defensible space", but conceded that he had drawn attention to an important theme.

Newman's work has certainly been influential, but in spite of some further research by himself and others (referred to below), the "prescriptions" of defensible space are still not clearly established. Newman's approach represents the Newtonian paradigm for science which see people's behaviour as subject to various external determining forces. The debate over the validity of Newman's work hinges essentially on whether it is physical (design) or social forces which exert the stronger influence. In his later work, Newman (1975) places more emphasis on social forces, and takes the position that design modifications to housing projects are only likely to succeed if there is also an adequate social involvement on the part of residents. Both physical and social forces have their part to play in the determination of a response to defensible space. Other researchers have reached the same conclusion (Wilson, 1978), but no adequate theory has emerged to explain the way in which these forces operate or interact with each other.

From the phenomenological point of view an adequate understanding of the relationship between characteristics of defensible space and territorial behaviour could only be acquired by reference to the social reality experienced by those involved.

Newman's research methods made no reference to such phenomena, and there is very little discussion in his book of the social or psychological processes which might be involved in people's responses to defensible space. This theoretical gap is filled by ideas which appear to have been imported from ethology. Newman suggests that territoriality and "sense of community" are latent in the individual, and can through the experience of defensible space be "translated into responsibility for ensuring a safe, productive, and well-maintained living space" (Newman, 1972, p. 3). Under the right conditions, stimuli in the individual's environment will "trigger" the territorial response. These conditions include on the one hand particular characteristics of physical design, and on the other certain socially produced conditions such as a developed sense of personal and proprietorial rights and a feeling of personal effectiveness on the part of the individual.

This implied biological determinism of territoriality based on an analogy between human and animal behaviour has been popularized by a number of writers outside the social sciences (e.g. Ardrey, 1967), but has been subjected to much criticism within these disciplines. Hillier (1973) writing in criticism of Newman, bases an indictment of his theory of territoriality on the anthropological evidence showing that defence of territory and demarcation of space are patterns of behaviour which are by no means universal among human cultures. He points to the attractiveness of such a theory to Western society, which places a high value on personal property rights; it can be used to justify these on the grounds that they are a response to innate and unchangeable human tendencies.

Such criticisms of Newman's implied theory can only be made from outside because his territorial theory was not operationalized in such a form that it could be tested. The only tests were of the hypothesized links between environment and behaviour. Methodological criticism and subsequent research have shown that these links are by no means clearly established. The emergence of social factors in addition to those of physical design as necessary conditions for a human response to defensible space weakens the original thesis, but provides no adequate alternative. The importance of both physical and social factors could be taken as support for the implied ethological theory, since the precise conditions under which a territorial response might be expected are not specified in advance.

Thus theoretical development towards a body of knowledge about the relations between people and buildings was inhibited in two ways by the way Newman's research was designed and conducted. First his theory about the processes linking defensible space characteristics with territorial behaviour was neither explicitly stated nor operationalized in such a way that it could be tested. Secondly, through restricting its data base to statistics about physical design and crime rates, the research design did not allow consideration or evaluation of any alternative theoretical model. In the face of conflicting findings no constructive conclusions worthy of generalization have emerged from the defensible space research, nor is it likely, within the paradigm used, that they will. The following section reports on a series of studies which attempted to rectify these shortcomings.

Studies of place conceptions: a phenomenalist approach

The research to be reported consisted of a series of studies by the author of the conceptions held by tenants in Local Authority housing concerning the outside spaces in their housing areas. The research originated from design evaluation work carried out for architects which showed that a consistent problem on housing estates was the nuisance which could be caused by children's play activity. Physical damage, and visual and noise intrusion particularly affected older residents and those who had no children of their own.

The problem has been highlighted by many studies, and a variety of solutions proposed. In most cases it does not involve criminal activity but arises from the general boisterousness of youth; children will play anywhere and everywhere that they can (D.O.E., 1973), and the impact is exaggerated by building at high density. It has also been suggested that parents are more liberal with their children than they used to be, and exercise less control over what they do and where they do it. Three main solutions have been proposed. The first draws on Newman's work and advocates the physical solution of creating "defensible space". The second sees high child density as the major root of the problem, and recommends that concentrations of families with similar aged children be avoided. The third suggests that better management of estates (e.g. by resident caretakers) is the answer. In the context of vandalism, several recent studies have advocated various combinations of these solutions (Wilson, 1978; D.O.E., 1977).

The present research sets out to explore the general problem of the way in which outside spaces are used in housing areas—particularly by children, and the extent to which residents exercise control over children's play in different situations. A social psychological approach based on an active model of man led to the central focus on individual conceptions of the outside spaces, and the exploring of such conceptions through listening to individuals' own accounts of related experience. Pilot research yielded the idea that the prime component of place conceptions was the concept of spaces as settings for activities. The appropriateness of a range of activities to a particular setting, together with a perception of what activities actually occurred there, were the most salient characteristics of outside spaces for the residents who were concerned with them. This finding is supported by other research on environmental conceptions (Canter, 1977).

The conception of one or more activities as appropriate or inappropriate to a particular setting is described in these studies as an "activity scheme". The term "scheme" derives from Bartlett (1950), to describe an organizing mental model which mediates between the physical environment on the one hand, and social and behavioural variables on the other, and which can be meaningfully linked to both. It was hypothesized that the activity scheme would serve a similar mediating function. In the context of defensible space, the scheme for a particular setting might be influenced by a perception of its physical design, but whether or not this influence was reflected in behaviour would depend on additional social and psychological factors.

Since the theoretical model incorporated the idea of the physical environment as a medium of communication between individuals or groups of individuals, the activity scheme was seen as the relevant measure of whatever meaning was communicated via the built environment. Thus if a housing architect was attempting to convey messages about activity to those who encountered his design through the use of a common spatial language, the extent to which these were successfully communicated would be reflected in users' activity schemes. For example, the defensible space characteristic of enclosure might be used to signal a degree of privacy in an outside space, with implications for what activities would be appropriate there; measurement of users' schemes would show whether this message was "read".

The studies also set out to investigate territorial behaviour, particularly in the control by residents of children's play activity, so that its relations both with physical design variables and activity schemes might be explored. Methods were chosen which were able to test Newman's hypothesis of a direct environment-behaviour link, as well as to investigate the possible mediating function of the activity scheme, its supposed derivation from messages carried by the built form, and other relevant social or psychological variables.

RESEARCH METHOD

Two Local Authority housing estates were chosen for the main studies: the Chalvedon housing area in Basildon New Town, and the Pollards Hill estate in south-west London. The design of both estates is characterized by the provision of outside spaces which were intended by their architects to convey a meaning of semi-privacy. In the case of Chalvedon, the housing fabric is punctuated by green spaces of about three-quarters of an acre in size, each surrounded on three sides by 40 to 60 dwellings, and on the fourth side by an access road. The spaces vary in the degree of through access provided, but all, in the stated intention of the architects, were designed for use primarily by residents of the surrounding dwellings, and this intention was formally expressed in the degree of enclosure and symmetry in the design. The study explored residents' conceptions of a variety of the outside spaces in the housing area, among which were included two adjacent green spaces, named for study purposes as Greens One and Two (see Fig. 1).

Pollards Hill employs the design concept of perimeter planning, with a continuous ribbon development of terraces surrounding a large central green space and creating a series of partially enclosed smaller spaces between the terraces which on the outside are hard-surfaced vehicle cul-de-sacs called closes, and on the inside counterform are grassed greens (see Fig. 2). Again, the stated intention was that these small greens (about the same size as at Chalvedon) should be semi-private and used primarily by residents of the surrounding dwellings. This intention was formally expressed in terms of partial enclosure and of surveillance. Closes and greens at Pollards Hill are very similar in terms of their surrounding built form, but, apart from common features of enclosure and size, rather different from the green spaces at Chalvedon. Therefore no attempt was made to draw direct comparisons between the outside spaces on the two estates. Comparisons were made within each estate between spaces with similar degrees of enclosure, but differences in spatial resource. Thus at Chalvedon the two greens varied in degree of pedestrian access—Green Two enjoyed through access from the road, while Green One did not; and in provision of play equipment—Green Two was equipped with better and more attractive play facilities than Green One. At Pollards Hill, comparisons were made between close (hard) and green (soft), and also between green (enclosed) and the larger central green space (unenclosed). These comparisons allowed analysis to be made of the relative importance of the different physical design factors in the derivation of residents' activity schemes.

The main method of data collection was the conduct of individual interviews with about 50 households on each estate. The Chalvedon study preceded the Pollards Hill one, and techniques tried out at Chalvedon were extended and formalized at Pollards Hill. In both studies activity schemes were elicited by a formal technique. A range of activities said to occur in the various outside spaces had been established from pilot studies. These were reduced to representative lists of 20 (Chalvedon) or 12 (Pollards Hill) activities which were presented singly to householders who were asked to rate each one on a seven point scale, according to how appropriate or inappropriate they thought its occurrence to be in each of the spaces under consideration.

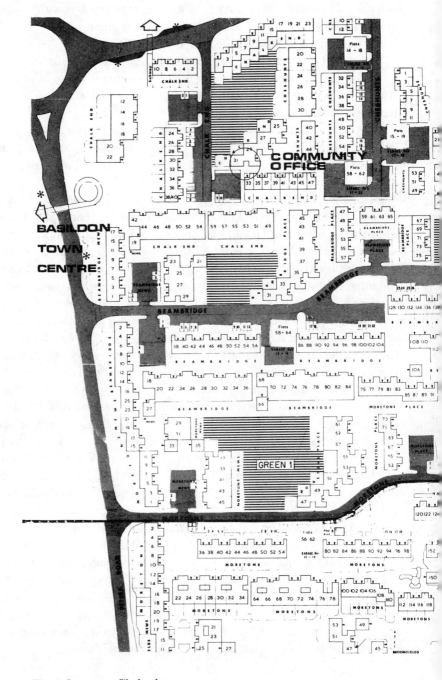

Fig. 1. Layout at Chalvedon.

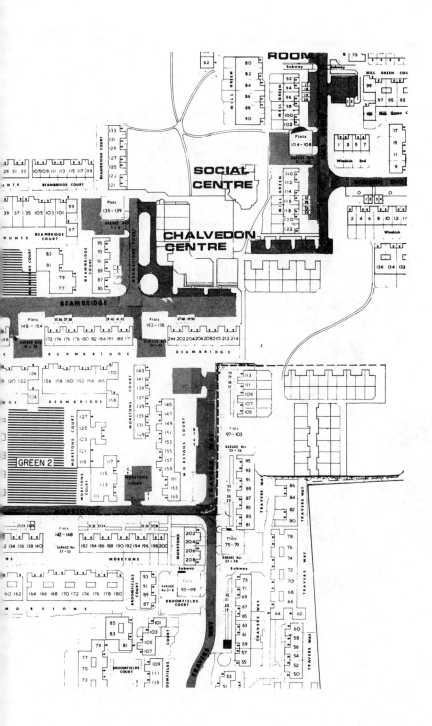

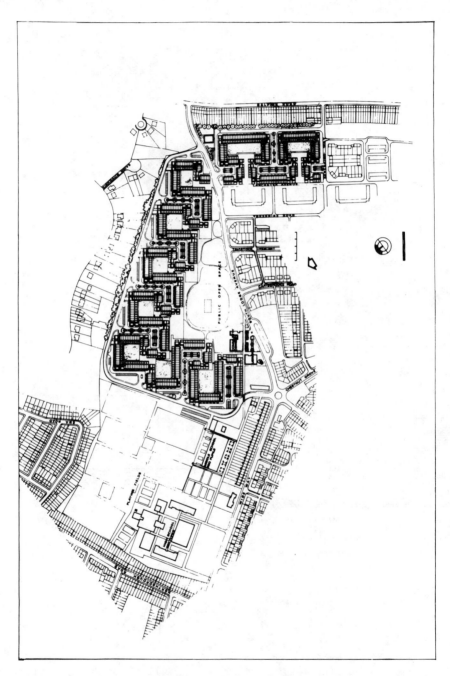

Fig. 2. Layout at Pollards Hill.

From these judgements of appropriateness, cumulative scales were formed which represent single dimensions of appropriateness of particular kinds of activity. Scales comprised of childrens' play activity items were labelled "play schemes", and indicated that residents' attitudes to children's play could be represented on a dimension of tolerance. An individual was allocated a scale score indicating his degree of tolerance of play in each of the spaces concerned, so that individual and group scores could be compared, and particular spaces could be characterized according to the average value of residents' scores in relation to them. The scalogram representing the play scheme at Chalvedon is shown at Fig. 3.

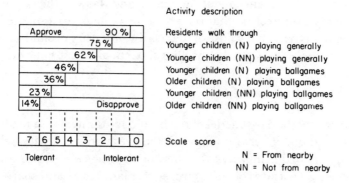

Approve	90%	Residents walk through
75%		Younger children (N) playing generally
62%		Younger children (NN) playing generally
46%		Younger children (N) playing ballgames
36%		Older children (N) playing ballgames
23%		Younger children (NN) playing ballgames
14%	Disapprove	Older children (NN) playing ballgames

Activity description

| 7 | 6 | 5 | 4 | 3 | 2 | 1 | 0 | Scale score |

Tolerant   Intolerant

N = From nearby
NN = Not from nearby

Fig. 3. Cumulative scale representing "play scheme" of Chalvedon residents for outside spaces.

It is worth noting that the majority of householders performed these judgement tasks with great ease. It had been established at the pilot stage that the appropriateness of activities was a generally salient consideration, and the main studies confirmed that based on their experience of the spaces concerned, most had clearly formed attitudes which they were ready to express. While doing so they were encouraged to comment freely, and after completion of the task the interviewer invited them to give their reasons for the attitudes expressed. These reasons, or accounts, were noted in detail and treated as primary data in seeking the derivation of activity schemes. Subsequent content analysis categorized the data so that counts could be made of the frequencies with which various reasons were given. High degrees of consensus, particularly at Pollards Hill, supported the idea that individual activity schemes have a social history, and derive from discussion and negotiation between users sharing a space: further comment will be made on this in the section "Understanding How Defensible Space Works" following.

In the Pollards Hill study formal scale measurement of a number of other variables was made, including expressed intentions to control children's play activity in the different spaces, which comprised the behavioural measure of territoriality, perceptions of the levels of activity normally occurring in the spaces, and various satisfaction measures. Reasons expressed for responses on these measures were elicited and recorded in the same way as for activity schemes. Most respondents were fluent in their comments about the spaces and the way they were used, conveying an impression that the phenomena being investigated were highly salient to them because of the relative intensity of children's play activity in spaces close to the dwellings, particularly at Pollards Hill.

RESULTS

From the hypothesized model of the built environment as a medium of communication, it was anticipated that residents' activity schemes would be derived primarily from their perceptions of the meaning carried by design features of enclosure, surveillance, size and shape of the outside spaces, as intended by the architects. However, the results of the studies showed that this theory required modification. Although in some cases the schemes were influenced by spatial meanings, there was another much stronger influence at work. This arose from the individual's perception of the spatial resources which the outside spaces had to offer, and by his knowledge of the extent of demand for use of such resources.

For example, at Chalvedon there was a significant difference between residents' average play scheme for the two greens. Green One was seen essentially as semi-private, in that it was regarded as appropriate for use by the children from the surrounding dwellings, but not by those from other parts of the estate. Green Two on the other hand, was regarded as legitimate for use by children from further afield, and by pedestrians passing through from one part of the estate to another; i.e. it was seen as semi-public.

In the reasons given for these expressed schemes (on which there was wide consensus), very few references were made to the formal characteristics of the greens. Most residents referred to the provision of Green Two with attractive play equipment which was not available in the nearby green spaces, and to the fact that Green Two provided a convenient short-cut between the shops and the main part of the estate to the north. Their knowledge of the way in which these facilities for play and for pedestrian circulation were distributed around the estate led them to judge that use of Green Two's facilities by outsiders was appropriate. In other words, they were placing social values on the spatial resources which Green Two offered—values which then influenced their activity schemes. The cognitive process by which individuals arrived at their activity schemes was evidently not just a mindless response to stimuli perceived in their environment, but a rational calculation of the various factors involved.

At Pollards Hill the findings were similar. Here the results of statistical analysis reinforced and validated the residents' own accounts. Average play schemes in relation to the closes and greens were primarily influenced by considerations about spatial resources, rather than by features of building form. The closes, much used for play, were generally regarded as inappropriate for this activity, and for two reasons. First there was a danger to children from vehicles; secondly, play tended adversely to affect the degree of amenity which residents expected at the front of their dwellings. In both cases, this exemplified a perceived conflict between the resource for play, and other resources for vehicles, and for amenity. The greens, intended to be semi-private, were thought of by most as semi-public: it was thought legitimate for children from other parts of the estate to use a green as long as this did not cause excessive nuisance. There was no significant difference between activity schemes expressed in relation to the small enclosed greens, and the large unenclosed green.

Figure 4 illustrates the nature of the two kinds of influence on the activity scheme. In the one case, meanings derived from a common spatial language are attached to perceived environmental cues, while in the other, social values are attached to spatial resources as a result of the individuals's perception of the distribution of and demand for those resources. These two kinds of influence represent quite distinct cognitive processes—the one based on communication, the other on rational calculation. The existence and dominating influence of the latter process

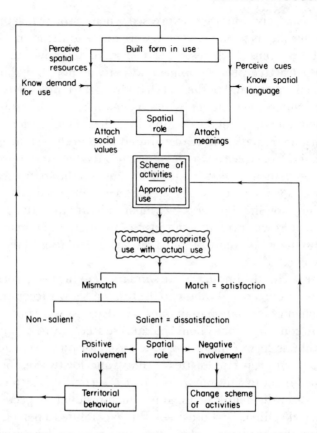

Fig. 4. Theoretical model for understanding the relation between defensible space and territorial behaviour.

in the reported studies became evident through the use of data from residents' own accounts of their behaviour, and led to a radical modification of the theoretical framework. Without the accounts data, the significance of physical design features, whether of building form or spatial resource, could only have been attributed to their communicative function, in support of the hypothesized model of the built environment as a medium of communication. Play equipment, for example, carries a message about its function. But residents' accounts indicated that it was not its communicative function which was primary in influencing activity schemes, but its function as a resource, the appropriate use of which was to be judged according to a rational consideration of the demand for it. The accounts method allowed realization that individuals are not merely passive recipients of spatial meanings, but through their experience of the built environment attribute social values to it, leading to cognitive schemes which are essentially socio-spatial. This has important implications for the defensible space thesis which will be drawn out further in the final section.

The schematic diagram in Fig. 4 also shows that activity schemes are mediated by an individual's role. In the studies reported, households were divided into two groups for analysis, defined as having positive or negative involvement with the outside spaces. Those with a positive involvement tended to be families with children who were the main users of the outside spaces for play; those with a negative involvement were generally older people whose children had grown up and left home. These two groups tended to vary in the social values they attached to spatial resources: the positive involvement group were generally more tolerant of play activity than the negative involvement group.

These variations in spatial role were also relevant to whether an individual householder was prepared to engage in territorial behaviour to control children's play. It was found that a key factor affecting territorial behaviour was the existence of a discrepancy between a householder's activity scheme—the way he thought a space *should* be used—and the way he perceived it was actually used. Where this discrepancy was salient to the individual (it was more salient for older people who were more affected by the nuisance of high levels of play), the size of it was strongly linked to expressed satisfaction. The more that actual levels of play exceeded desired levels, the more dissatisfaction was expressed. Given a salient mismatch between actual and desired levels, with resulting dissatisfaction, a householder was likely to take action to reduce the mismatch, or discrepancy. But whether he reduced it by territorial behaviour aimed at changing the way spaces were used depended on several further factors related to his spatial role.

Families with children were more likely to control the activity of their own and others' children. They felt that they had more right to do so, and that their controlling actions would be effective. Older people without children on the other hand felt less effectual, less right, and were less likely to behave territorially. The consequence for the latter group was that they were obliged to tolerate a mismatch between desired and actual levels of play, with accompanying feelings of dissatisfaction. In some cases it appeared that they had modified their activity schemes to match the reality of use of the outside spaces—a defensive reaction which was their only means of reducing a cognitive mismatch. Figure 4 shows diagrammatically these processes whereby territorial behaviour was found to be linked with activity schemes, spatial roles and expressed satisfaction.

CONCLUSION

The results support the general theoretical model of man actively pursuing particular social goals. The activity scheme clearly represents a goal which individuals sought to achieve with respect to use of the outside spaces; as such it functions as a mediating concept between built environment and territorial behaviour. Territorial behaviour could be explained in terms of an individual's activity scheme and his spatial role. It could not be explained purely in terms of characteristics of the built form. In the Pollards Hill study, Newman's defensible space model of direct links between design features such as enclosure and territorial behaviour was tested by correlating individual intentions to control children's play with the factor of enclosure of the outside spaces concerned. The correlation was low and statistically non-significant. The alternative theoretical model incorporating the activity scheme as a mediating concept was found to have some validity. But that part of it which postulated that the scheme would be derived from spatial messages communicated through the built form had to be modified to incorporate the second process of attaching social values to spatial resources. Such theoretical development within an applied research framework was made possible through the use of a phenomenalist approach which dictated the collection of data from residents' own accounts of their behaviour.

Understanding how defensible space works

The reported research suggests that experience of spaces and the way they are, or might be, used is a key element in understanding individual responses to the design of the built environment. In relation to defensible space, people do not "react instinctively" to perceived stimuli of enclosure or surveillance. Both resident and potential intruder may perceive these design features as cues and attach similar meanings to them based on a common spatial language. But this is only one of the psychological processes involved, and probably the less important one. Resident and intruder may also perceive in the physical design different sets of spatial resources. For the resident the setting concerned may be seen as a place for his children to play, for quiet amenity or for his own recreation. His spatial role implies a goal of using it for these kinds of activity, and the value which he places on these resources will be affected by his perception of his own and others' need for them, and by existing normal use patterns. In contrast, the potential intruder may perceive the space as offering resources for pursuit of his own, quite different goals. His designs for use of the space may include theft or destruction of property, or merely his own and his friends' recreation or convenient access. The value *he* places on these resources will be affected by their desirability to him and his perception of the norms of use. The resulting activity schemes of both parties will be a function not just of the characteristics of the physical design, but of these social considerations as well. The manner of variation between activity schemes will thus depend principally on the different spatial roles involved.

Further information about an individual's goals would be needed before any prediction might be made of whether he would act consistently with his activity scheme. The potential intruder might be dissuaded from intruding into a defensible space by his assessment of the probability of being apprehended, by the influence of others, or by the perception of more attractive or easier targets elsewhere. The resident might or might not "defend" his territory according to his strength of feeling of his own territorial rights, or his assessment of how effective his intervention might be. His defence might also take several forms. He might confront intruders or potential intruders in person, or he might reinforce the existing environmental cues in the setting with further material signs or symbols of his own. Both these kinds of action involve the introduction of changes to the physical environment, which in turn affect either the environmental cues or spatial resources (or both) perceived by the potential intruder. They may consequently change his activity scheme. The goal of achieving consistency between activity scheme and actuality for the resident may be a highly salient one, in which case territorial action will become more likely; or it may be less salient, in which case he may be content to live with a measure of inconsistency, or discrepancy.

From the designers' point of view, user behaviour is inevitably hard to predict. The conclusion of the present argument is that designers would do better to concentrate on the prediction of schemes of activity, which constitute a vital link between the built environment and associated behaviour. A knowledge of the spatial resources regarded as relevant to a particular situation by likely users, and the different values placed on these by those with varying spatial roles is an important part of the design process. This does not mean that no generalities are to be found between situations and between individuals. One of the characteristics of activity schemes in the studies reported was that they were shared by groups of individuals, and changed over time. At Pollards Hill there were indications of a continuing process of negotiation between residents, leading to greater consensus among individual activity schemes.

In the case of play, such negotiations apparently occurred as a result of the children's own activity. If their play in a particular space gave annoyance to other residents, those residents would be likely either to chase them off or complain to their parents. Disputes can, of course, lead either to convergence or divergence of the two parties' viewpoints. At Pollards Hill there was a marked consensus among the activity schemes of the different household types, with parents of children showing concern for the old people's amenity, and at least some of the old people showing considerable tolerance of noisy play. This estate has been occupied for about ten years. In contrast most Chalvedon residents had lived on their estate for only two or three years, during which time it appeared that much less community feeling had developed, less social negotiation had occurred, and consensus among activity schemes was much lower.

It is important to realize that activity schemes are not fixed, but have a social history and a life of their own. This carries implications for the roles of designer and applied researcher. Instead of thinking in terms of fixed relationships between particular design features and patterns of behaviour, the designer should be exploring and creating the physical conditions under which activity schemes can develop towards shared consensus on the appropriate use of housing space. The researcher's function is to study users' activity schemes and their social development, in order to feed back to the designer the success or failure of his physical solutions.

References

Ardrey, R. (1967). "The Territorial Imperative". Collins, London.
Argyle, M. (1967). "The Psychology of Interpersonal Behaviour". Pelican, Harmondsworth.
Ashworth, P. (1976). Some notes on phenomenological approaches in psychology. *Bull. Brit. Psych. Soc.* **29**, 363–368.
Bartlett, Sir F. (1950). "Remembering". Cambridge University Press, Cambridge.
Broadbent, G. *et al.* (eds). "Signs, Symbols and Architecture". Wiley, Chichester.
Buscescu, D. and Stringer, P. (1979). Place and two case-studies in Milton Keynes. Paper to the International Conference on Environmental Psychology, University of Surrey, Guildford.
Canter, D. V. (1977). "The Psychology of Place". Architectural Press, London.
Dept. of Environment (1973). "Children at Play". Design Bulletin No. 27. H.M.S.O.
Dept. of Environment (1977). "Inner Area Study, Lambeth. Housing Management and Design". Report by the consultants. D.O.E. ref.: LAS/LA/18.
Hall, E. T. (1968). Proxemics. *Current Anthropol.* **9**, 2–3.
Harré, R. and Secord, P. F. (1972). "The Explanation of Social Behaviour". Blackwell, Oxford.
Hillier, B. (1973). In defence of space. *R.I.B.A* Journal (Nov.).
Israel, J. (1972). Stipulations and constructions in the social sciences. *In* "The Context of Social Psychology" (J. Israel and H. Tajfel, eds). Academic Press, London and New York.
Joynson, R. B. (1970). The breakdown of modern psychology. *Bull. Br. Psych. Soc.* **23**, 261.
Mawby, R. I. (1977). Defensible space: a theoretical and empirical appraisal. *Urban Studies* **14** (2), 169–179.
Newman, O. (1972). "Defensible Space". Architectural Press, London.
Newman, O. (1975). Community of interest—design for community control. *In* "Architecture, Planning and Urban Crime". Report of N.A.C.R.O. Conference held on 6 December 1974. War on Want, London.
Proshansky, H. *et al.* (1970). The influence of the physical environment on behaviour: some basic assumptions. *In* "Environmental Psychology" (H. Proshansky *et al.*, eds). Holt, Rinehart and Winston, New York.
Proshansky, H. (1976). Introduction to 2nd ed. *In* "Environmental Psychology" (H. Proshansky *et al.*, eds). Holt, Rinehart and Winston, New York
Wilson, S. (1978). Vandalism and defensible space on London housing estates. *In* "Tackling Vandalism" (R. V. G. Clarke, ed.). Home Office Research Study No. 47. HMSO, London.

7

The Role of the Mass Media in Creating Exaggerated Levels of Fear of Being the Victim of a Violent Crime

A. N. Doob

A person does not walk alone at night because he or she is afraid of being a victim of a violent crime. A man buys a hand gun and keeps it loaded in his house in order to protect himself from burglars. A woman warns her daughter against taking public transportation at night because she worries that her daughter might be attacked. A mother does not allow her child to play alone in a park near the family home because she fears that the child will be molested by a stranger. Each of these examples involves what appears to be an important problem in our society: people are changing their lives and encouraging others to change theirs, because they are afraid of being the victim of a violent crime.

Fear of crime is apparently not a new problem in many societies. In the late nineteenth and early twentieth century in the United States, and in early nineteenth century Paris, there was apparently a rather serious concern about indiscriminate criminal attacks on innocent people (Conklin, 1975). Like many other social problems, we tend to think of the problem of crime as a recent one, brought on by the "evils" of modern society. However, as Conklin (1975) points out, "The idyllic image of a crime-free past shared by many is untenable in light of historical evidence". However, be the problem new or old, it would appear that people do, presently, fear being the victim of a violent crime. Hence, no matter what one estimates as the age of the problem, it does seem to be a problem at the moment.

In recent years, it appears that there has been a shift in "official" (political) attention from the offender in crime to the victim of crime.

Part of this shift is, of course, supported by summaries of research on at-tempts to change offenders into non-offenders (see, for example, Lipton *et al.*, 1975; Brody, 1976). The simple summary of these summaries is that attempts to change people by sentencing them to particular prison programmes are unsuccessful: correctional programs do not correct. This finding, then, combined with general attitudes about the causes of crime leads to calls for "concern for the victim of crime" rather than concern for the offender. When one looks at crime victims it becomes a natural next step to consider the general effects of crime on the community. Aside from anything else, this approach helps society view "criminals" as uncorrectable deviants where society has no recourse other than to help victims. In the past 15 years "victim surveys" have become an integral part of some countries' "war on crime" (see, for example, the programme of victim surveys in the United States). Part of these surveys, interestingly enough, often deals with "fear of crime".

As with all fears, it is difficult, if not impossible, to determine the amount of fear that is appropriate for a given amount of danger. Only at the extremes (e.g. the person who does not venture from his home be-cause of fear that a complete stranger will choose him as the victim of a violent crime) can we really say that a fear is truly exaggerated. At less extreme levels of fear, we have no way of scaling fear and actual risk in a psychologically meaningful way. Using a simple cost-benefit analysis, we might be able to show that the cost of activities forgone because of fear of crime is high. However, except by making some rather arbit-rary and questionable assumptions, it is difficult to combine this esti-mate with an estimate of the fear or anxiety avoided by deciding not to put oneself in perceived jeopardy. An alternative, but not entirely satis-factory, way of estimating exaggerations in an area such as this is to have people estimate the likelihood (on a scale of probabilities) of the occurrence of certain crime-related events. This, too, has its limitations since it assumes that the scale that is being employed has ratio proper-ties. As with many other such problems in social psychology, the issue of what constitutes exaggerated levels of fear can be avoided somewhat by looking at relative levels of fear of various people or groups of people in our society. In terms of the purpose of this paper, I would suggest that this, for the most part, should be sufficient.

The effects of high levels of fear of being the victim of a violent crime appear to be both psychological and behavioural. People not only worry about being the victim of a violent crime, but they arrange their lives in such a way that they avoid what they perceive to be dangerous activities. Recently, for example, Horace Cutler of the Greater London Council said that "In my view, there are tens of thousands of people in London who last night were afraid to open their front doors" ("London Evening News", 4 October 1978, p. 8). In a survey we did in Toronto, which is known to be one of the safest cities in North America, we found that approximately 39% of the people asked indicated that they "often" or "very often" decided not to walk alone at night because (they were) afraid of being the victim of a violent crime". In a similar vein, approximately 30% of our respondents answered "yes" to the question "Should women carry a weapon such as a knife to protect themselves against sexual assault". Approximately 22% of our respondents thought that "it is useful for people to keep firearms in their homes to protect themselves".

To the extent that these are exaggerations of certain problems, or exaggerated reactions to a problem, then there are important costs. Obviously, people's quality of life is likely to deteriorate if their activities are severely restricted by fears of going out. Similarly, there can be rather large, and often ineffective, investments of money to avoid or deter crime. One proposal to deal with apparent violence in some Greater London Council flats was to have "three or four policemen (living in) flats on different floors of buildings where there is trouble" ("London Evening News", 4 October 1978, p. 8). Fifty-four per cent of the respondents to our survey in Toronto said that they thought "it would be a good idea to spend more money on police patrols of (their) area of the city". A good deal of research would suggest that increasing police patrols will do little, if anything, to reduce the amount of actual crime in a neighbourhood. Furthermore, if one assumes that high levels of fear will tend to discourage people from going out on the street, then there exists the possibility that people's action (or inaction) will lead to a self-fulfilling prophecy: people avoid going out because they are afraid; fewer people, then, will be on the street or in public places; these streets or public places will then appear more dangerous, because they have few people on them, and, indeed, they may in fact become more dangerous areas because there are relatively few people around.

A somewhat separate question that can be asked is who benefits from this increased fear. In a certain way, it would seem that in North America there are two separate groups who appear both to encourage fear and to benefit from it: the police and the "protect yourself" industries. In many North American cities, apparent increases in crime rates are used as a justification for increased police budgets. More generally, there appears to be a conscious attempt by many companies to exploit fear of crime in the advertisements for burglar alarms, expensive door locks and such things as travellers cheques. It seems likely that in other areas, fears are created in order to "sell" some kind of economically or politically attractive solution.

Entertainment television as a cause of fear of crime

When we look for likely causes for exaggerated levels of fear of crime, entertainment television is likely to be seen as a reasonable culprit. For one thing, entertainment television is blamed for a variety of other social problems: increased levels of violence in our society, desensitization of people to violence, illiteracy, dyslexia, poor eyesight, obesity, the breakdown of moral and family values and probably other things as well. There are, however, some other more empirically based reasons why entertainment television is a likely contributor to high levels of fear. People watch an enormous amount of television; in North America it is not difficult to find people who watch 30–40 hours of television a week. Furthermore, in many North American cities, a large choice of programmes is almost constantly available; in Toronto, for example, we receive 16 different Canadian and American television stations. Social psychology is obviously not completely blameless in this area. We have published, in the past 20 years, numerous studies that suggest directly or indirectly that television is a cause of part of the violence in our society. Seldom have we or any other group tried to consider the benefits of television along with its costs. Finally, since we probably tend to think of high levels of fear of crime as being a new problem, we tend to look for recent changes in society. Relatively speaking, the advent of television is new.

For the policy maker, television is one of the few potential "causes" of society's problems that is theoretically within the control of government. Although it might be difficult to define what type of programming one wants to encourage or discourage, it is, theoretically possible to control television output since the number of people or organizations controlling television programming is small, and the access to television broadcasting is controlled by government. The same cannot be said of newspapers. Radio, it seems to me is somewhere between television and the newspapers in terms of how easy it is to control. However, at least for North America, television seems to be much more important in most people's lives than radio, and the fact that it is so heavily controlled does mean that its content can theoretically be changed.

In North American television, the picture of society that comes out over television is clearly distorted. Not only do the programmes not mirror normal life (or even normal problems), but the picture that it gives of such aspects of society as crime is clearly distorted. Violent serious crimes between strangers seem to be the rule on television, whereas most reported crime in society tends to be minor property crime (without violence). More importantly, from the point of view of understanding the importance of television in teaching people about their society, it would appear that the distortions of entertainment television are more likely to be seen as "true" by heavy television viewers than by light television viewers. Putting this differently, it has been shown that heavy television viewers are more likely to see the world as being like television than are those who spend less time in front of the television set (Gerbner and Gross, 1976a,b).

Going one step further Gerbner and his associates have suggested that watching a lot of television makes people afraid of the world they live in. This causal inference is based, for the most part, on a survey conducted in four American cities in which respondents were asked "During any given week, what are your chances of being involved in some type of violence: about a 50–50 chance, about a 1 in 10 chance, or about a 1 in 100 chance?" The answers to this were then correlated with the respondent's reply to the question "How many hours a day do you usually watch television?" Controlling for various other factors (e.g. age, sex, education, etc.) Gerbner showed that the relationship still held: those who watched a lot of television reported being most likely to feel that they had a high likelihood of being involved in some kind of violence.

Television viewing and fear of victimization: Is the relationship causal?

Obviously, the problem with any research such as Gerbner's is that the list of possible artefacts is infinitely long. Gerbner and his associates attempted to control for some of the more obvious socio-economic factors

that might have created the effect he reports. It occurred to Glenn Macdonald and me (Doob and Macdonald, 1977, 1979) that one rather obvious factor had not been looked at: the actual level of crime in the community. If one assumes that those people who live in high crime areas are
more afraid and that those who live in high crime areas watch more
television, it is easy to see how a correlation between television viewing
and fear could be created where no such relationship really exists. A
sample of people who are afraid and high television viewers (those living in high crime areas) combined with a sample of people who do not
watch much television and who report low levels of fear (those living in
low crime areas) would produce an overall correlation. However,
within the low or high crime samples, there might well be no relationship whatsoever between television viewing and fear of victimization.

The study that this analysis suggested was quite straightforward:
people living in high and low crime neighbourhoods should be sampled
separately. If Gerbner and his associates are correct, there should be a
relationship between television viewing and fear in each type of neighbourhood. If, on the other hand, the effect he reports is really due to the
more basic fact of how much crime there actually was in the neighbourhood, then there should be no effect of television viewing on crime after
the effect of neighbourhood is removed. This, then, was the study that
Glenn Macdonald and I did (see Doob and Macdonald, 1977 and 1979
for the details).

With the aid of the Metropolitan Toronto (Ontario, Canada) Police,
we chose four areas of metropolitan Toronto in which to conduct our
surveys: two were suburban, two were in the downtown area, with one
of each being relatively high and the other being relatively low in crime.
A random sample was drawn from each of the areas and respondents
were contacted by commercial door-to-door survey interviewers. They
were first asked to indicate, on a schedule of television programmes for
the previous week, which programmes they had watched. Then they
answered a 37-item fixed alternatives questionnaire. This questionnaire consisted of six questions dealing directly with the person's estimate of his or her own likelihood of being a victim of a crime; four questions dealing with estimates of the likelihood of particular groups of
people being victims; four questions dealing with the perception of
crime in general being a problem and there being a need for more police
personnel; two questions dealing with the necessity to arm oneself;
eight questions of a factual nature dealing with crime; three questions

dealing with society's response to crime; four questions dealing with the respondents' view of Toronto with respect to crime; three questions dealing with the respondents' prediction of their response to a request for help; and three questions dealing with media usage. The whole interview took approximately 45 minutes on average.

A factor analysis of the questionnaire results indicated that there was only one factor that accounted for a reasonable amount of variance. For the purposes of this paper, I will refer to the factor scores derived from this factor as "fear of crime". Nine questions had reasonably high loadings on this factor. Typical questions were the following:

> To what extent are crimes of violence a serious problem in your neighbourhood?
> What do you think the chances are that if you were to walk alone at night on the residential streets of your neighbourhood each night for a month that you would be the victim of a serious crime?
> Do you ever decide not to walk alone at night because you are afraid of being the victim of a violent crime?
> Is there any area around your home (i.e., within a mile) where you would be afraid to walk alone at night?
> If a child were to play alone in a park each day for a month, what do you think the chances are that he would be the victim of a serious crime?

Obviously, our analysis of the possible artefact in Gerbner's findings assumes that people who live in high crime areas will report more fear and will report watching more television than people who live in low crime areas. There was strong support for both of these assumptions: in both city and suburb those living in high crime areas watched more television and were more afraid.

Although Gerbner and his associates do not report measures of association between fear and television viewing, our calculations showed a phi and a contingency coefficient of about 0·13. Turning then to our data, the results were quite similar when pooled across neighbourhood: people who watched a lot of television were more afraid ($r = 0·18$). (The results for the amount of violent television—subjectively rated—are the same for this and all other analyses.) Thus the basic Gerbner findings were replicable.

However, when we turned to the relationship of television viewing and fear *within* area, the average correlation dropped to non-significance. Alternatively, when a multiple regression analysis was performed on these data using the fear of crime scores as the criterion, the amount of television watched contributed nothing after more basic factors such as neighbourhood, sex and age, had been entered into the equation.

In terms of fear, then, there seems to be little support for the notion that watching a lot of entertainment television will have any effect.

Entertainment television and the "picture of crime"

Earlier in this chapter, I mentioned that there were a fair number of other questions that were asked that did not weigh heavily in the fear of crime factor. Interestingly enough, some of these questions did correlate with the amount of television watched both across and within neighbourhoods. Although it is difficult, and obviously subjective, to describe the difference between these other questions and the "fear" questions, it seems to me that these other questions were of a more "factual" or "policy" nature. Thus instead of dealing with the likelihood of being the victim of a crime, they dealt with the actual incidence of certain kinds of crime as well as the steps that people ought to take to avoid being the victim of a crime. Examples of these questions are listed below. In addition, the correlation between the responses to the question and the amount of television viewing pooled across areas and the average within area correlation are given.

> How many murders do you think took place in Metropolitan Toronto during 1975? ($r = 0.15, 0.12$; high TV with high number of murders)
> Approximately what proportion of assaults in Toronto are directed against members of racial minorities by whites? ($r = 0.10, 0.12$; high TV with high proportion)
> During the last five years, how many people do you think were murdered in the subway? ($r = 0.15, 0.12$; high TV with high number)
> Would you imagine that you would be more likely to be seriously harmed by someone you knew previously or by a complete stranger? ($r = 0.12, 0.09$; high TV with stranger)
> Do you think it is ueful for people to keep firearms in their homes to protect themselves? ($r = 0.31, 0.20$; high TV with definitely yes)
> Should women carry a weapon such as a knife to protect themselves against sexual assault? ($r = 0.18, 0.17$; high TV with definitely yes)

Obviously, it is possible that some other artefact (other than neighbourhood) may account for these correlations. However, it seems plausible to suspect that entertainment television does contribute to the "picture of crime" that people have largely because there is no other major source of such information.

This analysis, then, suggests that "fear" is not causally related to the amount of television that is viewed, whereas the "picture of crime" that people have is much more likely to be related to the amount of television that people watch.

The news media, fear of crime and people's "picture of crime"

Various people have pointed out the problem in discovering effects of the mass news media. In an area of interest such as crime, we know that crime news is one of the most popular newspaper content areas for North American readers. Given this high level of exposure, it would seem likely that any dramatic event would be known to most publicly aware members of the community independent of whether they actually read newspapers regularly or listened to the news on the radio since such events would likely be talked about in normal everyday encounters. Similarly, of course, even if such informal exchanges of information did not take place, it would be virtually impossible to separate out the effects of the different media. Furthermore, effects, if they do occur, are likely to be small and cumulative.

All of this suggests that we should not be too surprised to find that the amount of exposure to television news, radio news or the newspaper does not correlate with fear of being the victim of a violent crime. The findings are simple and consistent: across or within neighbourhoods, there was no sign of a relationship between the amount of exposure to the news media and fear. Our rather standard way of looking at the effect of some event on people in social science research is to look for variations in exposure (created experimentally or observed naturally). In this case, for the reasons I have already mentioned, this may not be appropriate.

However, it still seems reasonable to suspect that news reporting does affect people's view of crime, even though it may not directly affect fear. The concern, of course, is that news gives people a distorted view of crime. Studies of the reporting of crime in the media (e.g. Davis, 1952) suggest that the nature and amount of crime reporting does not reflect what apparently is occurring in the community. Obviously, this is not too surprising, since news, by its very nature, is the reporting of the unusual. However, I think that the problem is somewhat more serious than that: dramatic crime is likely to "sell" the news and make it interesting for news readers, listeners and viewers. Hence there may be pressures to distort the news in the direction of making it more frightening. Roberts (1977) in a survey of Toronto newspapers' treatment of violence gives a number of such examples:

> In a report of a study showing that in the past 14 years only 13% of Canadian murder victims were strangers to their assailants, one newspaper (the Toronto "Sun") used the headline "Our murders break pattern" and quoted a police detective who "declared" that "statisticians and lawmakers were giving the public the wrong image" since according to his view of the matter in Toronto in the previous eight months there had been more murders by strangers (pp. 217–218).

In this example, it would appear that a story that could have been written in such a way as to reduce fear of strangers was written in a manner almost designed to have the opposite effect.

> In a story reporting the head of the Toronto Transit Commission's statement that "violence in the subways is an absolute non-issue" (based on statistics showing a very low level of violence of any sort), there were included "tips" designed to make a subway ride safer. These included checking for suspicious strangers and (for women) carrying a "rape whistle"—but not wearing it around the neck where apparently it is "handy for the strangling type of pervert" (p. 219).

Roberts gives numerous other examples of headlines and stories from the Toronto papers that appear to be designed to dramatize the frightening aspects of crime and to avoid mention of any context that might make the incidents reported understandable and not frightening.

This kind of news reporting would appear to be likely to distort a person's view of crime. The problem that Glenn Macdonald and I were faced with was how to find out whether this was the case. We settled on a rather simple technique, though like most methodologies, it clearly has its limitations.

Experiments on the presentation of news

Using each of the mass media sources of news (radio, television and newsprint), we created our own news stories. These news stories were shown/played to a sample of volunteer subjects, and they were then asked to indicate (on a written questionnaire) their views about that kind of crime.

Our specific plan was to create three variations on a news broadcast (or set of stories in the case of the newsprint experiments). We wrote a story about a murder. In one set of experimental conditions, the assailant was assumed to be a complete stranger to his victim. The second experimental condition was the same except that it also included a statement that stranger-to-stranger murders were relatively rare. The third broadcast did not include the story of the murder.

Our materials were quite realistic: the television newscasts were recorded in a Toronto television station by their regular news reader; the radio newscasts were recorded by a news reader of a popular radio station, and the newspaper stories were typeset in the format of newspaper stories.

We then were able to get visitors to the Ontario Science Centre to volunteer to participate in the experiment. They were exposed to one of the sets of stories (with the murder story embedded amongst three or four other stories) and were then asked to indicate what proportion of assault victims are total strangers to their assailants, whether they thought that they would be more likely to be seriously harmed by a complete stranger or by someone they knew, and what proportion of Toronto's murder victims were known, related to, or married to their killers.

The results are quite simple and straightforward: in each of the studies (print, radio, television) the very clear effect was that those who were given the "authoritative information" about the incidence of stranger-to-stranger murders appeared to accept this information, and feel it less likely that such crimes would occur generally or to them.

Putting crime in context then, and perhaps even giving people a more realistic view of the nature and incidence of crime, can have an effect on the way in which people view crime.

Summary of these findings

It would appear that the rather simple notion that entertainment television (or the news media generally) contribute in a simple direct fashion
to fear of being a victim of violent crime is probably wrong. At least in
the study that we did, there was no evidence that entertainment television was the culprit when one first took account of the neighbourhood a
person lived in and age and sex. However, in different kinds of studies it
seemed that entertainment television and the news media may contribute to a (sometimes distorted) view of crime.

At this point, however, the psychological relationship between this
distorted view of crime and fear of being the victim of violence is not
clear. It would appear that they may be rather independent factors.

In retrospect, this apparent independence does not seem too surprising. One might draw the analogy with cognitive and emotional components of attitude. Similarly, when one considers "fear of crime" in the
context of other fears, it should not be too surprising that the more
"emotional" aspect of this particular fear would relate differently than
the more "cognitive" component to outside influence. When one looks at
extreme phobias, it is not difficult to find people who "know" that they
should not be afraid of something that they find to be quite frightening.
However, it does leave us in the rather unfortunate position of not having found out much about the problem that we started off investigating.

Relevance for countries outside of North America

Perhaps before looking at the research that has been done on the relationship of the viewing of entertainment television to fear of violence
outside of North America, it is worthwhile to step back from this question and ask why it is one would even think that such results would be
generalizable (or transportable) to a different place. When one looks at
the question "Does viewing television make a person afraid" it is clear
that there are a fair number of unstated intervening variables that
would have to mediate the relationship if it did exist. In the first place
by "television" in this simple question, we really mean "entertainment
television" or, perhaps, more specifically "violent entertainment television". Why should we assume that this "independent variable" is the

same in different countries? Why should we assume that the phenomenon, even as it does exist, would not be specific to the particular kind of violence that is shown and available in large doses to the discriminating viewer in North America? Secondly, perhaps there are specific conditions that must exist before people will assume that their society is like the television they view. For example, it might be that only in a society where "crime on the streets" is an important political and social issue, would effects like those described in this paper be likely to be found. Looking at the "dependent variable" of this relationship, there is no automatic reason to believe that the "messages" on television outside of North America have anything whatever to do with the kinds of measures that we used in our studies and which Gerbner and his associates used in theirs.

In other words, the reason that one should be cautious about considering generalizing these specific findings is that none of the variables I have been discussing have anything at all to do with psychological processes. The variables that we measured in our survey deal with rather gross societal variations. Hence they might well have quite different meanings in different societies.

With this in mind, then, we can turn to the studies that I am aware of outside of the North American context. In a 1976 survey in Portsmouth (England), Piepe, Crouch and Emerson found essentially no relationship between responses to the question "How often do you think that violent incidents of any kind happen around here" and reported amounts of television viewing, after effects of social class and type of housing (owner occupied *vs* council flats) had been controlled for. Similarly, Wober in a much improved replication of Gerbner's basic study, failed to replicate Gerbner's findings in Britain. Using Gallup Polls Limited, Wober found no relationship between the amount of reported television viewing and responses to how trustworthy people were and the perceived likelihood of the respondent being robbed.

Wober (1981) concludes that

It should be accepted, therefore, that there is no evidence for a paranoid effect of television on British viewers, although the proposition has twice, and adequately, been put to the test. Two approaches are available for interpreting this situation. One is that what may be true in America is not true in Britain, for which difference it will be useful to explore the reasons. The second is that the Gerbner thesis has still not been demonstrated convincingly in America, and the effect exists neither there nor in Britain.

Clearly, my view is that Wober is correct in both explanations. The "fear" effect has not been adequately demonstrated in North America. However, for the other effects that we found, there is no compelling reason to expect similar findings in other countries. Essentially, this research shows that a "message" (television) has an effect (altering people's "picture of crime"), but this same message does not affect fear. When we move from one country to another, the message (and the context for that message) change, and the nature of the effect that is measured may also change.

This study in the context of applied social psychology

Probably the best reason for considering this research to be "social psychology" is that I was trained as a social psychologist (even though my collaborator in this research was not). A second possible reason is that the most available report of the research is published in a journal with social psychology in its title. These two approaches to the definition of social psychology suggest that almost anything that we do that involves humans or interacting (or co-acting) animals can be considered to be social psychology. A third, perhaps more reasonable reason for considering this research to be social psychological is that research on "communication effects" or "media effects" has been central to social psychology for the past 60 years.

But what, then makes this research "applied"? I think that it is studies such as these that point out the difficulty in making any kind of firm distinctions between applied and "basic" (pure?) social psychology. To the extent that we were looking at communication effects on fear, this work is clearly "basic". On the other hand, to the extent that these data have relevance in informing government policy on the media the research is clearly applied. I tend not to worry about this distinction. Rather I would prefer to ask the question: Does the research help us understand something important? If the answer is "yes" then that is sufficient.

From the funding agency's point of view, however, the research was clearly applied. The (Ontario) Royal Commission on Violence in the Communications Industry was interested in making recommendations about the possible regulation or control of the various media and felt that in doing this it had to have some idea about media effects. Having made the decision not to try to replicate the "TV causes violence" studies, the Commission made the decision that some aspects of media effects might be specific to the culture in which the media were available. "Fear" effects, which had been studied in the context of high crime cities in the United States probably seemed to them to be a good candidate for research in the Canadian context; hence their decision to fund this research.

The Commissioners obviously did not know what to expect from the research, and it may have even been an embarrassment to them, given that they had invited George Gerbner to speak before them. Obviously, however, I feel that they made a worthwhile decision to support research on this topic, and in the long run, it is possible that the applied question that this Royal Commission was interested in may have some small impact on "basic" or "pure" social psychology.

References

Brody, S. R. (1976). The effectiveness of sentencing: a review of the literature. H.M.S.O., London.

Conklin, J. E. (1975). "The Impact of Crime". Macmillan, New York.

Davis, F. J. (1952). Crime news in Colorado newspapers. *Am. J. Sociol.* **57**, 325–330.

Doob, A. N. and Macdonald, G. E. (1977). The news media and perceptions of violence. *In* "Report of the Royal Commission on Violence in the Communications Industry", Vol. V. "Learning from the media", pp. 171–226.

Doob, A. N. and Macdonald, G. E. (1979). Television viewing and fear of victimization: is the relationship causal? *J. Pers. Soc. Psychol.* **37**, 170–179.

Gerbner, G. and Gross, L. (1976a). Living with television: the violence profile. *J. Communic.* **26**, 172–199.

Gerbner, G. and Gross, L. (1976b). The scary world of TV's heavy viewer. *Psychol. Today* **9**, 41–45, 89.

Lipton, D., Martinson, R. and Wilks, J. (1975). "Effectiveness of Correctional Treatment — a Survey of Treatment Evaluation Studies". Praeger Publishers, Springfield, Mass.

Piepe, A., Crouch, J. and Emerson, M. (1977). Violence and television. *New Society* **41**, 536–538.

Roberts, J. A. (1977). Sampling of the treatment of violence by Toronto newspapers. *In* "Report of the Royal Commission on Violence in the Communications Industry", Vol. V. "Learning from the media", pp. 216–223.

Wober, J. M. (1981). Televised violence and paranoid perception: the view from Great Britain. *Public Opinion Quart.* (in press).

8

Towards a Renewed Paradigm in Movie Violence Research

J.-P. Leyens, G. Herman and M. Dunand

... The way in which communication is transmitted in various types of social structure is an obvious example where the individual and the group are interdependent

C. Hovland, 1951

The interest in aggressive behavioural effects of filmed violence started with two great American researchers. We all know them: Bandura and Berkowitz. However, neither were interested, at least in the beginning, in the effects of filmed violence *per se*. Bandura was studying imitation, especially aggesssive imitation; and the use of a videotaped model was a more economical and methodologically sound solution than a "live" model. Because there was no difference of effect between these two kinds of model, a new paradigm for studying the influence of filmed violence was created. As it arose within the framework of "social learning theory", it is no surprise that all the variables which have subsequently been investigated have concerned learning (reinforcements, generalizations, etc.). Berkowitz, on the other hand, was revising the old frustration-aggression hypothesis. He insisted on the presence of stimuli associated with violence; and aggressive films were precisely such stimuli. Again, it is not surprising that the factors studied in this tradition were concerned with their power to elicit more or less aggression (the meaning of the films, the moral justification, the anxiety provoked by the films, etc.).

Both the researchers and their followers immediately saw the implications of their experiments for the mass media violence problem. Data

This research was supported by Grant No. 2.4561.75 from the Fonds de la Recherche Fondamentale Collective.

were accumulated which showed that, under given conditions, aggressive films enhance, rather than decrease or fail to modify, the aggressive behaviours of viewers. But criticisms emerged, mainly from people in the television industry and in departments of communication. In general these criticisms were directed at: (1) the use of artificial films, (2) the unnatural setting of the laboratory and (3) the dubious validity of the means of measuring aggression.

At a time when relevance was fashionable if not compulsory in the American universities, experimenters answered these criticisms in the following way. They went to the field, to natural life settings, and showed regular commercial movies or television programmes to subjects—mainly children and adolescents—whose aggressive behaviours were observed in various ways. One study (Feshbach and Singer, 1971) found a decrease in aggression for some subjects in the violent treatment. Another one (Milgram and Shotland, 1973) did not find any effect.[1] While the results of yet other field experiments (Goldstein et al., 1975; Leyens et al., 1975; Parke et al., 1977; Stein and Friedrich, 1972; Steuer et al., 1971) were, in general, identical to those found in the laboratory: violent films or television programmes increased the aggressive behaviours of viewers, especially of those who were usually aggressive.

The conclusion of this stream of research seemed self-evident: because the results obtained in the laboratory and in the field converge, the problem is exhausted. Why not look at another problem? And indeed one notices that during the past few years there have been scarcely any papers on the topic in major social psychological journals. But we do not accept that conclusion. On the contrary we think that many aspects of the effects of mass media violence still need to be investigated. We know that such violence can have an effect upon viewers. Sometimes, researchers have found how this effect comes about, at a psychological level. But they have scarcely ever tried to answer the "how" question in terms of social variables.

This neglect has its origin in the theoretical issues (social learning and frustration-aggression) which led to the studies and to the experimental paradigms used in the laboratory: a single subject confronting a given film and just one confederate and/or experimenter whose behaviour is carefully programmed. Going into the field did not reverse the perspective. Actually, when experimenters left the laboratory for the field, they did not change their approach very much. They merely made slight modifications to the independent and dependent variables.

Overall the paradigm was borrowed from the laboratory. The films are still considered as the only source of influence, individuals are taken as the unit of analysis and, if they are distinguished, it is done according to their base-line aggressive behaviour. This last variable also reflects the laboratory situation in which subjects are made angry or not. Such an approach neglects the fact that individuals exposed to different treatments belong to particular groups which have their own dynamics. These dynamics may have an effect on their reaction to the films. Moreover, within the groups, members are not equivalent and they do interact while the independent and dependent variables are taking place. These two factors may also influence reactions to the treatment.[2] The wholesale transference of the approach from the laboratory to the field seems to us an obvious demonstration that researchers were holding firmly on to their basic assumption that all subjects are directly and immediately, rather than indirectly and in a mediated fashion, influenced by the violent films to which they have just been exposed. Among other things, such an assumption implies that each individual becomes a duplicate of any other individual and that the total audience is reduced to the sum of separate and equivalent units.

As long as the research was concerned with *imitation* (as a special case of social learning) and with the *frustration-aggression* hypothesis *per se*, that assumption of direct and immediate influence may indeed have been a useful one. But when studies are concerned with the effects of *filmed violence* as such, it seems to us that this assumption is actually harmful. Viewing a film or a television programme does not occur in a social vacuum. We rarely go to a cinema alone; we very seldomly watch television without companions (Maccoby, 1951). We belong to reference groups (Riley and Riley, 1951), we read newspapers, we sometimes discuss a programme beforehand, while it is on or afterwards (Codol, 1976); we see and hear the reactions of other viewers during a screening (Rabbie, 1978); and so on. Why not now systematically study the impact of such social factors, which make the social context of viewing and which may elucidate the real dynamics of influence? Why not take the example of Katz and Lazarsfeld (1955) who did not restrict their study to the mere characteristics of senders, receivers and messages, but investigated the interrelationship between the three in real-life settings and discovered the multi-steps flow of communication?

These ideas occurred to us at the completion of our own field study (Leyens *et al.*, 1975). We were looking at the effects of repeated exposure to filmed violence upon the behaviours of secondary school boys who were institutionalized because of inadequate home care or behavioural problems. These boys belonged to four rather autonomous cottages. Observations about their aggressive, active and interactive behaviours lasted for three weeks: a pre-film week, a film week (every evening members of two cottages saw a violent commercial film, while the others viewed comedies) and a post-film week. They were made during the midday and evening recreational periods while the members of each cottage interacted within their group. Additional individual and group measures were taken: cohesion and dominance conflicts in the cottages, status of dominance, popularity and usual aggressiveness of individuals within each cottage. Overall the violent films had an effect upon the viewers' aggressive behaviour; but some groups (cottages) were more influenced than others. Why? Some subgroups within a cottage (the most aggressive, dominant and popular) were more affected by the filmed violence than others. Why? All subgroups did not react at the same time. Why? As Parke *et al.* (1977) wrote in conclusion to this study and other similar ones conducted in the United States: "It is not only the stimulus side that needs more attention. The contexts in which our behavioural measures are obtained need careful study as well if we are not only to predict but even to understand the effects of movie violence in naturalistic settings".

We therefore suggest that a renewed paradigm[3] to investigate such effects should encompass the study of the social context of viewing. Nothing, however, can be more general than this proposal. How should one proceed? Given the seminal work of Lazarsfeld, Berelson, Merton and others, an obvious solution would be to follow the example of sociologists. However, they do not seem to be better off than social psychologists. In the 1951 autumn issue of the "Public Opinion Quarterly", the Rileys wrote:

> It is our conviction that sociological theory is now far enough developed to throw a great deal of light on the selection of media and programs, the interpretation of media messages, and the nature and extent of media influence. At the same time, however, operational techniques have lagged far behind this theoretical development.

The same claim is rephrased in 1953 by Freidson:

> Relatively little research has centered on the relation of social setting to the reception of mass communications.

Twenty-five years have passed since then, but it seems that the problem remains; according to the Edgars (1971),

> Perhaps the most serious of these gaps is the omission of the wider social context in which viewing takes place. The child watching a violent program is usually considered a completely privatized being, isolated before a staring eye that provides dangerous stimuli. Data on the number of hours spent watching television are not modified by considering who watches with the child, what discussion follows, whether the child ignores or rejects values and behaviour not reinforced in his normal circles of interaction, and so on. What appears needed is an integration of mass media research with sound sociological theory.

Assuredly, it would be a Promethean task to take into account the whole social context at once. Therefore the rest of this chapter will be devoted to several lines of research which our laboratory has been developing in recent years.

Decentration and focus on aesthetic qualities

According to Koriat *et al.* (1972) involvement is the most natural reaction immediately available to the spectators of a film. The social context, however, can alter that spontaneous involvement. Individuals may have been trained to look at special features of the film, rather than to restrict themselves to the raw story. A newspaper report may guide their attention towards specific characteristics of the film, and so on. We refer to that phenomenon as decentration. By that we mean *a process whereby the spectator of a particular film distances himself from the immediately available content of the film, and changes the probability of occurrence of the usual modal responses by altering the traditionally controlling variables.* The focus is still on the film, but on the "mediate" rather than on the exclusively "immediate" content. Decentrated viewers are not asked to neglect the film which they are watching, nor to perform another task completely apart from the film. The induction of decentration simply changes the *usual context of viewing,* giving the viewers *another frame of reference* from which to evaluate what they see. For example, spectators may be induced to enlarge their attention from the development of the plot and the films characters (the usual centration on the immediate content) to other aspects which previously were not always taken into account (decentration) such as the aesthetic value of the film, technical qualities, the Weltanschauung of the director, and so on.

Depending upon the type of decentration and the nature of the stimulus-film, it is assumed that not only will the viewers' overt behaviour (e.g. aggression) after the film be modified, but so also will such mediating variables as the meaning of the filmed stimuli, the arousal of the spectators and their identification with the hero.

To control the variables as closely as possible in the first series of experiments, we restricted the operationalization of the decentration process to a focus on aesthetic qualities which might be attributed to aggressive slides.

Cisneros et al. (1974) were particularly interested in the change of meaning of the stimuli. According to Gestalt principles, we expected that decentration would influence the immediate or usual meaning of the filmed stimuli. Indirect support for such a hypothesis is found in studies of coping processes conducted by Lazarus and his colleagues. Lazarus and Alfert (1964), for instance, showed their subjects a film depicting a ritual ceremony of very painful subincisions of the penis in an aboriginal tribe. While the film was usually interpreted as anxiety-provoking, subjects who received an orienting commentary denying the depicted suffering (e.g. "Think of the joyful experience of the adolescents who are being initiated into manhood") changed the meaning of the film accordingly. In the Cisneros et al. (1974) study, 44 Belgian military recruits were exposed to either aggressive or neutral slides. About half of these soldiers had been trained to look at the aesthetic qualities of the slides, while the remainder received no training or special instructions.

The hypothesis was validated. The semantic differential questionnaire which was administered immediately after the projection showed a change in the meaning of the aggressive slides. Compared to the others, subjects who had been submitted to the decentration training rated the weapons as significantly slower, weaker, better, less violent, less aggressive, less wicked and more familiar.

In a subsequent study, special attention was paid to aggressive reactions after the projection (Leyens et al., 1976). Forty-eight Belgian French-speaking military recruits participated in the experiment, 12 in each of the four experimental conditions. Two of these groups were shown, either aggressive or neutral slides without special instructions. The third group saw only aggressive slides, under decentration instructions (focus on the aesthetic quality of the slides), while the subjects in the fourth condition had to accomplish a subsidiary task (to give associations to the objects depicted on the slides). This last condition was a control for the effect of the intellectual task implied by the decentration; but, for the subsidiary task, attention was focused only on the immediate content. After the projection, all subjects were insulted by a partner and had to decide on the intensity (from 0 to 100) of electric shocks which they wanted to give him.

As can be seen in Fig. 1, the results were clear-cut. First, the "weapons effect" (Leyens and Parke, 1975) was replicated in the no-decentration aggressive slides condition. Secondly, decentrated subjects were no more violent than those who saw neutral slides. Apparently, this result cannot be attributed to the effect of an additional "intellectual" task upon aggressive behaviour, because the reactions in the subsidiary task condition did not differ from those in the no-decentration aggressive slides condition.

Obviously many practical questions are raised by the process of decentration. Although decentration did reduce aggression in the experiment just mentioned, this may not always be the case. What are the exact characteristics of decentration which can elicit a decrease or an increase in aggressive meaning and behaviour? Does decentration training have long-term effects; is it transferable from one film to another (whether similar or dissimilar); is it restricted to some individuals or is everyone capable of being decentrated; and so on?

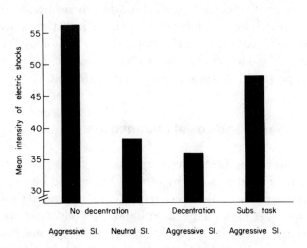

Fig. 1. Mean intensity of electric shocks as a function of decentration.

Social decentration and empathy

Certainly all these questions are important, especially in the light of potential applications of experimental social psychology. Unfortunately our population in the Army and at the University became so familiar with our topic of research that we had temporarily to interrupt the programme (this is also an applied problem for social psychologists)! As our next population, we chose very young children in the hope—fulfilled until now—that they would remain naive. Because Moscovici (1970) once wrote that the selection of psychological problems to be studied should not be foreign to the characteristics of the social environ-ment, we also altered our subject of concern somewhat. The new programme still dealt with social decentration but, this time, the meaning of the term corresponded more precisely to the one coined by Piaget.[4]

In one of the very few experiments which took the social context into account, Hicks (1968) showed that public disapproval by adults of filmed violence diminishes the aggressive reactions of children. Similar results have been obtained recently by Horton and Santogrossi (1978). What if, instead of disapproving, the adult were to focus the children's attention on the aggressor's malevolent act, on the consequences for the victim or on alternate courses of action? We assume that this induction of social decentration should increase the empathy of the young viewers and, consequently, should decrease their violent reactions. Other variables, such as their cognitive and moral development, are also being investigated to verify their links with empathy when embedded in the aggressive context. This new line of research has just started, with the collaboration of our colleague in Developmental Psychology, Mrs. Christiane Vandenplas-Holper. At present our hopes for this project are inversely proportional to the amount of data gathered.

Passive audience and social dominance

In the two preceding lines of research, the social context, or the audience, can be considered as *very active*. On the one hand, the experimenter, acting as a socialization agent, clearly instigated the focus upon aesthetic qualities and, on the other hand, the children trained towards decentration reacted in groups which were heterogenous from the point of view of chronological age and level of moral development. What about the role of a *more passive* audience?

A few studies (e.g. Balance *et al.*, 1972) have reported that the mere presence of a co-spectator can alter the impact of the message. However, as suggested by the experiment of Leyens *et al.* (1975), the investigation of the *quality of the audience* seems a more promising avenue of research.[5] In that field study, the individuals of the cottage most influenced by the violent treatment reacted very differentially. It appeared that the most dominant adolescents reacted more extremely and more rapidly at the beginning of the aggressive-film-week than the least dominant ones, who showed a slight increase of aggression only at the end of the film treatment. Our investigation was not aimed at explaining these differences, but several explanations are possible (Parke, 1974). Is it because submissive persons need a greater quantity of aggressive stimuli to provoke a reaction? Is it because the dominant members who "benefitted" from the aggressive films served as secondary models for their submissive partners? Is it because the dominant became such obnoxious boys, as a result of their viewing the aggressive films, that their victims had no other alternative than to retaliate?

Despite its lack of a definite answer, that anecdotal observation enlightened us about the role of the dynamics in the audience upon the one of the influence. As Doob (cf. the previous chapter) has clearly shown, the use of television is not indifferent to whether one lives in a peaceful community or in a high-risk section of town. Moreover, the implicit learning from television will be different. Consumers of violent television programmes in a dangerous environment will be more afraid of being themselves victimized than will other heavy consumers of television violence who have the luck to live in quiet and peaceful areas.

To study the role of the audience (the most obvious immediate surrounding) we followed the line suggested by the Leyens *et al.* study. We decided to study the reactions of very young children (4 to 6 years old) who were classified either as very dominant or clearly submissive. The first step of the programme included three phases:

(i) To study the differential reactions of dominant and submissive children when tested alone. In order to test systematically the effects of the social context of viewing, it is necessary to control as many as possible of the variables which are involved. Therefore, before investigating the effects of an interaction between dominant and submissive children on the reactions to filmed violence, one should know the reactions of these two categories of spectators when tested alone.

(ii) To study the differential reactions of boys when tested with a companion of the same or different status. Here a distinction is introduced between the *mere presence*—where a difference of status should not matter—and the *specific attributes* of the companion—where these same differences are of paramount importance.

(iii) To explain the potential differences noticed in (ii), in ways other than through the independent variables investigated up to now.

In the first study of this series (Leyens *et al.* in preparation), 4- to 6-year-old boys, selected by their teacher as really dominant or submissive viewed alone with a female experimenter one of the three nine-minute films that we produced for our purposes:

(a) *real aggression*: a dominant boy treats a submissive one badly.

(b) *neutral aggression*: a dominant boy treats a submissive one gently.

(c) *play aggression*: two boys of about the same status play aggressive games.

After the projection, all subjects were frustrated by a fictitious partner who did not want them to watch cartoons on his television set. The only reaction available to the provoked child was to darken his companion's set by pushing one of five buttons (i.e. from clear to completely dark).[6]

Manipulation checks showed that the operationalization of the variables was adequate. More importantly, the three films led to different levels of aggression, the real aggression film inducing the highest level and the neutral one the lowest. This result is particularly marked for the submissive children. As might be expected, when the film is neutral or when it depicts play aggression, dominant children tend to be more aggressive than submissive children. However, they do not react very much to the real aggression film. This may be due to a ceiling effect, the most obnoxious button being No. 5 which produces a dark screen for the frustrating peer.

A second experiment attempted to replicate the first set of findings, except that only boys in the third year of pre-school were used and the play aggression film was omitted.

Figure 2 shows the results for the third year pre-school boys in the two experiments. One can see that the parallelism is excellent. No effect of period is found by analysis of variance; but there is a main effect for the films ($F_{1,56} = 14 \cdot 8$; $P < 0 \cdot 001$) and one for the status ($F_{1,56} = 13 \cdot 8$; $P < 0 \cdot 001$), as well as a significant interaction between these two factors ($F_{1,56} = 4 \cdot 62$; $P < 0 \cdot 05$). As might be expected, the aggressive film leads to more violence than the neutral one and the dominant boys are, in general, more aggressive than the submissive ones. Finally, the significant interaction indirectly shows that *submissive children do not neces-*

sarily need a great amount of aggressive stimulation in order to react violently. In these two experiments, they were very sensitive to the aggressive film, even more than the dominant ones.[7]

Now, what about the effects of the audience? A third experiment confronted either a pair of submissive-submissive five-year-old boys or a pair of submissive-dominant ones with an invisible and frustrating partner (in the same procedure as before) after they had watched an aggressive or a neutral film. Several hypotheses are available to account for the reactions of the submissive boy who was to be the first to attack the annoying partner (i.e. before the independently obtained reactions of his submissive or dominant companion).[8]

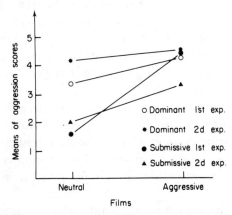

Fig. 2. Means of aggression scores as a function of the films and the status of the subjects.

One hypothesis is derived from Zajonc's (1965) social facilitation theory. According to his formulation, the *mere presence* of an observer should increase the probability of occurrence of dominant responses. In our context, and on the basis of the first experiment and of its replication, aggressive and non-aggressive responses can be considered as the dominant reactions of a submissive child after a violent and peaceful film, respectively. Thus, in terms of Zajonc's hypothesis, lone submissive boys should be less aggressive than pairs after the neutral film, while they should be more aggressive after the violent film. In either case, the status of the co-spectator should have no influence.

In recent years, however, Zajonc's theory has come under severe criticisms (e.g. Cottrell, 1972). Other hypotheses predict a differential effect according to *the quality of the audience*. One such hypothesis concerns social inhibition. The presence of a superior peer could diminish the self-concept of a submissive child who could then inhibit or restrain his spontaneous aggressive reactions. No such process should occur when the two boys have the same low status, as compared with when they are viewing alone.

The lack of empirical and theoretical evidence allows a third hypothesis to be drawn up, exactly opposite to the preceeding one, i.e. one referring to social disinhibition. The first experiment and its replication have already shown that, in the presence of a prestigious and encouraging experimenter, submissive subjects reacted strongly to the aggressive film. Why could not the submissive child take as his own norm the aggression he perceives to be present in his dominant peer? After all, there are two of them (one of them a boss in the class) to counter-attack the unknown annoying partner. Of course, when the film is neutral, this audacity should be lessened: no particular instigation is present. The same lack of instigation should preside over the conditions where the two boys are submissive.

In other words, the last two hypotheses concerning the quality of the audience predict the same results for the pairs of submissive boys. But the inhibition hypothesis suggests a diminution of aggression after the violent film on the part of a lone submissive boy accompanied by a more dominant one, while the disinhibition hypothesis predicts just the opposite.

The absence of theoretical background and of previous research evidence in the area prevents us from drawing up unequivocal hypotheses. What then are the empirical results?

Zajonc's mere exposure theory is definitely not confirmed. For all analyses, the *mere* (submissive or dominant) presence of a companion does not modify the aggressive behaviour of the submissive subjects.

The picture is strikingly different when one considers the quality of the audience (see Fig. 3). When the film is violent, the companion makes a great difference: the submissive subject accompanied by a dominant peer is significantly more aggressive than one escorted by another submissive subject (for the interaction between films and type of companion, $F_{1,47} = 3.65$; $P = 0.058$). In other words, the most instigating condition (in Berkowitz's terms) or the most disinhibitory one (in Bandura's terms) leads to a differential reaction on the part of our submissive subjects which depends upon their companion.

How may one explain these data? How is there such a difference

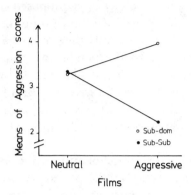

Fig. 3. Means of aggression scores as a function of the films and the co-observer.

when the film is aggressive and the submissive child has a dominant partner? Is this an illustration of the Marxist statement: a given society's culture is the culture of its dominant class? In other words, do the norms of the dominant boy become also those of the submissive one? Explanations in terms of ideology, disinhibition or instigation seem poor to us; they are *par excellence* the "deus ex machina". Faithful to Gestalt principles, we would like to use the Q-sort technique in order to have an idea of what are the processes followed by the different members in the various situations. Is it not plausible that to have a dominant rather than a submissive companion changes the whole meaning of the setting, the films, the frustrating partner, the punishment, and so on?

In the absence of a grand theory which could encompass all these problems, we are forced to proceed by small steps. Perhaps we do not use a sufficiently large range of small steps in experimental social psychology. This might have some pointers for applied social psychology.

Tentative remarks about the implications and applications of social psychology

Although they were working in the area of social psychology, Bandura and Berkowitz were searching for universal laws at the *individual level*.

The renewed paradigm which we have proposed concentrates on *inter-relationships between different individuals* (or groups of individuals) *and the social or physical environment.* Certainly the way we have tackled the problem is still very limited. In the perspective of a more ecologically-oriented psychology, one could imagine taking into account broader levels of the social context (see, for instance, Bronfenbrenner, 1977).

Now what is the relationship between our paper and the topic of the workshop: "European perspectives in the application of Social Psychology"?

Let us first consider the notion of application. It is obvious that the research reported here is not at all applied. We are not applied social psychologists; rather, we consider ourselves as experimental social psychologists who choose to investigate empirically and theoretically problems having implications for society; in the hope that such knowledge will be some day applied by others than ourselves.[9]

Such a position is certainly not rare among our colleagues in social psychology. We all want to study "real problems". To achieve that aim, many go into the field, hopefully to investigate so-called relevant, fashionable topics. But it is usually a matter of simply substituting measurement settings: they do the same research in the field as they would do in the laboratory. We hope that our paper has shown that such a mere substitution has little to gain in terms of improving our theoretical understanding of the problems being studied or their implications or applied solutions. Indeed, if one takes the trouble to do field research, one should profit from the situation and be particularly attentive to those factors that cannot, by definition, be obtained in the laboratory where everything is fixed. In other words, one should be especially sensitive to what one cannot control. In our field quasi-experimentation, we could not control the membership of the groups, the interactions between the members, the sanctions given by the counsellors, the hierarchy of dominance, and so on. It is precisely those factors that seemed interesting for the future of the research. As one of us (Leyens, 1979) has argued elsewhere, field studies (or more exactly the "va-et-vient" between the laboratory and the field) contribute probably more to theory building and to construct validity (i.e. sounder ecological problems) than they do to external validity.

There is another aspect to the problem. If we want to say something which has stronger societal implications and, therefore, more potential for application, we need more descriptive data than we have. What we usually do is to arrive first at theories, and then try to find adequate data to feed our innumerable theories so that they stay alive (i.e. in the literature) as long as possible. This is certainly useful for our *present theories*. Is it useful for the *societal problems* which we want to investigate? Here again laboratory experimentation can benefit a lot from field studies, provided that they are not only simple replications or duplications of the former.

A third remark about the implications and applications of social psychology concerns our professional duty as teachers. At least in Belgium, but probably in other countries as well, the academic market is completely frozen, especially in experimental (social) psychology. If, today, undergraduate and graduate students[10] collaborate with us in running laboratory experiments, tomorrow they will be confronted with other kinds of problems for which they will need other approaches. We think it is our professional duty, even as experimental social psychologists, to help them to find and try out these other approaches; and to do it not only with the aim of solving a problem, but also to gain theoretical knowledge. We think that this situation which has been forced upon us may eventually improve our theories as well as the implications and applications of social psychology.

This latter remark will be the only one to have a specifically European reference. Indeed, we do not consider our contribution and the reasoning behind it to be particularly European nor, for the same reason, particularly characteristic of any other part of the world. It is true that different countries have different problems and values and preferred ways of coping with and investigating them, but we are not yet ready to accept that geography *per se* can determine the functioning of our minds!

Notes

1. Possible methodological deficiences in the Feshbach and Singer study have been so thoroughly examined elsewhere (e.g. Liebert *et al.*, 1972) that it would be pointless to open the discussion again. On the other hand, the Milgram and Shotland studies probably constitute the best recipe available in the literature on how not to find an effect. Indeed, with the financial aid of a major television company, these authors chose the weakest instigating stimuli they could find and expected these to induce a real delinquent act.

2. The criticisms do not apply to the Milgram and Shotland and the Goldstein *et al.* studies. Their audiences were constituted by individuals who did not belong to a single existing group.

3. By paradigm, we mean an established way of asking questions and testing hypotheses in a given field. In this sense one speaks of the passive avoidance paradigm, the learned helplessness paradigm, etc. Compared to other possible meanings, this is assuredly a weak one. But let us hope that some day we will be able to write another chapter, entitled: Towards a new paradigmatic theory of movie violence research.
4. For a more detailed account of the notion of decentration and its implications for social development, see Vandenplas-Holper (1979).
5. Borden agrees with us when he writes: "With respect to aggressive behavior (. . .) the effect of an observer's presence is apparently more a function of *who* is watching than simply whether or not *anyone* is watching" (1975, p. 572).
6. The complete report concerning this new "aggression machine" will be presented elsewhere. Let us just say that its validity as an aggression measure is perfectly reliable. We are very grateful to Richard Robert, Paul Thibaut and Bernard Paris who constructed the apparatus.
7. To explain the reaction of the dominant children, we have already suggested a ceiling effect. Another explanation would be that the dominant boys are not accustomed to be annoyed by a peer. Because they resented such frustration so much, the films, aggressive or neutral, may have lost any impact upon them.
8. The data for the second attackers go well beyond our aims in this chapter. We prefer to present them later on in their global context in a paper of a more traditional format.
9. Fortunately, this happens sometimes in the area of mass media and violence in Europe. For instance, BBC television recently circulated a new policy guidance booklet which clearly takes into account the results of the most recent research. Swiss televison also devoted one of its favourite programmes to the problem of filmed violence and to our approach to this topic. As a final example, the French-speaking Belgian TV has tended to abandon the use of the "white square" warning to viewers that a film is either particularly erotic or violent, since Herman and Leyens (1977) published their data which demonstrated that the "white square" attracted a greater audience than no warning at all.
10. In our programme of experimental social psychology, most graduate students are foreigners—and especially Latino-Americans—who already have an academic position in their home country and benefit from national or international exchange grants. For Belgian students, the opportunities to undertake a Ph.D. are very limited and the academic vacancies after the Ph.D. are even rarer.

References

Balance, W. D., Coughlin, D. and Bringmann, W. G. (1972). Examination of social context effects upon affective responses to "hot" and "cool" communications media. *Psychol. Rep.* **31**, 793–794.

Borden, R. J. (1975). Witnessed aggression: influence of an observer's sex and values on aggressive responding. *J. Pers. Soc. Psychol.* **31**, 567–573.

Bronfenbrenner, U. (1977). Towards an experimental ecology of human development. *Am. Psychol.* **32**, 513–531.

Cisneros, T., Camino, L. et Leyens, J. Ph. (1974). La décentration: auto-contrôle de l'influence de la violence filmée. *Revue de Psychologie et des Sciences de l'Education* **2**, 301–316.

Codol, J. P. (1976). Une étude expérimentale sur l'influence de la critique cinématographique. *Cahiers de Psychologie* **10**, 83–98.

Cottrell, N. B. (1972). Social facilitation. *In* "Experimental Social Psychology" (C. G. McClintock, ed.). Holt, Rinehart and Winston, New York.

Edgar, P. M. and Edgar, D. E. (1971). Television violence and socialization theory. *Public Opinion Quart.* **35**, 608–612.

Feshbach, S. and Singer, R. D. (1971). "Television and Aggression: an Experimental Field Study". Jossey-Bass, San Francisco.

Freidson, F. (1953). The relation of the social situation of contact to the media in mass communication. *Public Opinion Quart.* **17**, 230–238.

Goldstein, J. H., Rosnow, R. L., Raday, T., Silverman, I. and Gaskell, G. D. (1975). Punitiveness in response to films varying in content: a cross-national field study of aggression. *Eur. J. Soc. Psychol.* **5**, 149–166.

Herman, G. and Leyens, J. Ph. (1977). Rating films on T.V. *J. Commun.* **27**, 48–53.

Hicks, D. J. (1968). Effects of co-observer's sanctions and adult presence on imitative aggression. *Child Devel.* **38**, 303–308.

Horton, R. W. and Santogrossi, D. A. (1978). The effect of adult commentary on reducing the influence of televised violence. *Pers. Soc. Psychol. Bull.* **4**, 337–340.

Hovland, C. (1951). *In* "Reader in Public Opinion and Communication" (Berelson and Janowitz, eds). Free Press, Glencoe, Illinois.

Katz, E. and Lazarsfeld, P. F. (1955). "Personal Influence". Free Press, Glencoe, Illinois.

Koriat, A., Melkman, R., Averill, J. R. and Lazarus, R. S. (1972). The self-control of emotional reactions to a stressful film. *J. Person.* **40**, 601–619.

Lazarus, R. S. and Alfert, E. (1964). The short-circuiting of threat by experimentally altering cognitive appraisal. *J. Abnorm. Soc. Psychol.* **69**, 195–205.

Leyens, J. Ph. (1979). Field research as contributing to theory building. Invited lecture at the 3rd Ökopsychologischen Kolloquium. Schloss Reisensburg.

Leyens, J. Ph. and Parke, R. D. (1975). Aggressive slides can induce a weapons effect. *Eur. J. Soc. Psychol.* **5**, 229–236.

Leyens, J. Ph., Camino, L., Parke, R. D. and Berkowitz, L. (1975). The effects of movie violence on aggression in a field setting as a function of group dominance and cohesion. *J. Person. Soc. Psychol.* **32**, 346–360.

Leyens, J. Ph., Cisneros, T. and Hossay, J. F. (1976). Decentration as a means for reducing aggression after exposure to violent stimuli. *Eur. J. Soc. Psychol.* **6**, 459–473.

Leyens, J. Ph., Herman, G., Dunand, M. (1981). The influence of an audience upon the reactions to filmed violence (in preparation).

Liebert, R. M., Sobol, M. D. and Davidson, E. S. (1972). Catharsis of aggression among institutionalized boys: fact or artifact. *In* "Television and Social Behavior. Vol. 5. Television effects: Further explorations" (G. A. Constock, E. A. Rubinstein and J. P. Murray, eds), pp. 351–359. Government Printing Office, Washington, D.C.

Maccoby, E. (1951). Television: its impact on school children. *Public Opinion Quart.* **15**, 421–444.

Milgram, S. and Shotland, R. L. (1973). "Television and Antisocial Behavior". Academic Press, New York.

Moscovici, S. (1970). Préface. *In* "Psychologie Sociale, une discipline en mouvement" (D. Jodelet, J. Viet and P. Besnard, eds). Mouton, Paris, La Haye.

Parke, R. D. (1974). A field experimental approach to children's aggression: some methodological problems and some future trends. *In* "Determinants and Origins of Aggressive Behavior" (J. De Wit and W. W. Hartup, eds). Mouton, The Hague and Paris.

Parke, R. D., Berkowitz, L., Leyens, J. Ph., West, S. and Sebastian, R. J. (1977). Some effects of violent and nonviolent movies on the behavior of juvenile delinquents. *In* "Advances in Experimental Social Psychology" (L. Berkowitz, ed.), Vol. 10. Academic Press, New York.

Rabbie, J. M. (1978). Mini crowds: an experimental study of audience behaviour. Paper presented to the General Meeting of the European Association of Experimental Social Psychology, Weimar, D.D.R., March 28–April 1.

Riley, M. W. and Riley, J. W. (1951). A sociological approach to communications research. *Public Opinion Quart.* **15**, 445–460.

Stein, A. H. and Friedrich, L. K. (1972). Television content and young children's behavior. *In* "Television and Social Behavior. Vol. 2. Television and Social Learning" (J. P. Murray, E. A. Rubinstein and G. A. Comstock, eds), pp. 202–317. Government Printing Office, Washington, D.C.

Steuer, F. B., Applefield, J. M. and Smith, R. (1971). Television aggression and the interpersonal aggression of preschool children. *J. Exp. Child Psychol.* **11**, 422–447.

Vandenplas-Holper, C. (1979). "Education et Développement Social de l'Enfant". P.U.F., Paris.

Zajonc, R. B. (1965). Social facilitation. *Science* **149**, 269–274.

III

Studies on Social Services

Introduction

The dominant impression of the previous part of the book and of much writing on applied social psychology is that there are psychologists who are prepared to term their work "applied" without any necessity or even prospect of its being put into application. It simply needs, in accordance with certain unstated criteria, to be "applicable". The final two chapters take a different stand on the question of application. Some of the major differences are that they are concerned with applying social psychology to whole fields of practice rather than just to specific issues, with professional aspects of social psychology, and with questions of education and training. The broad scope of these issues makes a progressive finale to this volume.

The previous chapter, by Leyens and colleagues, ended with a reference to the teaching of social psychology. They suggested that the needs of graduating students to find employment could not be met by a course devoted entirely to experimental social psychology. The teacher's duty was to be open to other approaches to social psychology so that students could be prepared for a variety of non-academic jobs.

Many of the potentially interesting applications of social psychology, as we have seen, are embedded in an interdisciplinary framework. Indeed much that might be called "applied social psychology" has now come to be categorized within other sub-disciplines of psychology itself—such as environmental psychology, psychology of law, feminist psychology, organizational psychology. As a result there is a wide range of opportunities for teaching social psychology to students of architecture, planning, law, women's studies, management studies and so on. Breakwell adds another example here—social work—which in particular highlights the missed opportunities of social psychology. Many other practical areas, the environmental and so on, have at least been incorporated into psychology. It is neglectful that psychologists have allowed social work to be almost entirely incorporated into sociology, and have not insisted upon the contribution that could be made by clinical, developmental and social psychologies, both in training and practice.

The contribution of social psychology to social work put forward by Breakwell is three-fold. In addition to its use in training, it includes analyses of the profession itself and of aspects of practice. Palmonari and Zani would add a fourth facet: the social psychologist *becoming* a social worker, or, in their terms, becoming a community psychologist. One reason why psychology has not taken its share of the social work profession has probably been simply the absence of a suggestive label. There is a tendency for macroscopic social issues to be taken as inevitably the sphere of sociology. Social psychology until recently has not tried to project an image of widespread applicability, being concerned rather with maintaining an image as a sharp, theoretical sub-discipline, able to hold its own with experimental and physiological psychology. Community psychology, as defined by Palmonari and Zani, does offer a label whereby the psychologist can gain a foothold in the social services. Their approach, in the context of reforms being carried out in Italy, is more pertinent to the British, post-Seebohm organization of the social services than is the more restricted social work model.

The implications for education of their scheme are fairly radical, given the present state of social psychology teaching. The community psychologist should have general skills rather than only specific knowledge. For example, he should be capable of working as a member of a team and of thoroughly immersing himself in the problem areas with which it is dealing. He should be active, rather than reactive: being required to take the initiative and creatively to invent *ad hoc* services to cope with a problem. Often he will need managerial skills. He will certainly have to be interested in and skilled at communicating with laypeople. (If potentially applicable social psychology is not used, it may often be because psychologists are unconcerned about communicating it to non-psychologists.) In many ways this profile is the antithesis of the characteristics of the stereotypical graduate psychologist, with his talents for reactive and detached analysis of problems by his own efforts. Much of his technical, methodological training guarantees that there will be a distance between the psychologist as "expert" and the ordinary citizen. And yet the training which one imagines the community psychologist in Italy might receive could well be the prescription for applied social psychologists in general. One would look for an education and training which is explicitly and concretely based on the community.

Despite the difference in focus of these last two chapters as compared to the rest of the volume, several important issues are reiterated. In particular, these chapters take a firmly non-individualistic stand; and emphasize the importance of the social and historical context of any problem. The idea that social psychology is a form of historical investigation is difficult to deny when one uses it to engage directly in the development or transformation of institutions such as the social services. There is no timidity about being drawn towards a relativistic position. Secondly, social psychological practice can be an opportunity both for applying existing psychological ideas and for testing theory. Both chapters refer to Tajfel's theory of intergroup behaviour. And thirdly, applied social psychology involves the practitioner in interdisciplinary work. In the case of social and community work the social psychologist cannot divorce himself from other areas of psychology, such as clinical, developmental or educational psychology.

In these two chapters social psychology assumes a more professional guise than elsewhere in the book, both in itself and as a means of analysing professional issues. The latter aspect is particularly manifest in Breakwell's contribution. If Palmonari and Zani emphasize the former aspect, it is in a relatively unfamiliar manner and one which is akin to several arguments in the second volume of this book. The reformed social services within which the Italian community psychologist would work are essentially decentralized and participatory. He should take on an emancipatory role: ultimately and ideally his clients would not need his attention, because they would have learned how to solve their problems and control their situation for themselves. Certainly he would see his knowledge and skills as something to share, rather than simply as instruments enabling him to act upon others and their problems. In many cases he would be satisfied with being an intermediary between other professionals or between them and their clients, rather than attempting always to be the prime mover and problem-solver. The professionalism would be so far removed from the more usual definition that he would be open to negotiating his role with other interested parties. Paradoxically perhaps, his attitude can be described as one of responsible deprofessionalization.

This approach to professionalization draws attention to a moral question which is pertinent to all applied social psychology. Much of the discussion in this book is of data, theories and disembodied social problems. But what is the impact of the data and problem analyses on people's lives? How often are they asked what they make of the psychologist's products? When he knows so little about how the results of an applied investigation might be used, can he be confident that they will be used humanely and to ends of which he would approve? Questions such as these suggest that ideology may be more immediately evident in applied than in non-applied research. The researcher has to be clear about what the role of ideology will be for him, and how he is to relate to the ideology of his clients, or sponsors and to that of his subjects. If he is interested in social action, he will want to identify a theory of social change consonant with his values.

If one attempts to generalize the picture of professionalism to other areas of applied social psychology, a question arises which is scarcely considered in this volume. Indeed, Breakwell goes so far as explicitly to refuse discussing it—the nature of social psychology itself. The professional or deprofessionalizing norms of the social psychologist will differ according to whether, for example, a positivist, hermeneutical or critical version of social psychology is adopted; or whether an emphasis is placed on individuals, social forces and institutions, or relations between individuals and groups as being the prime focus of social psychology. Many areas of social psychology, as treated today, would not fit Palmonari and Zani's assumptions. But the lesson is that social psychology cannot usefully be applied until it has been decided what one's assumptions are and examined their congruence or incongruence to the structure of one's problem area. It is satisfying to end this volume with such a major question confronting the reader.

9

Towards a Community Psychology in Italy

A. Palmonari and B. Zani

In Italy attempts are being made to reorganize the social and health services. The new system, founded on the principle of the decentralization of power, and aiming to actively involve more of the community in its schemes, is intended to replace the old system of assistance. One way in which the new system is distinguished from the old is that the social services are territorially decentralized, providing a system of "social security" which uses accessible resources to meet the real needs of the community. The fundamental principles from which the new organization finds its inspiration have been long recognized by the most progressive political forces, and are as follows:

Prevention: understood as the removal of the causes of accidents, illness, social unrest and psychic disorders, with the aim of establishing a balanced relationship between man and his environment;

The comprehensive and unitary nature of the services. This essentially implies recognizing the interdependence of the health and social services, so as to form a link between the different spheres of interest and avoid the tendency of the old system towards an over-emphasis on medicine;

Social management of the services, in the sense that it is the community which controls their organization and functioning.

Within such a scheme as this, it is most important that the work of the psychologist should not merely rely on the operative instruments of the clinical model, but should deal with social reality in all its complexity. Thus the psychologist must have new and effective courses of action at his disposal, inspired by accurate and sound theoretical work.

From this point of view, it is interesting to consider the American model of community psychology (Zax and Specter, 1974; Golann and Baker, 1975). It has various limitations which it is worthwhile analysing.

The limitations of American community psychology

A critical consideration of American community psychology will help us to reconsider the merits of the project for the reform of the social and health services in Italy.

One must recognize the part played in American community psychology by the belief that the work of the psychologist should aim to modify the relationship between the individual and the environment and the characteristics of the environment itself, since it is here that the root of psychic disorders and the alienation of man from himself is to be found. The knowledge that this is the case has illuminated the most important objective in primary prevention: it has demonstrated the urgent need for a reform of the training and practice of social workers. In particular the psychologist, having once realized the limitations of the clinical model (from which his work in the social services has always found its inspiration), has become aware of the necessity of not confining his preparation to clinical psychology, but of working in close contact with social reality in all its complexity, and not only with single individuals extrapolated from the context of their history.

However, there are certain limitations in the way in which these realizations have been translated into practical community psychology: (a) on a general political level, (b) with regard to social policy, and (c) with regard to the theory and correct use of the social sciences.

(a) On a general political level, although it is often recognized that it is necessary to bear in mind all the forces interacting within a community in order to analyse it, essential structural factors, such as the distribution of power and wealth, are ignored. As a consequence of this, fundamental social "problems" are often considered as "dysfunctions" of the social system, as though the relative power of different groups were not at the root of these problems, and as though, in order to solve them, it were sufficient to remove the difficulties impeding the functioning of the system with technical instruments. However, an analysis of social context which purports to be thorough should recognize the roots of the essential social problems at a structural level (and in particular in the uneven distribution of power), and bear in mind that an intervention at such a level cannot be technical, but must be political, aiming to construct a new balance of power relationships. The clearest indications of these limitations in the "community approach" to the analysis of society is that the concept of "class" is rarely used, whereas frequent mention is made of "groups".

(b) On the level of social policy, the weakest point appears to be the lack of a comprehensive policy which could give a clear but unitary sense to the various elaborate and specialized projects. Thus it is difficult to discern any kind of consistency between the different courses of action, let alone to identify the necessary instruments for obtaining a significant result. Klein's recent work on the "New Towns" (1978) exemplifies this point. The difficulty of constructing a habitat which respects the needs of the family, of ethnic groups and of different cultural groups is, indeed, a very real one. However, in practice it seems that the political nature of the fundamental problem is not recognized. It seems that there is no comprehensive policy to promote the participation of the community in the management of such schemes, let alone in the selection of effective measures for the prevention of maladjustment. For example, the importance of taking social measures in order to give young people the possibility of meeting one another and of occupying themselves autonomously is recognized, but the social response to these needs consists in providing them with the same, well-known, obsolete youth-clubs.

Indeed, one often has the impression, reading the American literature on community psychology, that the measures taken have been conceived in an incoherent way, using schematic, rather than clear, comprehensive logic. Thus one is left with no points of reference for a precise definition of the desired objectives, or of the most suitable instruments for obtaining and evaluating the results.

(c) We can also find various limitations in community psychology's theoretical and practical use of the social sciences. The main fault, in our opinion, is the way in which use has been made of the assumption (an assumption which is not incorrect in itself) that the social environment directly influences psychic disorders, cultural handicaps and mental deficiencies. In practice this is too simplistic an assumption. A well-known example is that of "culturally disadvantaged children". The influence of the environment on this phenomenon is obvious, but the problem has been tackled by dealing only with individual cases, as though, in order to overcome the handicap, it were sufficient to stimulate single subjects by perhaps placing them in "special" classes at school. The same is true with the attempts made to involve the family in offering less limiting conditions for socialization. Measures have been taken which assume that all that is needed is a "school for parents" (in which parents are taught to bring up their children more expertly) for the family to be able to offer better conditions for socialization. However, this is an oversimplification which is not compatible with the complexity of reality, and it has, indeed, led to repeated failures. Only in recent years have people begun to ask in what respect "disadvantaged" children differ in a school context from those who came from more privileged families. From such inquiries it has been confirmed that the difference *is not accounted for* by cognitive deficiencies in the "disadvantaged" children; though as yet their deficiency in learning has not been explained. However two factors come into play here:

(1) linguistic differences: a wide-ranging discussion has developed which has demonstrated that the language used by children from the lower classes is a "different" but not "inferior" variety of the standard language; it has its own system of equally complex rules (Bernstein, 1971; Robinson, 1972; Giles and Clair, 1979);

(2) differences in behaviour with regard to school motivation and application (Donaldson, 1978).

However, even with this knowledge, we cannot say that we have at our disposal a precise conceptual elaboration of the problem which we wish to tackle, of the reasons why certain forms of social intervention are successful in some conditions but not in others, or of the reason why some active measures, when taken, produce a result very different from the expected one.

Even more evident is the oversimplification on which the programmes of "parent education" are based. In fact, the research which has been carried out shows that such programmes do not influence those aspects of the behaviours of the mother which, according to recent studies of the psychology of development, are important for the socialization of the child (for example, the way in which she speaks to him, how she expresses her affection, and how she plays with him). Moreover, even though these aspects of the situation have been studied, there has been no systematic research on the social and motivational variables which affect the acceptance or rejection of a situational change.

The most important point to notice, then, is that the body of critical studies on these matters has developed not within and as a result of projects such as the ones mentioned, to verify and if necessary restructure them, but rather outside them, allowing other schemes, which repeat the very errors criticized, to be realized at the same time.

The lack of communication between the sphere of social action and that of social research seems strange, but it is certainly very frequent. Several factors come into play here.

Above all, a part is played by the persistent behaviouristic prejudice that every "controlled" change in the environment (and a specialized scholastic programme or a course for parents can be considered as such) must necessarily give a specific and foreseeable result. Because of this belief, when a scheme fails, instead of examining in depth and in a more precisely conceptual way all the elements of the situation, there is a tendency to adjust the scheme so that every aspect of it can be noted and controlled. By doing this, aspects of the intervention, such as the attitudes of the subjects treated, their social representations of the assistance which is offered to them, and their motivation for becoming involved, are ignored. This inevitably renders the initial hypothesis fallacious.

Secondly, a part is played by a general lack of recognition for this area of the human sciences, and by the refusal of the administrative bodies concerned to undertake an exploration of the theoretical ground which this type of practical work requires. Nor, on the other hand, do the "experts" in the social sciences feel the need to provide those administrative bodies responsible for the projects with the detailed information they require.

Thirdly and finally, a part is played by the conceptual separation of research (even applied research) from practical work. This almost always results in a well-defined, institutionalized barrier: the two spheres of action (theoretical and practical) do not exchange information. Both proceed in a rectilinear way, blind and deaf to the feedback which could correct their courses. If it is borne in mind that in order to overcome the limitations of community psychology, it has been suggested that one adopt the remedy of behaviourist technology (cf. Nietzel *et al.*, 1977, on behavioural community psychology), the risk of a greater rift between these two spheres of interest appears even more imminent.

Having thus commented on American community psychology, we are now in a position to consider the project for the reform of the work of the psychologist in the social and health services in Italy.

If it is examined carefully, one can see that the project for the services, as delineated by the reforming measures, is founded on a general political vision of the situation and has assumed the form of a comprehensive project of innovatory social policy.

The course the reform movement has taken, in fact, was born not only from the realization of the necessity of rationalizing the chaotic state of the social assitance, security and social health system in Italy, but also from the recognition of the importance of decentralizing political power, and of directly involving the community in decision-making and in the control of the social services. The project for effective social policy is inserted in this general scheme and aims to treat the social services as a unified and integral body. The process of elaborating the social services is backed by many working-class movements which have participated, and, indeed, continue to participate in it. It is, on the other hand, opposed by numerous other forces, which are present in all institutions and movements. These forces see, in the possible realization of the project, the risk of losing the privileges they have consolidated, of having to change the style of their work, and of having to face up to exigencies which they consider troublesome and meaningless. Often these movements of resistance claim to be the only guarantee of rationality and efficiency in the social services.

Another important obstacle in the way of a reform is the unsuitability of the cultural milieu for a confrontation of the problems which the process of reform itself implies and creates. A lack of this kind is felt in the technical, administrative and political spheres. For the scheme to be carried out, therefore, there must be a very serious undertaking: a new culture must be constructed. All new initiatives, if they are not managed correctly, run the risk of becoming rigid institutional meshes, which rely on bureaucracy and have the sole aim of maintaining and perpetuating the establishment. Can social psychology be of any help in this process of cultural construction which is necessary in order to reform the social services?

We are convinced that it can, bearing in mind only the precise limits within which the social sciences are able to facilitate and contribute to the change. And we are convinced that, in order to make a significant contribution, the psychologist must possess a wider range of skills than those acquired by traditional clinical training.

The new ways in which the psychologist may intervene in the social and health services

For the psychologist to work in the new social and health services the following aspects of his work must change: (a) the objectives of the work, (b) his work methods, (c) the field of the intervention and (d) his skills.

NEW OBJECTIVES

The new objectives are the promotion of welfare and the improvement of the quality of life of the whole community, and no longer only the cure and rehabilitation of those affected pathologically. This also implies an efficient system of prevention. That is, the analysis of the specific needs of the area concerned in order to discover the causes of the problems and the factors which constitute the elements of risk for this specific economic and social organization.

This statement in itself indicates the necessity of linking the social and health services. Social factors influence health and illness (somatic and psychic), as well as the process of the active establishment of man in his environment.

Objectives such as these can only be considered emancipatory if they are attained in conjunction with a political project founded on the principle of the decentralization of power and the active participation of the community. Without it they can only be attained at the risk of dangerously increasing the power of social technicians.

WORK METHODS

An objective as complex as this can only be attained by planning the interventions in a rational and efficient way. In the sphere of planning, the psychologist, together with other social workers, performs an active function, not only in the management of the institutional instruments which have already been tried, but also by planning new forms of intervention capable of dealing with the problematic situations which are characteristic of the specific social context. This requires research which is aimed at a deeper understanding of the area in which the work is being carried out, to systematically reveal the needs and dangers present and to verify the effectiveness and efficiency of existing social services.

It is obvious that team work is the answer for correct programming, planning and research. It is beyond the specific skills of individual workers to maintain a close link with the comprehensive political project and to follow its objectives in a strict and suitable sequence. Thus the team must assume responsibility for making decisions in close collaboration with the politicians who are responsible for the services. The relationship that is established between this team and the politicians, however, will not be one of subordination, but rather a reciprocal relationship aiming to translate cultural ferment into precise and concrete political moves.

THE FIELD OF INTERVENTION

The work of the psychologist can no longer be exclusively aimed at establishing a "relationship with the client" (usually a person with some difficulty or a need to be helped and cured), following the medical model which has hitherto inspired his work. He should rather direct his attention towards different expressions of community problems; those coming from groups who voice needs and suggest changes, and those from the institutions within which the social services function. There are two reasons for this: first because the promotion of social welfare involves establishing relationships with groups and institutions as well as with single individuals; and secondly because it takes into consideration the wider social context from which they originate.

HIS SKILLS

Because he aims to carry out such complex interventions, the psychologist must possess numerous skills, some of which he will share with other social workers, and some of which are more specialized. The psychologist must:
(1) know how to adjust his methods to the typical problems of the social context in which he works in such a way as to reveal its social needs and help to find adequate technical and organizational solutions for them. He must therefore know how to carry out research which is relevant to the present, and which aims to examine and transform real situations.
(2) establish real communication with his clients, encouraging and listening to their requests for change and revision in their particular sphere of interest. The psychologist should not simply passively register the needs of the community, but should rather be an active interlocutor: able to listen, but also to put forward concrete plans of action, to struggle for their realization and to alleviate the tensions which the dynamics of the reform movement create. He must become the eye and ear of the community in such a way as to translate those needs expressed by the area into concrete projects.

(3) favour a change of attitude, in an emancipatory rather than manipulative way (in the sense intended by Holzkamp, 1972).

(4) intervene in a specialized way in specific situations: by making observations, counselling and supporting work groups through helping them to play a more active part in the general scheme. He must, of course, also carry out therapeutic and rehabilitative interventions. He must continue to help those people who have immediate problems to be solved, otherwise the emphasis on prevention becomes an escape from concrete problems.

(5) contribute to the training of other social workers by supplying them if necessary with the means to verify the work carried out in institutions (creches, nursery schools, clinics, etc.) and in direct contact with the community. Thus the psychologist should share his knowledge with others, transmitting scientific and technical learning, destroying myths, and giving everyone access to that information which is necessary for solving problems but which, in our culture, tends to belong exclusively to the "authorized personnel".

The proper training of the psychologist is crucial in order for him to be able to work in this way. He should acquire both specific technical competence and conceptual skills, so that he is able to formulate social interventions. This really implies redefining the professional role of the psychologist. He must now become involved in political issues; he must be capable of attending to new situations arising from the activity of the social services, of interpreting them and of evaluating the methods to use in dealing with them. At this point a problem arises. By which criteria can the psychologist define the nature of his work? Roughly speaking there are three professional models available to him.

The model of the independent professional

This label is usually associated with the profession of lawyers, doctors, etc. but it is also assumed by other practitioners, with or without university degree. According to this model, the practitioner ought to identify and characterize his work by professional criteria, whatever type of need he is coping with.

The bureaucratic model

This can be thought of as the system of dividing work hierarchically be-

tween managers and executives which is used in many large organizations. According to this model, the most efficient criteria for the worker
to follow lie in his faith in the instructions which are given to him, and in
his attempts to carry them out exactly. The hierarchical superior controls the quality of the work accomplished.

The model of the "political activist"

This model has only recently appeared in Italy and was adopted particularly frequently in the first stages of the renewal of the social and
health services. It is endowed with different and unrelated meanings although it is essentially based on the idea that the value of professional
skills is minimal in the realization of plans which are considered to be of
an essentially political nature. According to this model, the task of the
social worker is essentially to carry out political instructions, renounc-
ing whatever power could derive from his own skills.

The reorganization of the social services demands a new vision of the
problem, over and above all these models. The work so far undertaken
uses a theory of social needs (or at least the desire to understand social
needs) as a point of reference. This indicates that the essential task is to
facilitate the passage of each member of the community from a situation
of deprivation to becoming actively involved in changing his own position in the social system and that of the group to which he belongs.

A vision such as this recognizes the fundamental importance of politics in putting plans into action, and relies on using all the creativity
which professional competence guarantees in this field. Thus the activity
of each practitioner is in no way predetermined, and every aspect of it is
subject to negotiation: his relationship with politicians and with the
community (paying particular attention to local culture), the translation of political plans into realizable schemes, and the continuity and
security of his own work.

In the first place, however, it is necessary to prove obsolete the
simplistic way of thinking which considers that it is possible to define
criteria of professionalism simply on the basis of categorizing them as
belonging either to the bureaucratic model or to the model of the independent professional.

Some examples

It might be useful at this point to present some concrete examples of the way in which the psychologist can intervene in spheres which are not traditionally his own, that is in planning and realizing preventive social interventions.

An interesting example is that of the "family guidance clinics". This service, recently established in Italy, aims to provide social and psychological assistance for expectant mothers, couples and the family in general. In order for this to provide a true alternative to the traditional gynaecological consultation, it is necessary to concentrate on preventive action. The psychologist, then, should not simply intervene when asked to do so by the doctor in psycho-pathological cases or in "difficult cases"; but he should, for example, discuss with the doctor himself how the gynaecological examination is conducted. He may also, in a general discussion with all the staff of the service, raise the matter of how to tackle the first interview, given that this is a particularly delicate moment for the patient which may affect him subsequently and change the public image of the social service.

It is important for the psychologist to involve himself in other enterprises and dedicate himself more fully to the community. For example, he may hold discussion sessions for particular groups of women, initiating the formation of the groups, providing them with continuous support, and so forth. However, these measures alone clearly represent a mere reorganization of the services. The psychologist must also promote the scheme by extending his activities further afield. He must attend public meetings and attempt to clarify the significance of such consultations, the services which they can offer and the way in which they function. He must initiate debates on relevant subjects; plan programmes for sexual education in schools or for social and health education on a regional basis. He must collaborate with the other social services to form a more united network, and so forth.

Another instance in which the intervention of the psychologist can be particularly effective is in deciding on preventive measures against the segregation of children. The most important form of social activity in this sphere lies in ensuring that the basic services are functioning correctly: creches, nursery schools and subsidiary services in part-time elementary schools. The collaboration of the psychologist with the people responsible for such services is particularly important. He should help to plan and manage them, to evaluate the climate of relationships which grow up within them, and if necessary he should help to undertake their improvement. However, ensuring that these services are functioning correctly is not the only measure to be taken against the lack of social integration in children. There are also the more extreme but fairly frequent cases of children who must find a completely new social environment (orphans, children whose parents are separated and therefore unable to look after them, children whose parents are considered incapable of looking after them).

The solution to which recourse is still often made is that of institutionalization, even though the unsatisfactory and harmful nature of this measure is quite widely recognized. Because of their great need for special care it is frequently the youngest children who are taken into an institution, with especially harmful consequences for them. It is the job of the social worker to find satisfactory solutions for these extreme cases. However, since there are no standard procedures to follow, any form of social intervention in this sphere must necessarily involve inventing *ad hoc* services which are capable of meeting the needs of the child until he reaches a degree of self-sufficiency. A few solutions have already been explored: for example, the arrangement of a service placing single children on a long-term basis in especially chosen families, or establishing a family-group (where two or more children are entrusted to a married couple), an apartment-group (here the emphasis is on the establishment of a relationship of equality between the children accommodated and the adults responsible for them), or "foyers" (groups of adolescents). These plans require the active involvement of the psychologist, in planning them, in choosing the members of the staff, and in encouraging the community to accept the arrangements. It is also important for the psychologist to help in the management of these schemes, to help the staff to solve any interpersonal problems which might arise and to systematically evaluate the way in which the projects are proceeding.

The provision of a service of this sort, integrated into the community, requires both politicians and practitioners to formulate a new way of dealing with reality and to open up a new cultural perspective for the whole population.

Another important aspect of the work of the psychologist is that he must make contact with the different groups within society who are aware of important social needs, but who are unable to express them in immediately intelligible terms, or to present them in the right places. The psychologist can intervene in order to allow the group to follow up the problem, helping its members to get over the technical difficulties which may prevent further progress, particularly if they are unclear themselves about their objectives. He may also help by deciding on a project for the group which the members themselves can organize within, or in close contact with, the social services.

A pertinent example is that of parents who may already be aware of problems arising at school and who wish to become involved to make the school more capable of responding to the needs of their children. The psychologist can present himself as an intermediary ready to understand these needs, to promote meetings between parents, and to involve the teachers as well. He can try to collaborate with them to draw up a programme of discussions on topics of common interest (for example with the aim of realizing a plan for health education). The psychologist can prove useful in arranging the meetings and debates, in contacting people qualified to speak on various topics, in encouraging the teachers to make the problems dealt with the subject of further discussion in class with the children, and finally in finding methods for evaluating the project with all those involved.

Finally, one must not underestimate the role of the psychologist in passing on techniques to other groups of social practitioners (for example, rehabilitation therapists, nurses and teachers). In this way he can help them work together and master the specific skills of his own profession (e.g. the accurate observation of the behaviour of children in a nursery), clarify the function of the institution in which they work, and encourage them to use certain rehabilitative techniques. For example, teachers are not trained to deal with psychomotor disturbances such as some writing and reading difficulties. These complaints arise fairly frequently in schools and early, systematic measures taken by the teachers could help to cure them. The psychologist could supply the necessary information, showing the lines which the teacher should follow in his dealings with the child, giving constant advice and concrete examples of the way in which he should proceed so that the teacher may both overcome any difficulties that might arise and evaluate the results obtained.

Applying social psychology

We have seen that the new organization of the social and health services in Italy demands that the work of the psychologist should be conducted in a very different field of action from that of the traditional clinical field. We have supplied some examples to show how this new way of working can be effective in real situations and we have associated it with a new way of understanding community psychology (c.f. also Palmonari and Zani, 1980). However, at this point it is important to ask whether these new methods merely amount to the empirical application of ideas which belong to the vast field of psychology and which are simply guided by common sense, or whether they offer a useful area in which to verify the theories elaborated in academic circles and by research.

We feel that in modern European social psychology some theoretical ideas have been developed recently which have significance for the practical work of the psychologist. We will try to show how two of these theoretical contributions might be usefully employed.

THE CHANGE OF STABLE SOCIAL NORMS

The problem

In every culture stereotypes and sometimes prejudices exist alongside the many other genuine values which constitute the most generally recognized aspects of local life. Let us consider the highly complex systems of communication and of interpersonal and intergroup relationships which constitute the social network on which the life of the individual depends. Often social control imposes itself on this network and sometimes there is a total intolerance of differentiation and an insensibility towards the introduction of new elements. If the psychologist wishes to carry out innovatory interventions, he must understand the culture of the community in which he is working in depth, in such a way that he can anticipate how certain enterprises will be received, understand the meaning of certain unexpected reactions, and avoid conflict with the community. It may, in fact, happen that in order to attain some fundamental objectives new elements are introduced which are not welcomed by the local community. In such a situation it is necessary to modify certain deep-rooted beliefs and certain patterns of behaviour which are taken for granted.

A useful theory to follow in social intervention

Social psychology has studied the question of the modification of perceptions, judgements, opinions and the values which are at the basis of social behaviour, under the rubric of "social influence". In our opinion the "interactionist" model of Moscovici (1976) helps us to understand the process of social change which results in innovation more completely than does Asch's paradigm (1951), which was pre-eminent in this area until a few years ago.[1]

In Moscovici's model systems of power are not considered simply as "given facts", but are always seen as resulting from the confrontation of different social agents and the negotiation between them. Interactional exchanges, even when they occur between agents of differing status, always imply a reciprocity which ensures that each one has the possibility of affecting the system. Thus it is possible for theoretical innovations introduced by a minority group to become widely accepted. This "minority influence" depends on the meanings attributed by everyone involved in the situation to the behaviour of the minority group when it confronts and negotiates with its interlocutors.

What is important is not the alternative propositions of the minority group themselves, but the organization of these propositions. Because of this their mode of behaviour is of the utmost importance. It is, in fact, by behaving consistently that a minority can become influential and its opinions can become widely accepted. Consequently they finally provide an alternative model which is *consistent* within itself; and which *competes* with the dominant model. This assumption of an alternative position on the part of the minority group creates conflict not only with the majority group, but also with the very large social groups which are dominated by the latter, and which take the current definition of reality for granted. Thus the minority group has to find a way of offering a true alternative in its strategy, taking up a position of strong opposition in its dealings with the majority group and encouraging dealings and negotiations with the dominated groups.

From this theoretical position we can see a few indications of what the aims of the psychologist should be in his work in the social services. We consider the most important one to be of a methodological nature. When it is clear from a political point of view that a certain belief is definitely preventing the attainment of the objectives which are essential for reform, it is necessary to create a definite pole of opinion, opposing the existing one. One must affirm with resolution the existence of an alternative and be able to adopt practical methods which are consistent with such a position, while keeping open at the same time as many channels of communication as possible with those people who might not initially understand the meaning of the operation.

At this point we can discuss as a concrete example the problem of deinstitutionalization and the struggle against the social rejection of individuals. This represents one of the major objectives of the new social services. The problem has arisen of how to close down progressively more of the total institutions which cater for children, old people and the mentally ill. It is necessary to create social infra-structures which dispense with the need for more institutions, and which favour the expansion of the process of deinstitutionalization. However, it is also necessary to construct a cultural milieu which offers an alternative to the institutional one. It is necessary for the whole community to understand that the problems of children, old people and the mentally ill must be faced up to by everyone, even if it involves altering one's present style of life. These problems should not be dispensed with by classifying and institutionalizing the disadvantaged groups. The enterprise must provide a true alternative to the existing situation and this is the point of departure for affecting a change.

The fact that it is local organizations which promote this form of social policy is certainly helpful; but it does not guarantee in itself the renewal of the social services. On the contrary, it seems that in this area the old functional formulae, according to which the segregation of the weakest members of society is a necessary evil, are being reintroduced. The theoretical and practical problems of finally eradicating such a way of thinking can only be solved by the initiative of social groups who share the political ideals of the local organizations, but who are able to arrive at a way of thinking which provides an alternative to the traditional methods of offering assistance to children and old people.

The psychologist has the problem of adopting methods of work which are equal to the complexity of the tasks he must undertake. They should take into account the necessity on the one hand of remaining loyal to the institution to which he belongs; and on the other hand of encouraging and supporting the groups which offer an alternative to that same institution. One can appreciate that he must continually negotiate about the nature of his intervention with the administrators and politicians, and with the other social groups who are affecting, or who are affected by, the reform of the social services.

INTERGROUP RELATIONSHIPS

The problem

It is important to pay a great deal of attention to relations within the team of practitioners and to their relationships with politicians and with their clients. Otherwise the renewal of the social services runs the risk of being impeded by communication difficulties. However, one cannot treat this problem as though it were merely a matter of establishing suitable interpersonal relationships. In the situations we are concerned with relations of this kind are usually affected by more far-reaching social factors.

In fact, because it is generally desirable to involve a cross-section of the community in the social services, the people involved are often inspired by different ideals. They are, however, asked for the benefit of others to simply accept certain principles and to allow the clients to make an autonomous choice. Nevertheless, certain ideological or political inclinations influence the criteria according to which responsibility is handed out, results are judged, and knowledge is passed on. Sometimes the practitioners who realize that their ideals differ from those of the majority feel themselves excluded from the most important enterprises and claim that those who belong to the same party as the administrators are given preferential treatment. Sometimes, whether rightly or wrongly, a practitioner is regarded as the confidante of a local councillor.

It is necessary to study these problems in more detail, bearing in mind first, that they are not merely caused by personal differences, and, secondly, that they cannot be immediately accounted for by lack of political involvement.

A theory to help understand intergroup relations

It will be useful at this point to consider recent discussions of the level of analysis on which social psychology should concentrate. Normally social psychology is thought of as the study of relationships between individuals; the results which it produces are mainly relevant to this interpersonal level. However, it is important to bear in mind that, in the analysis of social behaviour, other more far-reaching factors play a part, such as ideology and social representations (Doise, 1978). By taking these factors into consideration it is possible, in our opinion, to avoid two potential mistakes: either being reduced to an unsatisfactory analysis in terms of intra- and interpersonal concepts; or avoiding this only to give a general deterministic interpretation of the environmental-structural influences involved.

Here we need do no more than clarify the significance of social representations in determining behaviour. The individual, when faced with a task which involves establishing relationships with other people and/or groups, is not only influenced by aspects of the direct interaction. He is also influenced by his own organization of mental images, expectations and convictions about the course the relationships will take, about the attitudes of the other people involved, the relations between them, and the underlying motives for their present behaviour. Social representations thus constitute a sort of naive theory about the nature and organization of more or less limited aspects of social reality, which is shared by the members of certain groups. By means of these representations individuals can make a fairly simple interpretation of reality, which they know is shared by their own and other groups. Thus they arrange a basis from which to evaluate the phenomenon of reality and by which to guide their behaviour.

The theoretical development of the problem of relationships between groups given by Tajfel (1978) has a place in this general scheme. Under what conditions are relationships between individuals determined by the fact that they are members of groups, rather than by the direct relationship itself? Group membership will have a determining influence if, in a given social situation, they feel themselves to be members of a group which is seen to be a separate entity, distinct from the mass, if they attribute to their membership of this group positive and negative values which they know are understood by others who are not members, and if membership of the group assumes a more or less emotional significance. On this basis, in the same social situation, members of a group will enter into relationships with others and consider them as members of other groups. This process will vary from one extreme at which the individual may consider every person with whom he has a relationship as a member of a different group, to the other at which he may discount these factors entirely and be influenced merely by the interpersonal relationship itself.

Let us return to the concrete problem which we started with. If we bear in mind the essential characteristics of the theoretical model we have presented, it is easy to find a solution to this problem by considering it as dependent on individuals' membership of certain groups. Thus one avoids an interpretation which reduces everything to personal limitations, and to the equally inadequate interpretation that lack of political involvement is responsible. It can happen that when there is tension between two groups who theoretically should collaborate, the enterprise of one group is greeted negatively by the other simply because it has originated within the rival camp. If one does not wish to admit, or is unable to understand, this very simple fact one runs the risk of rationalizing and legitimizing personal reasons for not collaborating (which are connected with social representations), so that new reasons for conflict are found. This can be true of two political groups (two parties, or streams of thought within the same party, etc.) or of two professional groups (doctors and psychologists, for example, or psychologists and sociologists), when each group perceives intergroup differences and is encouraged to differentiate between the groups. However, it may also happen that such a situation arises from the various roles and administrative positions of the members of the same group.

It is quite wrong to try to explain this problem with reference to the individual alone. It is very important for the psychologist to make intergroup mechanisms explicit and to demonstrate the extent to which social factors affect the individual.

The examples we have given form the basis of our conviction that social psychology can reveal new areas in which the psychologist can intervene in the local social services. In the same way the other social sciences can also make valuable contributions to community work. However, a further exploration of this problem is certainly necessary, so that practitioners can become more actively involved in the formation of a new theoretical system of social relationships. This is already beginning to develop, thanks to the new political and institutional settings. But sometimes insurmountable problems are found in the form of deep-rooted prejudices, in sectarianism and ignorance.

Note

1. The explanation of the phenomenon of influence given by Asch, and subsequently taken up by others, does not make explicit the importance of power relationships (although they are seen to be important in determining changes). Instead it considers that interpersonal relationships are entirely responsible, taking for granted that influence derives from finding oneself high on the scale of social prestige. This model,

which Moscovici has called "functional", can account for pressures towards social conformity and also for social change which results in innovation; but these processes are only considered possible if they are initiated from above, promoted, that is, by those who have more power. Theoretically it is not admitted that a minority group might be capable of influencing and introducing innovation in the system of power.

References

Asch, S. E. (1951). Effects of group pressure upon the modification and distortion of judgement. In "Groups, Leadership and Men" (H. Guetzkow, ed.). Carnegie Press, Pittsburgh.

Bernstein, B. (1971). "Class, Codes and Control". Routledge and Kegan Paul, London.

Doise, W. (1978). Images, representations, ideologies et experimentation psychosociologique. Soc. Sci. Inform. 17, 41–69.

Donaldson, M. (1978). "The Children's Mind". Fontana, London.

Giles, H. and Clair, St. R. (eds) (1979). "Language and Social Psychology". Blackwell, Oxford.

Golann, S. E. and Baker, J. (eds) (1975). "Current and Future Trends in Community Psychology". Human Sciences Press, New York.

Holzkamp, K. (1972). "Kritische Psychologie". Fischer, Frankfurt.

Klein, D. C. (1978). "Psychology of the Planned Community: The New Town Experience". Human Sciences Press, New York.

Moscovici, S. (1976). "Social Influence and Social Change". Academic Press, London.

Nietzel, M. T., Winett, R. A., McDonald, M. L. and Davidson, W. S. (1977). "Behavioural Approaches to Community Psychology". Pergamon Press, New York.

Palmonari, A. and Zani, B. (1980). "Psicologia Sociale di Comunita". Il Mulino, Bologna.

Robinson, P. (1972). "Language and Social Behaviour". Penguin, Harmondsworth.

Tajfel, H. (1978). Intergroup behaviour. In "Introducing Social Psychology" (H. Tajfel and C. Fraser, eds). Penguin, Harmondsworth.

Zax, M. and Specter, G. A. (1974). "An Introduction to Community Psychology". Wiley, New York.

10

The Holly and the Ivy: Social Psychology and Social Work

G. M. Breakwell[1]

The contribution which social psychology can make to social work seems to lie in three areas:

SOCIAL PSYCHOLOGICAL ANALYSES OF SOCIAL WORK ORGANIZATION AND PRACTICE

Such an analysis would treat social work as yet another social institution whose objectives can be interpreted and whose methods can be examined through social psychological theory and techniques. One of the interesting things about such an analysis is that it can exist in a vacuum. The analysis, completed by the theorist, can remain unknown to the practitioner or, if known, it may be unacceptable. There is no inevitability about the practical value of practically relevant analyses. Even where such analyses lead to policy suggestions, implementation depends on factors other than how justifiable those suggestions are. If they could ever be delineated, these factors themselves could be amenable to social psychological analysis. The important thing is that, whether or not the analysis influences practice or policy, it can still be made. In the last resort, these social psychological analyses of social work are by social psychologists for social psychologists.

SOCIAL PSYCHOLOGY IN TRAINING SOCIAL WORKERS

In the training of social workers, social psychology can operate at two levels:

(a) social workers can be taught social psychology as an element in their course;

(b) teachers of social work can use social psychological theory and methods to make their teaching more effective.

Teachers of social work may thus end up by using social psychology simultaneously as a content and a means of education.

SOCIAL PSYCHOLOGY IN SOCIAL WORK PRACTICE

Social workers operate in many contexts but they are always embedded in complex organizations, working with clients located in complicated familial and financial networks and in combination with other professionals who adhere to very diverse ideologies. Utilization of social psychological techniques in such situations by social workers can be very valuable in predicting what actions are necessary and what consequences are likely. In this case, the social worker does the social psychological analysis for himself and to promote the interests of the client.

What is really being discussed above is what might be called the *social psychological approach* (SPA). All social activities can be analysed in social psychological terms, those adopting the SPA are committed to doing just that. If one really wants to, it is possible to analyse anything from a social drink to a social movement in social psychological terms. Of course, it is possible to analyse the same phenomena from many other approaches and it is not necessary to claim primacy for the SPA analysis. Its primacy is irrelevant as long as it proves catalytic and convincing, and, of course, it will sometimes be neither.

The pragmatic application of SPA to social work in the three realms outlined above is the central focus of what follows. However, a warning is in order: the discussions are selective; no attempt has been made to provide exhaustive descriptions of all that social psychology might contribute in these realms. Selection was moulded by the desire to examine the impact of new theories of social functioning and the importance of cultural differences in social work organization.

Social work ideology and organization

There is no monolithic structure to social work. Social work in the U.S. is very different from social work in Britain. The differences mean that a single analysis cannot be universally applied. However, the self-same differences enable us to see how an analysis might be evolved. The comparison of social work in the U.S. and Britain pinpoints those ideological features which are most amenable to social psychological analysis. Since ideology shapes practice, the dynamics of its evolution need to be examined.

In Britain, the British Association of Social Workers (BASW) is arguably the most representative organization of social workers. Though most representative, it is by no means totally representative, so that, in using BASW's pronouncements on social work ideology, it should not be assumed that this is the total picture. But, to paraphrase an old adage, half a picture is better than none.

In 1977, BASW published "The Social Work Task" which was an attempt to define the task of social workers, the ethics they should employ and the models of manpower deployment which should be adopted. In this document, BASW defined social work:

> Social work is the purposeful and ethical application of personal skills in interpersonal relationships directed towards enhancing the personal and social functioning of an individual, family, group or neighbourhood, which necessarily involves using evidence obtained from practice to help create a social environment conducive to the well-being of all.

Repeatedly, BASW claims that "central to the practice of social work is the worker's use of self in enhancing a client's personal and social functioning through the medium of interpersonal relationships". BASW does not say exactly how the worker should use the "self" or specify the techniques which should be used in "the medium of interpersonal relationships". The statement revolves around the desire to establish a global ideological stance for social work rather than a precise theory or methodology. BASW seems to think that to define social work one needs to define its ideology rather than its practices.

Nevertheless, the ideology outlined indicates fairly clearly what are not to be regarded as social work tasks and practices: social workers are not administrators of legislated provisions of the social services—they should not be dishing out bath aids to the disabled, carting runaways back to detention centres or sorting out social security claims. Social work, BASW admits, is less to do with materialism and more to do with "applied love". Social service workers—administrators—give practical help; social workers help with human relationships. Social work "involves the creative application of skills derived from values to help meet individual needs through interpersonal relationships between worker and client" (BASW, 1977, p. 10). To put it even more bluntly and repetitively and at the risk of swamping the reader with quotes, "provision of help and aid does not necessarily imply social work. Only if personal skills informed by professional values are used in the context of interpersonal relationships as an integral part of the helping process can that process be described as social work".

Of course, such statements beg the major questions like what constitutes need; where are professional values lodged and how do they relate to personal values; what constitutes an interpersonal relationship and how does it relate to larger scale intergroup relations; and, most importantly, what are these personal skills which are destined to work such wonders. Where it realizes that these questions exist, BASW evades them with clever use of the taxonomic diversion. The taxonomic diversion involves listing types of need and sorts of social work roles without ever showing what they mean in practice. A taxonomy of the possible is no explanation of the actual.

Perhaps a social psychological analysis can contribute an explanation to the question of why the most influential social work organization in Britain should be offering a specious definition of social work. An analysis of sorts can be achieved through the use of theories of social identity and intergroup behaviour which are being evolved in Europe (see, for example, Tajfel, 1978). The main thrust of these theories can be summarized—though the summary camouflages many diverging trends in the work being done in the field. To put the idea simply, and to unashamedly erode its subtlety, people need to feel satisfied with the social identity which they derive from their group memberships; if they are not satisfied with it, they act to make it more satisfying. Depending on ideological and material circumstances, the person may either seek to change his group memberships ("the social mobility option") or to change the group ("the social change option"). The initial evaluation of a social identity and the strategies enacted to change it intimately involve what have been called "social comparison processes" (Festinger, 1954; Suls and Miller, 1977). Identities are valued in relation to other identities. The status of a group is derived from its relation to others. Where a satisfying social identity cannot be achieved through social mobility, for whatever reason, then social change must involve a movement in the status relations between groups. Efforts after social change normally involve unilateral attempts by groups with low or insecure status to change the criteria of status attribution; the dimensions of intergroup differentiation or the structure of group boundaries. It is predicted that, in the search for a positive social identity, a group will seek to differentiate itself from other groups along any continuum of comparison where they can gain some sort of advantage (if not objective then a subjective one). *The group will cling to dimensions of differentiation which are valuable and which they can call their own: these are the things which make it unique and superior.*

The ideological stance of BASW seen in the light of this framework becomes more comprehensible. In truth, BASW is in the business of marking out a territory for itself; establishing the professional domain and ethos of social work. BASW is engaged upon the task of differentiation. It needs to simultaneously draw the line around what is unique to social work and to invest those unique characteristics with value. The problem is that, as BASW admits, none of the roles occupied by social workers are unique to social workers. Moreover, where other professionals can point to a technology or an institution they can call their own, social work has neither. In the past, social work has possessed no unique method and the social worker has had no unique system of knowledge to administer. The doctor has his drug, the surgeon has his knife; both have an accumulated wisdom in the use and efficacy of their tools. BASW has gone in search of an equivalent tool and skill for the social worker. They came back to the "self" and "personal" skill. BASW have made the very absence of a professional tool and set of skills the hallmark of social work. The social worker, having no overt tools, uses himself. If Man is differentiated from other animals by the fact that he makes and uses tools and the professions are differentiated by their use of different tools and the systems of knowledge and rules they imply, social work is distinguished by its abandonment of tools and the absence of systematic knowledge.

Finding that the other "caring professions" had occupied institutions and taken possession of technologies of social problem-solving, BASW actually had two alternatives. The intergroup theories described earlier would predict that it must seek to erect for social workers as a body a distinctive and positive identity. But it could do this in two ways. BASW might have claimed that social work was unique in its eclecticism—in the breadth of the techniques and tools it was able to employ. In fact, BASW rejected this in favour of a claim to elitism through the notion that only social workers use their "self" to solve social problems.

It is interesting that they should adopt the least tenable alternative, but not surprising. Since its establishment, social work has been harried by claims that it could do nothing more than was already being done more efficiently by others. In claiming a specialized tool and skill for social work, no matter how ethereal they may seem, BASW is fighting for its corporate existence. Had BASW been stronger and more secure to start with, it might have been able to argue that social work did not need to lay claim to any unique skills or knowledge. The National Association of Social Workers (NASW), the U.S. counterpart of BASW, was originally stronger and has evolved a very different ideology for social work. In the U.S., social work ideology revolves around an integrated methods approach (Goldstein, 1974; Pincus and Minahan, 1975). Any method that proves practicable is used, the art of social work lies in their integration. It may well be the case that in practice British social workers are equally pragmatic. The main point here is that the organ which represents them nationally claims that they are not mere opportunists and that this response is predictable in terms of intergroup theory.

Intergroup theory also predicts other developments in social work organization as prescribed by BASW. These developments revolve around the deployment of labour. Part of BASW's battle for a superior status for social work is exemplified in attempts to get more social workers qualified—to get social workers to complete a recognized social work course. The attempt to standardize such training courses is largely a function of wishing to be seen as a profession with a recognized body of knowledge to communicate to initiates. It is interesting that in the U.S. such accreditation of courses was abandoned as early as 1960. Perhaps where a profession sees itself as secure it is unnecessary to reify the trappings of professionalism.

BASW's concern with a standardized professional qualification goes hand in hand with attempts to differentiate between the roles of qualified and unqualified social workers and social work assistants. The professionalization of social work involves the erection of training standards, but it also involves criteria for manpower deployment. BASW has thus set out criteria which would control what sorts of cases qualified social workers should deal with. Essentially, they should get the most complex and most important or dangerous cases. Again, BASW is sharpening the edge of the difference between its social workers and all others and again this edge is carefully placed to achieve kudos.

This growing trend in the division of labour is supplemented by
further specialization. After the Seebohm report (1968), the Social Services in Britain were reorganized to eliminate specialization by social
workers. There were no longer to be psychiatric, adoption or geriatric
specialists. Social work was to become "generic"—a single social
worker being asked to deal with psychiatric, geriatric, child care, and
many other, less easily classifiable, problems. Since 1974 (Otton, 1974;
Birch, 1976) efforts to reintroduce specialization have been increasing.
Since, at the time of writing, only 38% of social workers are qualified it
has been argued that they need to specialize in order to cope with the
volume and range of work to the best of their abilities and according to
their preferences. BASW has indicated the generic social worker as a
Jack-of-all-trades and master of none. Since they wish social workers to
be seen to have mastery it is not surprising that they should support the
notion of specialization, even though they do not claim to be able to de-
lineate the skills which each type of specialist must possess and which
will differentiate him from other types of social work specialists. On the
basis of the original definition of social work given by BASW the thing
which differentiates one specialist social worker from another, whatever it turns out to be, will lie within his or her "self".

It is ironic that on both fronts BASW's attempts to set up a positively
valued professional group seem likely to backfire. By locating the
unique essence of social work within the social worker's "self" and in
the intangible interpersonal relation with the client, the very definition
of social work militates against the growth of consensual practices or established data in social work. If the tool is the "self" and there is no
theory of the "self", the tool must be used randomly on the basis of intuition rather than fact. Who is to say that the "self" which is one social
worker's tool has any similarity to the "self" which is another social
worker's tool? Moreover, why should we assume that either can communicate with the other? BASW seems to be talking about social work
as if it were a sort of magic rather than a form of social science. Now, believing that you are a magician can be pleasant for a short time—until
you find that the spells do not work. One wonders how long the magus
ideology can survive in social work. Certainly, the fact that it simultaneously embodies a doctrine which separates social workers and calls
for ever-increasing specialization (without foundation in methodology)
is likely to accelerate its decline and fall since it helps to fragment the
profession and thus threaten the security which it craves.

Of course, it is not necessary to use the SPA to produce a critique of BASW's ideology and programme for social work. BASW would probably be able to produce such a critique for itself. Purely on the basis of personal contact with social workers, one might be able to argue that every social worker with a modicum of fieldwork experience knows the limitations of that ideology and programme. The advantage of using the SPA is that it gives reasons for the evident inadequacies; it precipitates the discussion of the hidden motives which necessitate BASW's course and it can predict changes in that course.

Obviously, the analysis of the development of social work in terms of social identity and intergroup theories might be extended. The intention here, however, was not to provide a comprehensive analysis but rather a limited exemplar of how SPA might provide an incisive orientation for the analysis of professional movements. The tendency in the first half of this chapter is to apply social psychology to understand how practitioners make themselves ready to face such a worldly problem. The objectives of these two types of application of social psychology are slightly different and the articulation of the social psychological analysis with the subject matter is considerably different. These two types of application cut into different stages in the process of problem-solving. Certainly, the approach to application which is adopted above could be said to answer no existent worldly problem, but it is equally certain that it may help other people to solve problems and it may act to solve problems which are merely beginning to develop. Its contribution may be indirect. In a way, it is an anticipatory analysis—suggesting where and why a branch of social problem-solvers may have problems of their own.

Social work training

In order to understand the possible contribution of SPA to social work training it is necessary to have some idea of what that training is. Responsibility for the direction of training in social work lies with the Central Council for Education and Training in Social Work (CCETSW). In November 1975, in a booklet entitled "Education and Training for Social Work", CCETSW enumerated what a social worker requires:

Knowledge of: a. human development and behaviour
            b. society, its development and regulations
            c. social, economic and cultural institutions
            d. the interaction of these

Ability to: a. apply this knowledge
            b. use oneself in serving individuals and groups, community and society.

The objective is to intervene when called upon to "help people, whether individuals or groups, to have sufficient control over their own lives to increase their opportunities for personal choice and self-realization". CCETSW is quick to point out where this right to intervene originates:

> The social worker derives his mandate to intervene either from statute or from those who engage his services. These two forms of authority impose limits on the extent and nature of social work involvement in social problems.

Adopting this justification of intervention means that the problem of deciding when to intervene is avoided in most cases. It cannot be avoided, however, when the demands of the individual client and the demands of statutes which mediate society's expectations are antagonistic or even mutually exclusive. For example, should the social worker intervene to remove an elderly lady from her home and relocate her in a hospital or a geriatric institution against her wishes because the statutes demand that she be protected from her desire for isolation? The situation is not an unusual one for the social worker to face: the two sources from which his mandate comes make simultaneous and contradictory demands. In the last resort, in these situations, the individual social worker has to decide between client and society.

The decision which the individual makes will be dependent upon the value system to which they adhere. CCETSW in "Values in Social Work" (1976) faced this issue. They argued that the ultimate value in social work is a "respect for persons" and the BASW Code of Ethics is quoted:

> basic to the profession of social work is the recognition of the value and dignity of every human being irrespective of origin, status, sex, age, belief or contribution to society. The profession accepts responsibility to encourage or facilitate the self-realisation of the individual person with due regard for the interests of others.

Cloaked in the humanism of this statement is the recognition that social work can never be neutral. It takes sides and offers the respected individual "self-determination, acceptance, confidentiality and individualization". In answer to the perpetual question of whether social workers are agents of social change or social control CCETSW says that the social worker is neither: authorization comes from both society through law and the client through consent. Nevertheless, the individual social worker operates in relation to specific problems according to his own unique value system which according to CCETSW is derived from his group membership. Faced with the old lady who does not want to move, the social worker chooses between law and consent in accordance with values.

Training can have a large impact on value systems. The disciplines taught on courses have built-in models of the nature of Man and assumptions about the structure of the social world which mould values. CCETSW argues that psychology has a particular role to play in changing values. For instance, psychoanalytic approaches lead to a belief that Man may have some control over his fate but that this is limited severely by those unconscious and uncontrollable ingredients of his nature; behaviourism would lead to the conclusion that he has no control whatever over his destiny; and humanism would offer the perception of Man with total self-determination. These three precepts about the nature of Man will certainly infect social workers who adhere to any one of them with very different ideas about the responsibility which men have for their actions and with different notions of how to evaluate or help others. There are, of course, other world views which influence values: Marxist, Buddhist or Christian ideologies for instance. Adherence to any world view can influence values and through them influence the sort of social work done. The interesting thing about the views of Man that psychology may provide is that they not only influence values, they also contribute a technology for changing what might be disliked in Man's actions.

Underlying much of the CCETSW analysis of what social workers are doing and why they do it is the assumption that training for social work must be both theoretical and practical. In January 1975 in a paper on "The Teaching of Community Work" it stated explicitly that "students gain more from fieldwork than theoretical studies" and that there is an "inevitable tension between education and practice". They condemn most training courses as "too theoretical". Yet CCETSW recognizes that the social worker needs to be able to study, organize, form policy, implement policy and evaluate its implementation. In this the contribution of social psychology is specified (CCETSW, 1975b, p. 34): it

> provides the student with a basic understanding of the biological and cultural bases of human personality with some reference to key theories of personality and socialisation processes

The key theme is the "interrelationship between individuals and the various groups in which they interact" and it is recognized that social psychology provides valuable tools of analysis. CCETSW emphasizes the study of social perception, attitude formation and change, communication, human groups and role behaviour. However, it is difficult to know whether CCETSW's recommendations are followed by those who actually run the courses.

The courses which have evolved to train social workers are diverse. They differ in length and in the type of candidate they accept. In 1979, in "The Certificate of Qualification in Social Work", CCETSW describe six types of qualifying courses for social workers:

a. 1 year course for graduates with relevant degrees (what is considered relevant depends on those running the course—sometimes a degree in psychology is considered irrelevant)
b. 2 year course for graduates with irrelevant degrees
c. 4 year undergraduate course
d. 2 year nongraduate courses for people over 20 years of age who have some experience relevant
e. 3 year nongraduate course for 19 year olds
f. 3 year course for people with family commitments (what constitutes a "family commitment" is unspecified)

These courses also differ in location; some are run by universities, others by polytechnics or colleges or training centres. They also differ in the material taught, though most cover, at least cursorily, social philosophy, sociology, psychology, social policy and administration and medicine and law as they relate to social work (Snelling, 1974). All courses require students to go out on "placement" to gain practical experience in the field.

Regardless of there differences, these courses all serve to gain for the successful student recognition as a *qualified* social worker. Qualified social workers are differentiated from unqualified social workers and assistants—who may be doing identical work—but who have very limited prospects of promotion and are paid considerably less. Unqualified social workers can be sent on qualifying courses of one or two years duration which may be full or part time by their local authorities. With government cutbacks in support to the social services the chances of unqualified social workers being sent on courses have been severely reduced.

Until recently, unqualified social workers who were not sent onto CQSW courses would receive no formal training. Now the Certificate in Social Services has been introduced (CCETSW, 1978b). This involves assistants to social workers in the residential field, community services or in day care who have some responsibility for the client but not total responsibility and also specialist staff in the social services (like mobility officers for the blind). The object is to make sure that these are able to support the qualified social workers but there is no idea of putting them on an equal footing with social workers. As the CCETSW (1978a) report states "their role is part social work but they are not social workers".

For the qualified social worker there are also post-qualifying courses designed to serve three ends: to keep the fieldworkers abreast of new developments; to extend their existing knowledge and practice skills; and to extend the knowledge base of social work by feeding back their experiences to the teachers and coming to be competent consumers of research themselves. In June 1978 there were 30 such post-qualifying courses with 350 places, each lasting at least one term.

In this move towards greater training for so-called "unqualified" workers and continuing education programmes for professionals Britain is following the U.S. where both professionals and paraprofessionals receive formal training; where courses tend to be located within operational community agencies; and where these shorter courses are responsive to changing demands of the community (CTCP, 1973).

The responsiveness of British courses to changing community demands is a little difficult to gauge since data on the exact structure of courses is difficult to obtain. We know the generalized principles CCETSW lays down, but not how these are translated on individual courses or by individual teachers. It is therefore difficult to generalize about the contribution which social psychology is allowed to make to these courses—so much depends on whether the course team has a social psychologist and whether that social psychologist is an enthusiastic Freudian, a social skills exponent or fond of encounter groups. However, whether or not the structure of social psychology taught should be left to the arbitrations of chance is not at issue here—all higher education succumbs to that particular problem, it is the price paid for academic freedom of conscience. What is at issue is what social psychology is likely to be being taught on these courses. While concrete evidence is unavailable, there are clues as to the probable nature and impact of social psychology on these courses.

There are two sorts of clues: the first comes from the history of psychology's involvement in social work; the second comes from the history of social psychology in Britain. Social work in Britain has been traditionally centred around casework—the intensive involvement of a social worker with a client and their family. The social worker relied on personal relationships with the client and personal skills to solve the presenting problem. In casework, psychology offered two sorts of understanding. The first was through psychoanalysis and the second through behaviourism. Most social work courses, even when integrated methods and systems analysis have been introduced, still teach a form of psychology which serviced older forms of casework. Psychoanalysis with its fundamental emotional and sexual explanations, and behaviourism, with its simplistic tenets of behavioural control, are still the meat and drink of CQSW psychology. The intricacies of other aspects of modern psychology like information processing or cognitive-developmental approaches are omitted. Their relevance to the problems of social work is not immediately apparent and their omission may seem reasonable. However, this emphasis on the simpler and relatively outmoded (because unsupported) claims of psychoanalysis and behaviourism means that the psychology which is taught on social work courses is fundamentally *asocial*. An emphasis on the social nexus is not demanded by these approaches and this militates against any fundamental reliance on social psychology.

Now, the second clue as to the position of social psychology on courses comes from the history of social psychology itself. Until quite recently, social psychology in Britain, as in the U.S., has focused on the individual. In examining the relationship of the individual to the social context, the emphasis has been upon inter-individual activity—social psychologists studied communication in dyads (particularly non-verbal communication), impression formation in dyads and the way in which two people become friends. Inter-individual phenomena were studied and explained in terms of intra-psychic or interpersonal variables. The interrelation of the individual and the large scale social institutions and social ideologies which surround him were not perceived as the domain of social psychology. Even when essentially social concepts like attitudes were studied they were treated as personality characteristics of the individual to be measured and changed; their social origin or purpose was left unconsidered. When group leadership was studied the question asked was whether there was a certain sort of personality which made a good leader. The fact that Fiedler came up with a contingency model of leadership led others to seek to disprove this disconcerting finding rather than to build theories of group functioning upon it. All the larger scale analyses were left to sociologists who, with notable exceptions, studiously avoided psychology. If the sort of social psychology taught on social work courses reflects this historical tendency in social psychology it, too, should be largely interindividual, emphasizing work on social skills (Trower *et al.*, 1978) and therapeutic group work (Bion, 1961; Douglas, 1978).

It cannot be expected that the current movements in social psychology to focus on social group processes and intergroup relations will have permeated the teaching of social workers—especially when given the emphasis on behaviourism and psychoanalysis which is the social workers' other legacy. Yet it is precisely those approaches which treat with the individual inside a social milieu which may serve social work best. There is a wide range of work now emanating from social psychology on social influence processes (Moscovici, 1976), social representations (Herzlich, 1973), intergroup conflict (Billig, 1976), socio-linguistics (Halliday, 1978) and the more amorphous notions of ethogenics (Marsh *et al.*, 1978), all of which would be valuable to a social worker who has to be able to influence and withstand influence, mediate conflicts, communicate across many boundaries, and understand the nuances of ritual and rule in diverse communities. Some work provides more holistic analyses and more comprehensive understanding than the social psychology that preceded it, which tended to fragment an event in order to understand that fragment in all its depth and complexity. The social worker faced with an oppressive caseload and financial stringencies may need to know what a raised eyebrow means in the interplay of nonverbal communication. But it may be rather more reassuring to know that he or she is aware of what may trigger a large-scale community dispute and knows how to avoid it by the use of manipulative influence processes. The argument is not, therefore, that interindividual or intrapsychic analyses should be abandoned but rather that there should be a speedy inclusion of work in social psychology which spans the intrapsychic to the intercultural in its levels of analysis and explanation.

Such a change in orientation is already being called for by social workers themselves who regard their role as an agent of social change rather than personal change. Community workers are seeking to establish themselves as an independent entity (Association of Community Workers, 1978) with their own methods and training—a training which includes a grounding in the sorts of theories which a truly *social* psychology can provide. CCETSW is responding to this call; but so must the individuals in charge of courses before anything can be achieved.

Of course, the sort of social psychology which is taught will ultimately depend on the goals which social work erects for itself. As long as the objective is the rehabilitation of the client with individual problems, emphasis will be upon individual psychology. If the focus should turn to questioning the social origin of the problem and the social context in which it exists, then social psychology may be valuable. The interesting thing here is that it is not a matter of whether social work is an agency of social control or social change which determines the value of social psychology; it is a matter of whether social work is dealing with individuals in isolation or in their social context.

Moreover, the value of social psychology to social work depends on whether social psychologists will turn their attention to the problems of social workers. There is some antipathy amongst social psychologists to remove themselves to the realm of practice; there is a tendency to want to be scientific. Social work allows none of the control or latitude for manipulation which is necessary for "science". Theorists in social psychology will have to make the step beyond safety to speculate and synthesize before they can provide more than generalized and global suggestions to social work practitioners. Perhaps such a dangerous step cannot be made by a theorist and must be made by practising social workers who apply social psychology, test it and change it to suit their own ends. To do this, of course, the practitioners have to be taught social psychology in the first place.

Social work practice

So far there has been no consideration of how a practising social worker
might use a social psychological analysis. It is time to turn to this now.
There are obviously many realms where social psychology might be
used. A taxonomy would be tedious and would not show the important
point which is *how* social psychology might help. However, an example
would serve this purpose well. The example used here is modelled on
the experiences which Rowett (1979) had when administering a group
home for three mentally handicapped men in North Yorkshire.

Since the MIND (National Association for Mental Health) campaign to return psychiatric patients to the community, many experiments have been made in rehabilitation. Patients who had been incarc-
erated in psychiatric hospitals for many years, for no better reason than
that there was nowhere else for them to go, have been relocated. Some,
after a period of retraining for everyday life in short-stay hostels attached to hospitals, have been placed in "group homes". Group homes
normally consist of three or four ex-patients living together in a house
which has been donated by the Local Council or some charitable organization. The inhabitants of the group home are self-sufficient, cooking and cleaning for themselves, even though they may be too disabled
to keep a job. The role of the social worker attached to these group
homes is to cope with any problems that might arise—to smooth out
any financial difficulties, to mediate between the occupants and the organization that funds the home, to encourage good relations amongst
the occupants and to keep an eye on their activities in the community at
large. Since the concept of the group home is relatively experimental,
the role of the social worker is fluid.

It is precisely in these areas where expectations have not coalesced
that social psychology can contribute most. Essentially, the social
psychological approach (SPA) can be used to interpret the relations between the men within the group home and the relations between the
group home and the community. The SPA could elucidate why the
three original occupants of a group home might not want a further new-
comer to join them; it might show why stereotypes and discrimination
prevailed in the relations of the occupants with their neighbourhood; it
might illuminate the marginality of the group home within the community and predict the consequences of such marginality. Theories of
group dynamics would provide clues to the analysis of each of these
problems.

SPA would also predict that occupants, once established, would not wish to move on. If such a prediction had been available when the group home concept was first formulated there would have been no illusions about using them as staging posts to complete independence. The SPA was not adopted and the prediction was not made and now many tragically static group homes exist where the dependency of hospital has found simply a new location. It also means that the hope that initiated the schemes has floundered—the type of patients who can benefit from this new sort of sheltered existence have been exhausted and the funds to establish more group homes are not available. SPA could also have predicted that relations between the group home and the community would not be easy. It would predict the pressures that would build on the funding authorities to close group homes or to restrict them to the most "normal-looking" of the mentally handicapped. It would thus have predicted the possibility of creating "ghettos of the disabled" (Tyne and Williams, 1978) and the backlash locally against the social services who are seen as the originators of these marginal communities (Hughes, 1978). It is interesting to consider that a little foresight bred of SPA might have prevented the Dawn House Affair. Residents of a Birmingham community accused social workers of deliberately deceiving them into agreeing to a rehabilitation and assessment centre for the mentally disordered by representing it as a hostel for the mentally handicapped. Whatever the council inquiry and the independent social work inquiry concluded about the actions of the social services in that case, the community backlash is predictable and could have been anticipated in advance by social workers who adopted a broad social perspective on their activities.

Within the example chosen it can be seen that SPA can help at two levels: the everyday running of a single group home and the evaluation of the policy to initiate group homes in the first place. It is an approach which can be adopted by the individual social worker in the field and it will provide a method of looking at material and chunking data; it can provide a relevant model for the analysis of data which will lead to predictions and anticipation of consequences; but, most importantly, it may lead from an understanding of why a thing happens to how it may be initiated or prevented in the future. In these ways SPA might help both practising fieldworkers and those who formulate large-scale policy. The emphasis moves from blind experiment and intuition or the enthusiasms and expediencies of the moment towards consistent analysis and evaluation.

In conclusion, it would not go amiss to explain the title: the holly and the ivy. The relation of social work to social psychology is akin to that of the ivy to the holly: a symbiotic relationship. Social psychology can provide a framework for interpretation and a technology for action to social work; social work can offer a vast array of data to social psychology.

Obviously, problems which surround any application of social psychology will be found in attempts to use it in social work. Social psychologists can make their analyses to their heart's content, but to have impact their recommendations must be implemented and translated into immediate policy by social work authorities. Similarly, a good analysis is only possible if access to data is available, the social psychologist is again dependent upon social work authorities to provide such access. Asking for access is asking an awful lot because it signifies the loss of power over knowledge; knowledge which might be dangerous in the hands of someone else. This *is* asking rather a lot, even if one is offering sustenance in return. In this case, the hand that feeds you can only do so if you give it the food in the first place—in this situation, you begin to wonder whether you would not be just as well-off feeding yourself and biting the intermediary's hand. Of course, this is why the possibility of social workers trained in social psychology doing their own social psychological analyses and deriving policy from them is so encouraging.

Note

1. I would like to acknowledge the help that I received from Colin Rowett, Senior Social Worker, Broadmoor Hospital, Berkshire, England in producing this chapter.

References

Association of Community Workers (1978). "Towards a Definition of Community Work". ACW, London.
BASW (1977). "The Social Work Task". BASW, 16, Kent St., Birmingham, B5 6RD.
Billig, M. (1976). "Social Psychology of Intergroup Relations". Academic Press, London.
Bion, W. R. (1961). "Experience in Groups". Tavistock, London.
Birch, R. (1976). "Manpower and Training for the Social Services". HMSO Publications, London.
CCETSW (1975a). "The Teaching of Community Work". CCETSW, Paper 8.
CCETSW (1975b). "Education and Training for Social Work". CCETSW.

CCETSW (1976). "Values in Social Work". CCETSW 13.

CCETSW (1978a). "Opportunities for Post-Qualifying Study". CCETSW, Leaflet 8.

CCETSW (1978b). "The Certificate in Social Services". CCETSW, Paper 9.1.

CCETSW (1979). "The Certificate of Qualification in Social Work". CCETSW, Leaflet 2:1.

CTCP (1973). A continuing-education program for mental health professions. *Hosp. Comm. Psychiat.* **24**, 683–86.

Douglas, T. (1978). "Basic Groupwork". Tavistock, London.

Festinger, L. (1954). A theory of social comparison processes. *Hum. Rel.* **7**, 117–140.

Goldstein, H. (1974). "Social Work Practice: A Unitary Approach". Univ. S. Carolina, Columbia.

Halliday, M. (1978). "Language as Social Semiotic". Edward Arnold, London.

Herzlich, C. (1973). "Health and Illness". Academic Press, London.

Hughes, W. (1978). The Dawn House Affair. *SWT* **9**, 46, 6–8.

Marsh, P., Rosser, E. and Harré, R. (1978). "The Rules of Disorder". Routledge and Kegan Paul, London.

Moscovici, S. (1976). "Social Influence and Social Change". Academic Press, London.

Otton, G. (1974). "Social Work Support for the Health Services". HMSO Publications, London.

Pincus, A. and Minahan, A. (1975). "Social Work Practice: Model and Method". Peacock, Illinois.

Rowett, C. (1979). The story of Billy. *SWT* **11**, 9, 16–18.

Seebohm, R. (1968). "Report of the Committee on the Local Authority and Allied Personal Services". HMSO Publications, London.

Snelling, J. (1974). Training social workers. *Proc. roy. soc. med.* **67**, 943–45.

Suls, J. and Miller, R. (eds) (1977). "Social Comparison Processes". Wiley, New York.

Tajfel, H. (ed.) (1978). "Differentiation Between Social Groups". Academic Press, London.

Trower, P., Bryant, B. and Argyle, M. (1978). "Social Skills and Mental Health". Methuen, London.

Tyne, A. and Williams, P. (1978). New colonies? *Apex* **6**, 1, 8–10.

Author Index

Page numbers in italic indicate where names are mentioned in the reference lists

Subject Index